Designing Complexity

The Methodology and Practice of Systems Oriented Design

By Birger Sevaldson

Designing Complexity

The Methodology and Practice of Systems Oriented Design

By Birger Sevaldson

COMMON GROUND

First published in 2022
as part of the *The Constructed Environment* Book Imprint
doi 10.18848/978-1-86335-262-8/CGP (Full Book)

Common Ground Research Networks
University of Illinois Research Park
2001 South First St, Suite 201 L
Champaign, IL 61820 USA

Library of Congress Cataloging-in-Publication Data

Name: Sevaldson, Birger, author.
Title: *Designing Complexity. The Methodology and Practice of Systems Oriented Design/* by Birger Sevaldson
Description: Champaign, IL: Common Ground Research Networks, [2021] |
    Includes bibliographical references. | Summary: "This book is a complete
    description of the background, theories, practice and methodology of
    Systems oriented Design (SOD). Since 2006 the author has been in the
    forefront of developing a new generation of systems thinking in design.
    He took initiative to the RSD conferences and the SDA network and the
    definition of the pluralistic emerging field of systemic design. SOD is
    one of the major directions in the field of systemic design. The book is
    the result of 15 years with design research and development for a
    growing community and increasing attention to systemic design. Systemic
    design is today the most comprehensive and powerful approach to help
    making design become better at coping with the increasingly complex
    challenges that we face in our society. The book is essential in helping
    designers to make the change to become more useful and able in the
    future"-- Provided by publisher.
Identifiers: LCCN 2021037799 (print) | LCCN 2021037800 (ebook) | ISBN
    9780949313614 (hardback) | ISBN 9781863352611 (paperback) | ISBN
    9781863352628 (adobe pdf)
Subjects: LCSH: Design--Methodology. | Design--Philosophy. | System design.
    | Complexity (Philosophy)
Classification: LCC NK1520 S447 2021 (print) | LCC NK1520 (ebook) | DDC
    124--dc23
LC record available at https://lccn.loc.gov/2021037799
LC ebook record available at https://lccn.loc.gov/2021037800

Cover Illustration Credit: Palak Dudani, 2018

Table of Contents

All figures will be available at high resolution on:
https://www.systemsorienteddesign.net/designing-complexity/figures

Acknowledgements

It took me a long time to write this book. It results from years of work, inspiration from students and colleagues and professionals from the design industries and other areas. Therefore, many more people should be thanked here than those mentioned. I want you to know that you are not forgotten. Yet, it is appropriate to mention a few of you, especially.

I am thankful to the Oslo School of Architecture and Design (AHO), especially Rachel Troye, chair of the Institute of Design, for her continuous support and never losing faith in this project.

Special appreciation to Design and Architecture Norway (DOGA), especially Benedicte Wildhagen and colleagues, for their early support and encouragement and the following years of collaboration. Demonstrating the usefulness of SOD in projects of high complexity in the public sector has been essential for the further development of SOD.

I am also thankful to Halogen, the design company that has adopted our methods the most, made them their own and developed them further. Especially CEO Lillian Olsen, Adrian Paulsen and others have been supportive, inspiring and essential in keeping the connection with the world outside of AHO, demonstrating the commercial application of SOD.

Special mention to Andreas Wettre for countless inspiring conversations over many years and for making me think twice and be critical of my assumptions. Bringing gigamapping to the leader groups of many companies has been very valuable in developing this concept.

I appreciate the help of Jonathan Romm, who has been standing by through different roles over the years, especially in bringing SOD to professional application and helping with the development of SOD education.

Michael Hensel deserves special mention for years of collaboration and the most eloquent discussions and conversations. Without our prior partnership with the OCEAN Design Research Association, I would never have reached this point.

I also thank Marie Davidova for her innovative and enthusiastic application and development of SOD in the design of sustainable and regenerative environments.

I am also grateful to Harold Nelson, who gave me crucial inspiration and encouragement, especially in the early days.

Tore Gulden from the Oslo Metropolitan University has been a collaborator and inspirator for many years. I appreciate the criticality and the diversity in his contributions.

I am grateful to the colleagues at USN, the University of South East Norway and the Norwegian Industrial Systems Engineering (NISE) research group, especially mentioning Kristin Falk and Gerrit Muller. Our collaboration through H-seif research projects has been critical in demonstrating the application of SOD in advanced technological industries.

The SOD team also played a significant role in their crucial contributions and in providing such an excellent environment for the development of SOD. I am grateful to Tobias Luthe, Abel Crawford and Haley Fitzpatrick and before mentioned, Andreas and Jonathan, and former colleagues Linda Blaasvær and Manuela Aguirre.

The master's and PhD students, who have courageously thrown themselves into explorations of complex messes, humbly enduring the frustrations and coming out at the other end with innovative and inspirational solutions, also deserve my gratitude.

I also acknowledge all readers of this text, mentioning Manuela Aguirre, Marie Davidova, Andrew Morrison, Alex Ryan, Peter Jones and especially Gordon Rowland for their excellent and critical reviews.

Thanks to Peter Jones for his continuous support and editorial review and Macy Siu for her great editorial work. I also need to thank the Systemic Design Association (SDA) for providing such a rich and diverse environment of colleagues, keynotes, ideas and conversations over the last ten years.

Finally yet importantly, I am thankful to my wife, Liv, for her criticality and support throughout this long writing process.

Foreword

This book is the generous sharing of a life of thinking and action taken by an accomplished academic and professional, who is a highly successful scholar-practitioner in the fields of systems and design, particularly Systems Oriented Design (SOD). It is an invaluable resource for those who want to work with professional systems designers and those who are professional systems designers themselves working with, and in, complex environments.

This book is exemplary in the way that theory and applications are presented in depth and breadth. It successfully integrates the many case studies presented as examples of scholarship and praxis in unified actions as response to complex challenges. In addition, a diverse background of the many traditions of systems from academics, theorists and practitioners is presented as an informed pallet upon which Systems Oriented Design stands. At the same time the book provides a palette of tools, methods, and approaches that are not only extremely interesting but useful in practice.

Professor Sevaldson presents both his stance and his approach to Systems Oriented Design (SOD) which is invaluable for understanding his examples of what SOD is and what it can become. He presents his values, understandings, beliefs, assertions, and assumptions in clear transparent terms. He presents the theories, methods, and tools that he and his associates have utilized or developed over an extended period of time refining and applying the Giga Mapping method.

The book is a valuable professional level resource for those who are just becoming interested in the field, as well as those who have been active participants in the field for some time. The three parts of the book are fluidly interrelated. The parts are exceptional expositions on their own, but become even more effective in their interplay creating a synergy of ideas and experience. By providing a comprehensive overview of the provenance of systems and design with an inventory of SOD methods and tools which lead to the many examples of SOD in practice gives newcomers as well as veterans access to the dynamic and evolving field of SOD practice.

Another valuable aspect of this book is that it champions visual inquiry and communication as essential to understanding and engaging with complexity. In a world dominated by linear text, this book provides a wide variety of visual methods and tools allied with relevant holistic means for accessing or making meaning in dynamic, complex settings. This kind of approach is essential in SOD and other systemic design domains. In fact it is essential to thinking and understanding complexity in general and deserves greater appreciation and utilization. This book provides a good introduction to how visual thinking and communication leads to success when dealing with complexity—the book is exemplary in this aspect.

This book is a milestone in the developmental timeline of serious thinking and practice in both systems and design, and most importantly in their integration. It will become a standard in the field.

Harold G. Nelson

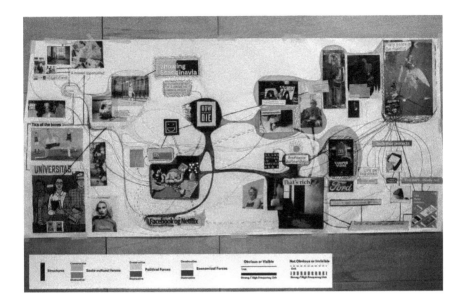

Systems do not only consist of material stock and flows, cause and effect relations and energy exchange. All systems are subject to interpretation. We might consider the boundaries of the systems, including associations, symbols, emotions, narratives, beliefs, cultures and power structures. Often these immaterial forces are stronger than what is concrete and quantifiable. (*Cover image: Gigamap by Palak Dudani 2018*).

Read This First

The title of this book, "Designing Complexity," seems to be an oxymoron in itself. The traditional purpose and role of design has been to solve problems, to find order, to organize, and to simplify. Yet, the concept of designing complexity goes against these established beliefs because complexity is not something that can be designed away. Let's admit it: it is not possible, through design, to solve complex situations in such a way that they are no longer complex. In general, it is not possible to tame, order, and completely remove complexity through planning. It is in the nature of complex problems that new issues will arise during the process of "solving" them. Any attempts to tame it might backfire, often resulting in issues that are more severe than the original issues that we try to fix. The word "complexity" in itself represents the answer to this dilemma. Complexity comes from the Latin word, *complexus*, which means embraced, encompassed or plaited. Cutting, sorting, and taming the relations in a complex system will either kill the system or result in something entirely different that is assumedly unplanned and unintended. Similarly, cutting the threads of a weave will result in destruction. Nevertheless, we can learn to navigate, cope with, interact with, influence, and change a complex situation. Hence, the title of this book: *Designing Complexity*.[1]

Needless to say, writing a book on designing complexity is in itself a complex task. First, one must leave behind the notion of absolute prescriptions. There is no one "right" way presented in this book. Instead, there are many experiences, approaches, and perspectives that are collected and presented throughout the book. The foundation that grounds these perspectives is design, with its practices, competencies, skills, and theories. Design is the main lens through which the theme of Designing Complexity is looked upon. The framework that is used to collect these practices, methodologies, and theories is called Systems Oriented Design (SOD). SOD is a design methodology and design practice that is especially geared towards understanding and working with complex systems. It is influenced by a number of systems theories yet it remains true to its origin, the core of designing.

---

1. It is necessary to mention Ranulph Glanville's article *Designing Complexity* (2008), where he proposes a different view on the topic. He argues that we choose to perceive situations as complex in contrast to this book, where complexity is seen as a feature of the world yet observed and interpreted by constructivist minds. While his paper is highly theoretical and philosophical, this book attempts to address the praxeology of designing complexity.

SOD is a "dialect" in a bigger field called Systemic Design. There are many dialects in Systemic Design. What distinguishes SOD is that it is more rooted in design practice than most others. However, the differences are of little importance. The reader might want to explore other approaches and mix tools, methods, and approaches however they best fit.

Systems Oriented Design was mainly developed at the Oslo School of Architecture and Design (Norway) starting in 2007. One can also say that SOD represents the "Oslo-School of Systemic Design"

SOD is a living methodology. All elements of SOD are interdependent and situation-dependent. None of them are set in stone, and many of them need to be adapted, combined, and redesigned according to the situation. SOD does not provide an orderly, linear design process that is presented in steps to follow.

As such, this book is also not entirely orderly or linear. After many attempts, I settled with organizing the text into three parts that might seem more or less logical:

> **Part One** provides an overview and framework for getting the big picture and a sense of the field with its fluid boundaries.

> **Part Two** presents theories, philosophies, and the academic context of SOD. These are the things that hold the framework together.

> **Part Three** presents the practices of SOD and develops this into praxeology the reflection on practices. These are the things that flesh out the content and real-life practice of SOD.

I look at these three parts as complementary texts that, as a whole, weave together the complex theme of Designing Complexity. I see this clearly through the image of a Persian rug; Part One is the frame or the warp[2], Part Two is the weft, and Part Three resembles the knots, creating the content, colours, and patterns of SOD. The parts do not necessarily build upon each other. Though the nature of the text is linear, it is not a requirement to read the book in a linear way. The reader might pick specific sections and weave his or her own understanding of designing complexity. There is no given starting point of exploration, just as in the case of admiring a Persian rug.

---

2. The warp in a knitted rug consists of the longitudinal threads. The first one sets up. The weft is made of the horizontal threads that are interwoven with and crossing the warp.

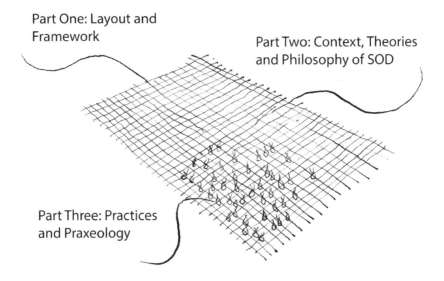

Part One: Layout and Framework

Part Two: Context, Theories and Philosophy of SOD

Part Three: Practices and Praxeology

Figure 1: The book is organized like a Persian carpet weave where the warp provides the overview and framework, the weft holds it together by relating to theories and philosophy, and the knots represent the application and practice that form larger patterns together.[3]

Not only for Designers

This book is written at the outset to help designers becoming better at dealing with complexity. However, this opens up a question: who is a designer? Especially in the intense change processes we are in the midst of, where the design professions diverge and converge into new forms, becoming more transdisciplinary and migrating into ever new fields this question gets harder to answer. We see today designers with a design education working in new fields and new roles, and we see designers without a traditional design education working inside the core design fields. In addition, we see many people working in the field who don't define themselves as designers but who work in designerly ways, inspired by the migration of design thinking into the management and business world or by being participants in teams with designers and other professions.

---

3. All figures included in this book are available at high resolution on:
https://www.systemsorienteddesign.net/designing-complexity/figures

This book is heavily geared towards the designers' professional competencies and a main statement in this book is that these competencies are important for developing new systems approaches in design practices. However, this book addresses all types of designers, those trained in the core ability and those adapting to designerly ways of working, as well as those working with design in the widest meaning. This does not mean that the designerly ways are watered down. On the contrary —it should help those without the core competencies to better appreciate the particularities of the profession and it should also help the professionally educated designers to better understand and appreciate the others and to be integrated into this advanced designerly way of working.

The book is practice heavy. Yes, it can be read by academics and strategists as well. Part Two, in particular, is geared towards an academic discussion of systems thinking at large and systemic design and SOD in particular.

The Purpose of this Book

The purpose of this book is to help change our way of designing so that it can meet the increasingly complex challenges of our world today and in the future. Design is about change, but it is not the only significant domain that is involved in changing and forming our societies. Other domains, including politics, economics, and engineering are equally important. However, if we look at the principal approach of designing rather than at the field of design, it might indicate a generic approach to design that can be valuable across other domains. The generic value of designerly approaches is recognised and reflected in the current interest in design thinking. More precisely the purpose of this book is to crystalize and describe design processes that are better adapted to change in our complex society across scales and levels and beyond the domain of design.

Not only have designerly methods spread to business management but the civic aspect of design has risen a lot in the last decades and ever new aspects of the civic society are addressed through design. Design has shown the potential to contribute to ever more complex societal fields, and to deal with ever more important issues such as sustainability, public services, and policy design.

In these situations, the designer's abilities come into play. Most central is the ability to negotiate and weigh multiple contradictory requirements, needs, parameters, and at its best, to generate win-win solutions. Design is on the move beyond serving consumerism. New horizons have opened up for us where we can find powerful roles for doing good. However, in order to develop this beyond a rudimentary stage where outputs are uncertain and the effects are not very well accounted for, we need a methodological change. We need to become better at embracing complexity and at the same time take more responsibility for our actions. This change is only in its beginning, but it is desperately needed. The very way we change our world has to change. The way change has been induced so far is through singular interventions, some having a disruptive character. However, rarely have the creators of disruptive change been held responsible for the unintended effects of their disruptions. We cannot afford this type of change processes any longer. We need deep insights into the potential systemic effects of big data, autonomous technologies, social networks etc.

The book's focus is to communicate, discuss, and teach SOD as a methodological approach in the field of Systemic Design. Its purpose is to cultivate methodology and practice for responsible advanced design processes. It is based on the skills and knowledge of design professions, and merged with an eclectic approach to systems thinking, bringing an advanced form of design thinking and systems thinking to designers and beyond.

Why is this Book Needed and What Does it Address?

The world is becoming an increasingly complex place to live in, relate to, and influence. This applies to many fields, and design is no exception. In the field of design, the transformations towards increased complexity have a substantial impact. Two tendencies drive this phenomenon. The first is higher information density. There are increasing demands for more knowledge and expertise, and pressure to follow trends in culture, technology, society, science, politics etc. The second tendency is a shift towards ever-wider contexts for design. New applications and fields for design are rapidly emerging. This introduces the need for adaptability, flexibility, as well as interdisciplinary and transdisciplinary collaboration.

We are now faced with an increased attention on sustainability. We need to focus both on the individual user's needs and desires, as well as on the larger social and economic systems, while accounting for secondary and tertiary consequences of our actions at the same time. Being responsible requires consulting a growing network of stakeholders, experts, users, and even non-human actors. We are now beginning to see the downside of being solely user-centred. We need to train our side vision, our antennas, and have empathy for those outside the primary user group; we need to understand the backbones and the dark corners of the systems we design. For the practicing designers, these challenges and requirements emerge both within the client's needs and organisation, but also through government regulations, customer surveys, focus groups, user involvement, and requirements for sustainability.

The making of artefacts has become globalized and is moving across cultures and economies in an unprecedented way. As designers, we need to address issues of social, economic, and ecologic sustainability, and must always remain cognizant of other cultures and ways of living. The consequences of our actions are becoming increasingly crucial and also increasingly difficult to comprehend.

On the personal level, many designers find it increasingly unbearable to submit to the traditional role of the designer. As mentioned, seen from a cold business perspective, the role of the designer is to increase sales and consumption. In the long term, this has devastating consequences. The growth-based economy has to change, and designers have the choice to either close their eyes to these consequences, or try to find other modes of operation.

It is perhaps a response to these numerous challenges that designers are moving into new realms like social design, design activism, organisational design, and policy design. The notion of design has expanded, and the belief that design can make a difference is growing. Unfortunately, there are many failures caused by shallow insight into the complexity of the problems that are being addressed. However, design has the prospect of being much more useful amidst the growing complexity of our world; in fact, there is need for it to manage even higher levels of complexity. This challenge is realized and taken on in several fields like service design and social design. To a large degree, these new design fields deal with systemic issues, and are involved in the design of systems. However, these efforts are limited to their fields and framed by their perspectives. What is needed instead is a general overarching approach to deal with complexity in design. This approach needs to be both powerful and flexible. It needs to fit the "designerly way" of knowing and working, which implies that designing is an activity for the production of knowledge. Furthermore, it needs a theoretical root-perspective, one that is not obstructive to the design process. Lastly, this approach needs to be able to flourish and grow instead of being defined and frozen, so that it can be a living process that continues to develop as rapid changes pile up.

As a response to these challenges, we have kick-started a new community that nurtures a renaissance of systems approaches in design. This movement is pluralistic and contains different approaches and practices. This emerging field is called Systemic Design (Jones & Sevaldson, n.d.). and is organised in the Systemic Design Association[4]. This community shares the belief that systems approaches provide the needed platform for coping with the challenges ahead in a substantial manner. SOD is one approach in the field of systemic design. In this book, I will refer to systemic design whenever I discuss issues regarding the whole field, and refer to Systems Oriented Design or SOD whenever I discuss issues particular for SOD, including the techniques, methodology, and mindsets specific to SOD. SOD is related to design practice. We are not asking designers to re-educate themselves, but to realize that designing is inherently systemic. From that position, there is still a lot to learn and to train and to rethink. This book is here to help with this process.

---

4. The Systemic Design Association (SDA) is a democratic non-for-profit association. See www.systemic-design.net

How Does this Book Address these Topics?

First, this book provides an overview of the issues and elements of SOD. You do not have to be in the business of saving the world to benefit from reading this. SOD can be useful for all professional designers who work with even the simplest design tasks. It is not a magical cure, but it can help you do things slightly better. It can also be useful for other professions, like engineering, management, or even policy making that engage in Design Thinking and other design-like processes.

This book suggests that there is synergy between designing, design thinking, and systems thinking. A relatively simple methodology based on better integration between those domains has great potential to deal with the issues mentioned above.

Rather than presenting a new orthodoxy with rules and prescriptions, I suggest a dynamic methodology with emphasis on flexible use of methods. Methods should be used and developed according to the projects at hand. This implies that SOD is a methodology without fixed methods. The theories and methodology of SOD are addressed particularly in Part Two. Rather than prescribing methods SOD puts emphasis on skills, mindsets, and the development of competencies. From the years of experimentation in classrooms and in businesses in the Oslo region[5], there are certain practices, techniques, and tools that have proven to be useful. These are the praxeology of SOD, which are compiled and explained in Part Three of this book.

How to Read this Book

This book reaches out to a broad audience of designers, design professionals, and others who work with design, as well as scholars involved or interested in the development of the emerging field of Systemic Design. It is also relevant for managers, engineers, and other planners who engage in design thinking. This book can be read in slightly different ways by different readers depending on how you decide to prioritize the three parts according to your needs and preferences.

Part One: An Introduction to and Overview of SOD

Part One provides an introduction and overview of the combined knowledges, challenges, and approaches of SOD. This part is meant to provide an overview for beginners and people who are curious and want to learn while starting up with

---

5. The Oslo environment springs out from the Oslo School of Architecture and Design and includes the OsloMet University as well as some design companies, public organisations and other institutions.

practicing. Many notions, topics, and questions are touched upon without deep elaborations. Most of the touched upon issues are unpacked in Part Two and Three of the book.

Part One puts an emphasis on the change of mindset. How can one change from being an object oriented designer to become a systems oriented one?

Further, Part One also provides for a minimum of theoretical background and overview. However, the main purpose is to give the minimum of necessary insight, tools and framework to begin practicing SOD processes. The most central tool of SOD, Gigamapping, is explained, discussed, and exemplified. The most important framework, the Rich Design Space is discussed in the same manner. All of these issues are elaborated further in the following parts of the book. The chapter ends with examining a case in detail.

If you are curious about SOD and Systemic Design, and wondering what it is, then this part is for you.

Part Two: Contexts and Background the Theories of SOD

Part Two provides much of the background, history, theories, and applied philosophy of SOD. Part Two theorizes, connects, and situates SOD in the emerging field of Systemic Design, and also maps out its relations to other fields and the systems world at large. It describes what the particular contribution of SOD is and how this can make a difference. In particular, it describes how the core competencies of design can be useful for the next generation of Systems Thinking.

Part Two discusses in depth why the systemic turn is needed in design and how the normal way of practicing is breaking down in the face of the environmental crises, social issues and globalization. It goes through the structural, ethical and cultural challenges that the design field is exposed to. It also discusses the rapidly changing field of design when it diverges into new specialities and converges into new transdisciplinary modes of working and migrates into new fields.

We also briefly discuss the history of the systems field, why it has failed in design and what parts can be applied in design, as well as how these parts need to change to fit to the field of design. Further on we deliberate on what design can contribute to the systems field. We go through a very condensed history of systems thinking in design, and investigate designerly concepts relevant to systems thinking like the notion of composition, Gesamtkunstwerk and Gestalt. After introducing systemic design as the emerging pluralistic and flourishing field, for design we position SOD in that field.

If you want to gain a deeper understand of SOD and why Systems Thinking is important to contemporary design, then this part is for you.

Part Three: Practices and Methodology

This part reads like a textbook for SOD. It describes and discusses the practice, methodology, and praxeology of SOD.

It starts with looking at the limitations of methods and methodology, and proposes the use of praxeology as an alternative ways of describing how to do things. This is discussed in the light of concepts and models of SOD. Further on, we go through several core perspectives and concepts in SOD, including the problems of, for example, defining the boundaries of systems we work with. Realising that there is no clear and clean methodology to offer, we discuss Lindblom's idea of muddling through, and how we can improve sense making and sense sharing when designing for complex systems.

The bulk of this chapter is dedicated to praxeology with gigamapping at the centre. The discussion includes analyses and evaluation and how creativity fits into the picture. The SOD process is then explained as a complex layered and hybrid design process with an element of very rapid learning.

The elaborated discussion on praxeology of SOD ends with a down to earth summary and rules of thumbs for how to gigamap.

If you want to become an advanced practitioner of SOD, then this part is for you.

Part One

An Introduction to and Overview of SOD

Introduction to Part One

Complexity

There is no singular agreed definition of complexity. Complexity is often described through examples. (Mitchell, 2009, pp. 3–12). Looking at the attempts to describe the principles of complexity through examples and derived principles, one often gets the feeling that these principles are incomplete and skewed according to the author's knowledge domain. Mitchell, for example, emphasises the phenomena of interaction of unintelligent low-level entities that produce higher level intelligent phenomena by following simple rule sets[6]. Discussing complexity in social systems, as interaction between highly intelligent entities is obviously much harder to cope with. Mitchel describes complexity as numerous individuals following simple rules (p. 12). In social complexity, numerous interacting highly intelligent individuals follow numerous intricate and diverse written and unwritten rules and, in addition, they will break those rules at will. This book addresses that level of complexity. From this we can derive the following generic principles that should be applicable to all systems:

1. Complexity emerges from the interaction of many entities within a system and the interaction of the system and its parts with the environment.

2. Complexity is a feature of systems that operate over time.

3. Complex systems produce emergent phenomena. Their result is more and different than the sum of their parts.

4. Complex systems adapt to the environment and change over time.

5. Complex systems might challenge and change the rules they operate from. This is especially evident in social systems.

---

6. Melanie Mitchell is a highly acclaimed professor of computer science. Her emphasis on unintelligent entities following simple rulesets seem to be a result of the domain framing she operates within.

6. Complex systems challenge the orthodoxy of planning since while we plan the systems change.

Designing complex systems means designing in a new way, partly giving up control, partly leaving the planning / executing mode and work over time with systems as they change. It also means designing on multiple levels and catering for secondary effects, nudging and triggering more than imposing, and to let things grow and flourish rather than construct and harness.

Throughout this book, we will return to many aspects of the issues briefly touched upon here —at the beginning of a journey into a different mode of design, Systems Oriented Design.

Systems Thinking and Design: Changing Mindsets

Designers generally do not relate to systems approaches, which are seen as difficult, cumbersome, and alien. It is therefore necessary to address the mindset that is needed to understand the value of SOD.

When talking about systems, people often think that systems refer to something specific, something that is not directly related to them. However, the term "systems" is commonly used in everyday language (e.g., "the system doesn't work,", or "I don't understand the system") to address problems in large systems like the government. The term is also used to refer to smaller things, like computer systems, or other technological or organisational systems.

The everyday use of the term is as correct as any other more specific use. In fact, the everyday intuition behind the meaning of "systems" is a good starting point for understanding systems. Specifically, systems is a way to describe everything that is interconnected. Then you might ask, what is not connected in one way or another to something else? This means systems are everywhere, everything is part of systems; we are systems, and we are part of numerous systems, whether biological, technological, or societal. For now, we can base the further development of the arguments on this simple realization that systems perspectives are a universal way to look at the world. However, keep in mind that systems theories are many and diverse, and there exists a large body of research and academic publications. Though not entirely precise, we can say that Systems Thinking covers many, if not all, models, approaches, and theories in the systems field. If there were one sentence that embraces all the different approaches and theories to describe what Systems Thinking is, I would suggest:

Systems Thinking is the philosophy, art, and science of interconnectedness.

Therefore, SOD is not just another design specialization or sub-field of design. Rather, it is a perspective and mindset for an overarching worldview that helps us better understand how things are linked together. This worldview is applicable to any design task from large-scale, complex, societal and governmental change projects, to seemingly simple, small-scale objects.

We will return to these issues. However, I suggest five changes in mindset to start thinking like a systemic designer.

1. Systems are everywhere.

2. We must look beyond the object.

3. Systems are dynamic.

4. We must look at the Gestalt of the system.

5. Designing means working with systems.

The First Change in Mindset: Systems are Everywhere; Everything Can Be Interpreted in the Context of Systems.

While keeping in mind the everyday use of the term "systems," we need to think of systems not as something detached from us like when we say, "the system does not work" in reference to, for example, the waste management system, or the public health system. Instead, we need to think of systems as being everywhere, and understand that everything is part of numerous systems. We could start with looking at ourselves. We are embedded and interlinked in intricate biological systems, and our bodies are complex biological systems in their own right. We are part of social, technological, economic, and cultural systems. When buying food at a grocery store, we are interacting with hundreds of systems; each and every product is the result of complex systems of production, transportation, and trade. When we pay for our groceries, we engage with complex payment systems. Our interaction with the staff at the store is part of an institutionalized system of a working community. When leaving the store, we walk out into systems of climate regulation, interacting with architectural systems that shelter us from the outdoor weather systems. When we enter our car, we immediately become entangled within a large and immensely complex transportation system. As we drive, we engage with a road system, which is built according to guidelines and research conducted by a technological knowledge system, maintained by a renovation system, and regulated by a surveillance system.

This mind game of unraveling the complexity in seemingly mundane and simple everyday objects and processes inevitably trains our sensitivity for understanding systems.

The Second Change in Mindset: Look Beyond the Object; Move Attention from Object to Relations[7]

Following the first change in mindset, the second change is to look at objects merely as symptoms of systems. Every object is a result of intricate systemic processes. They play roles in complex systems, and they will decay and decompose as a result of systemic processes. For example, an apple will rot because of processes involving the apple being a biotope for a series of microorganisms. Looking beyond the object helps us understand them better, in terms of how they came to be, how they operate, what roles they play, how they are connected to other objects, and how they will end their existence. These are all necessary insights when designing for sustainable human use and interaction.

We have only scratched the surface with the example of our trip to the grocery store. Every single product that we buy can be deconstructed to expose complexity within layers of frameworks and perspectives. A bag of rice can be understood in terms of its geographical origin, its supply chain, the agricultural and biological technologies involved, as well as through the lens of cultural, historical, political, and economic perspectives, etc. We could go on like this forever. In the end, everything is somehow interlinked.

The switch from looking at the world as a composition of objects, to looking at the world as interlinked entities with constantly changing, dynamic relations is impossible to maintain in everyday life. Instead of perceiving the full depth of systems involved in a everyday process like cooking dinner we see only the surface. This implies that we see the object rather than the systemic relations and processes. For example, the rice that I bought from the grocery store for my dinner casserole will come together with many other ingredients in my cooking pot. Together, they will form a composition of flavours informed by cultural preferences and my abilities as a chef. My final casserole dish will contain dozens of ingredients from different regions of the world. These ingredients will also play different roles in the composition of the meal; some will be the main source of nutrition, while others will contribute to flavour. Each of the ingredients is the result or symptom of very complex production, transportation, and trade processes. When cooking, we utilize a large number of tools, technologies, and techniques, each with similarly complex histories of construction and production.

---

7. The phrase, "look beyond the object" is borrowed from John Thackara (1988).

As mentioned, we do not have the capacity to constantly keep track of these myriads of interrelations. Instead, we objectify things, and understand them as singularities instead of interlinked processes. Rather than understanding the world as a continuous web of relations, we look at it as an accumulation of objects. This helps us to look at one object at the time to save our brain capacity for activities other than navigating the complexity of everyday life. These objects are also called archetypes, clichés, and schemas. We are so good at objectifying the world that we do the same with processes, for example, cooking dinner. We talk effortlessly about it and talk about it like an object, the object of "cooking dinner". Everyday cooking is a common activity that only when one wants to learn more and get more advanced to expand one's repertoire, one dives into its intricate systemic interrelations, its cultural heritage, and its full repertoire of techniques and practices.

The Third Change in Mindset: Systems are Dynamic; What Seems Stable is Just Moving Very Slowly

The third change in mindset is about time. Again, our natural coping mechanism for dealing with complexity in the world is objectification, which results in simplification. Objectification is dependent on the assumption that the conceived objects are fairly stable. We assume that an apple from our grocery store will be the same apple tomorrow. In fact, this is a perceptual error because the apple has inevitably changed since yesterday. The apple is its own dynamic system. Interaction with the environment, temperature, and humidity leads to slight changes in its weight, skin, and internal composure. The changes are very small, but consistent. In addition, the apple must interact with a myriad of microorganisms that are feasting on it. Eventually it will turn into a rotten apple, and at some point, it will cease to be an apple altogether.

The same goes for every conceivable component in our universe. Mountains are only seemingly stable because they move very slowly. However, we cannot understand them without understanding their processes of composing and decomposing.

This constant shift is apparent in everything. With each motorized cycle of an electrical engine, it undergoes slight changes. Overtime, it will wear out, and eventually it will break down. However, the same process works the other way around. An apple blossom will transform into an apple, and an electrical engine will only become an electrical engine when its components are combined.

The exact moment that an apple stops being an apple and starts to become mere organic material is not possible to pinpoint. But this blurred boundary is connected to the perceived gestalt of the apple, more than its features and composition.

This leads to the fourth change in mindset.

The Fourth Change in Mindset: Look for the "Gestalt" of the System Rather than Understanding the Sum of its Fragments

Note that a car is conceived as a car regardless of whether it works or not. Even if it is broken, it is still a car for anybody who recognises the concept and schemata of a car. If we break it down into separate parts until it is unrecognizable as a car, we are left with a pile of parts that could potentially become a car. The exact point when it stops being a car is impossible to define. However, we are capable of recognising an incomplete car, even if it lacks major parts. In our mind, we have a picture of the whole and we fill in the missing pieces. This is known as the phenomenon of Gestalt.

"Gestalt" is a German word that is loosely translated to English as "to shape, figure, or form". The notion of Gestalt is central in Gestalt psychology, which deals with the active perception process that combines parts, structures, and fragments into a whole based on the relationship between these parts. Seeing an overall shape or Gestalt of a system is an active perceptual process of visual thinking and interpretation. We can discuss the delimitation between perceiving systems as entities in an external world or as perceived representations. However, thinking and perception are interlinked and inseparable (Arnheim, 1969). We will return to this discussion later. For now, since Gestalt is a constructed perception, we will discuss it as representation and interpretation.

So, independent of its functionality, the components combine to become a whole that is different from its parts. Despite the fact that we know a car is a very complex technological system, we are able to recognise it even from a simple line drawing. The phenomenon of Gestalt is well known in design, but it is largely ignored in Systems Thinking. Systems are mostly analysed from the accumulated functionality of their parts, through for example modelling and simulation. Less frequently, they are seen as a whole, as a Gestalt. Exceptions are very well-established archetypical systems such as the abovementioned car.

It is a misunderstanding that we need to know all the parts of a system in order to be accountable for it. We can never have a total overview, but we can get a sense of the Gestalt of a system instead of striving for a full account of all its details and interconnectedness. This approach has several advantages and some weaknesses. For now, it is sufficient to point out the following:

- Looking at the whole Gestalt of the system(s) at hand maintains an overview perspective. It avoids the reductive approach of many other systems approaches where systems are reduced to a limited amount of elements and relations.

- Looking at the whole of a system allows the seamless integration of categorically different data types qualitative, quantitative graphics, and diagrams, as well as different systems models can be compiled in the same Gigamap and related.

- This approach encourages a view of the systems as designed artefacts, which allows for seamless transition between understanding systems, describing them, and designing them.

- This perspective makes it easy to share conceptions of systems through "sense-sharing"[8].

These points are quite difficult to grasp in a summary, and we will return to them in depth later. For now, a short example should be sufficient to grasp the idea:

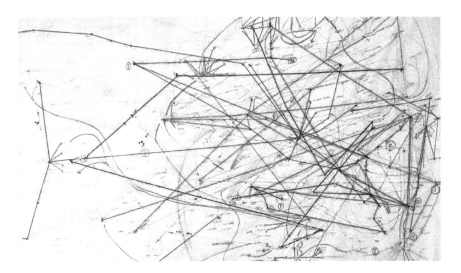

Figure 2: Mapping out relations for a task of building social housing on the Chalmers Campus, Gothenburg (From a 2015 SOD workshop at Chalmers School of Architecture, created by students Karin Backlund, Maxwell Kevin Otieno, and Evelina Peterson).

Figure 2 shows a type of map that is central in the methodology of SOD a Gigamap. This is a particular Gigamap compared to the one in *Figure 3*, which is

---

8. The concept of Sense Sharing will be treated in part Three.

orderly and easier to access. The first map is messier, tentative, chaotic and less accessible for outsiders. Yet it communicates a particular sense of this system. It is chosen to demonstrate the argument of looking at the whole Gestalt of a system.

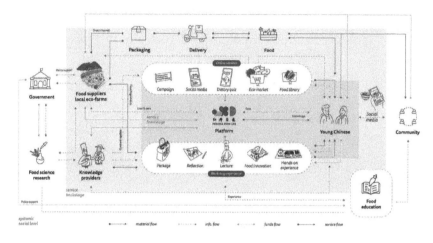

Figure 3: Gigamap of a service system. Panacea Food Lab. Designing for change of food culture among young Chinese (Zijun Lin, 2020).

A Gigamap is a very extensive map that includes large amounts of information across different scales and categories. The aim is for it to function as a rich picture, a collaborative device, a memory enhancer, and a learning device when designing for very complex situations.

The Gigamap in *Figure 2* shows several of the above-mentioned changes in mindset. This particular gigamapping process started with a mapping of specific entities or objects, similar to a mind-map but less hierarchical. The case was a proposal for an intervention in the campus of the Chalmers Technical University in Gothenburg, developed by students of Chalmers Architecture. The entities that were defined in the process were linked together by drawing lines that represent the network of relations that exist between them. From the start, the objects were named and written in relatively small text, with emphasis being put on the relations instead. This first object-oriented network map was then covered with a layer of transparent foil to add additional information. In this case the information was an in-depth exploration of the relations and the whole systemic network. Further analyses of existing relations then led to a new layer of relations marked by colour-coded threads, indicating a move from object-oriented to relation-oriented design. At this stage, the map is messy and overloaded with information. It can no longer be read as singular elements and their interconnections, but instead requires a holistic reading of the picture or figure of the system, the

Gestalt. The map is a process tool and not meant for communication beyond the people who produced it. For them, the map is comprehensible also on a detailed level. But the point is that at this stage, the map helps them share a sense of the Gestalt of the system, meaning its structure and shape, its level of complexity, and other such overarching features.

The Fifth Change in Mindset: Designing Means Working with Systems; Designing is Potentially the Best Way of Dealing with Systems

An awareness of the notion of Gestalt leads to the realization that our conceptions of systems is a construction, or rather, a design[9]. We actively create the Gestalt of the system we work with through the design process. We need to change our minds to realize that Systems Thinking is a form of design, and that design is inherently systemic (Nelson & Stolterman, 2012, 74). Design is, whether consciously or not, always dealing with systems change. Unfortunately, design education at large and the design profession do not sufficiently advocate this view. As such, design work has often failed. Failing, in this case, means a failure to meet the project goals because insufficient attention was given to the circumstances, conditions, and environment (the systems) surrounding the problem; failing also refers to the issue of generating new problems elsewhere in the system during the process of solving the original problem. Therefore, we need to develop a better sensibility for systems in design. This needs to be fully integrated into the design process so that there is a natural flow in a process that is unified, rather than adding a component to the design that feels alien and is disruptive to the design process.

Systems Approaches in Design

Systems approaches have been around in design for a long time, but it is only through the emergent movement of *systemic design* that it has developed in a way that combines systems theories with design practice. Systemic design is a field with many different approaches. It forms the surrounding environment of SOD.

In the academic context, many design researchers have historically been aware of Systems Thinking. Systems approaches in design have been suggested by Alexander, Banathy, Buchanan, Fuller, Rittel, Nelson, Rowland, Bistagnino

---

9. We will dive deeper into the discussions of whether systems are real world phenomena or mental constructs for interpreting the world in Part Two.

(developing Systmeic Design since 2000), Ranulf Glanville, Wolgang Jonas and others (Alexander, 1964; Banathy, 1997; Bistagnino & Campagnaro, 2014; Buchanan, 2001; Cross & Cross, 1996; Fuller & Snyder, 1969; Ranulph Glanville, 1994; Jonas, 1996; H. G. Nelson & Stolterman, 2012a; Rittel, 1972; Rowland, 1999). Yet, insight into Systems Thinking is fragmented, and historically there has been little impact on design practice. Systems approaches were often regarded as detached from design, as a specialized knowledge field, as opposed to the overarching umbrella they are meant to be. In design practice, systems approaches were often seen as too technical or too rigid to be used in a design process. Discussions around Systems Thinking in design have mainly been geared towards theoretical discourse and normative prescriptions for design practice; they have largely failed to demonstrate, disseminate, and analyse the application of an integrated systemic design methodology. There is a step between learning Systems Thinking and being able to implement it in design work. One needs deep insight, experience, skills, and competencies gained from practicing systemic design. Systems theories and models are hard to apply directly and unchanged into the design process. Until recently, systems approaches have been imported into the design domain, rather than assimilated. This is probably the main cause for its lack of impact.

Importing views and methods alien and disruptive to the design process does not work without frictions because designing is a visual and cognitive process where creative flow and synthesis is more at stake than in most other planning activities comparable to design. Creative practices are convoluted processes that are easily disrupted. Instead of importing external systems views, if we look at design as a potentially systemic practice, we can reinforce the "systemness" of design[10]. Through this, we can achieve a systemic design approach that originates from, and is seamlessly integrated with design. With this fundament in place, we can relate to and be inspired by the rich world of existing approaches to systems and their many theories and models. The emergence of systemic design is not so much about integrating external systems theories into design, as has been tried before. It is more about nurturing the inherently systemic practices of design and to integrating existing theories into design by re-interpreting them and modifying them so that they become useful without interrupting the design process. Instead of submitting to one or the other orthodoxy of systems theories, this results in a pluralism of theories and methods in design, and a flourishing field of real world practices[11]. This means that despite the above-mentioned limitations, today's designers do have a very good starting point. They are especially well-suited to

---

10. Harold Nelson emphasises the inherent systemic nature of design (H. G. Nelson & Stolterman, 2012a).

11. A pragmatic, eclectic and critical application of multiple systems theories and approaches is propagated in Critical Systems Theories and well elaborated by Gerald Midgley (Midgley, 2000)

cope with the complexity of the real world: they are trained to analyse and synthesise complex interlinked problems through designing; to shape, envision, and ideate solutions from complex and fuzzy starting points. Designers are creative people trained to come up with new solutions to difficult design problems. In addition, there are several concepts from art and design that are particularly useful when developing a systemic design practice. Amongst these we already mentioned the holistic approach and the idea of the Gestalt. We can add aesthetic form-giving that seeks the balancing of numerous requirements, and excellent communication skills through sketching and visualization and not least, the way designers think when they design. (Rowe, 1987)

Towards Systemic Design

The notion of design has moved from simple problem-solving and designing singular artefacts to designing for complex interactions, services, and social systems. Such systems are made out of numerous actors, relations, and operations. One could say that design has moved from problem-solving to designing for situations. At the same time, Design Thinking [12] has become accepted as an alternative approach in business and leadership for dealing with complex problems and developing innovative concepts with a better understanding of the users (Brown, 2008; Brown & Katz, 2009; Liedtka & Ogilvie, 2011; Lockwood, 2010; Martin, 2009a; Oster, 2008). This is both a divergent and convergent move of design and it opens up a lot of opportunities. Yet there are several shortcomings in this, which are addressed by systemic design.

The valuable feature of Design Thinking is its ability to widen the scope of a design inquiry to include human aspects and to derive innovative user-oriented solutions from a complex outset. This seems related to Systems Thinking. However, in the migration of the designer's inherent everyday activity we might call design thinking from the realm of design to business and management, something has been lost. Design thinking became detached from design practice, the skills, experience, and competencies that designers accumulate over long training and years of practice. This is what makes up design thinking as it was described by the design scholars who defined it (Buchanan, 1992; Cross, 2011; Goldschmidt, 1994; Kimbell, 2009; Lockwood, 2010; H. Nelson, 1994; Rowe, 1987). Design thinking is closely related to Reflexive Practice (Schön, 1982) and Research by (through) Design (Frayling, 1993; Sevaldson, 2010), which are both based on an intimate relationship between the acts of reflecting and designing.

---

12. I chose to use capital letters for Design Thinking as a proposed method for general use and small letters for the more undefined and generic use of design thinking as an integral part of the process of designing.

Design practice contains both a manual craft component like drawing skills and aesthetic judgment, as well as cognitive skills for planning, organizing, analysing, innovating, engaging and meta-reflecting. It is hard to draw an exact line between the art, the craft, and the cognition of design. Designing is not merely a craft, but it is also a particular mode of thinking and investigating the world how it is and how it ought to be. Visualisation is central in this activity. This reflective component of designing is the real design thinking.

Current design practices, including the inherent, real design thinking, and the type of branded Design Thinking, which has migrated to other areas, are not well-grounded to address high-level complexity. Furthermore, neither design practice nor design thinking uses visualisation extensively and sufficiently as a process tool to embrace complexity. In some new design fields like service design, visualisation has taken steps forward, but their scope is still too narrow to grasp more of the system, its environment, and landscape. Therefore, chances for radical change remain undiscovered, and deep systemic innovations tend to be absent. All these practices within and outside of the design field need to widen their scope to deal with interrelated issues in a more responsible way. They need to increase the amount of information and perspectives that are reviewed and involved. This means coupling vast amounts of data, information, insights, and knowledge with design and creative processes. In fact, it means organising and even creating this knowledge through design.

Regarding the interdisciplinary nature of design, there is not one particular approach in Systems Thinking that can fully meet the needs present in design, nor can systems approaches be successfully integrated into design "as is" without alteration and further development (as mentioned earlier). Systems Thinking cannot migrate into design "uncontaminated". This indicates a transformation not only of design, but also of Systems Thinking, which needs design. It is ultimately the synthesis of design and Systems Thinking that will change both, and generate something new.

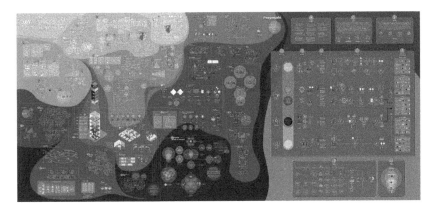

Figure 4: Last iteration of Gigamap of the organisational structure, culture and operation of a design company in Oslo (Angel Lamar, 2019).

We need to find a mode of Systems Thinking that is immediately accessible for designers, one that breaks the methodological constraints and shortcomings of particular systems approaches. Designers must be allowed to operate freely, yet critically, in the space between design and systems approaches. The preconditions for developing systemic design requires that a systems approach for designers be generative rather than purely descriptive. As well, it should engage the designer's skills and integrate Systems Thinking as a design process. Systems Thinking in design must function as a mode of design for dealing with super-complexity a methodology that can integrate large amounts of diverse information in order to facilitate the design of holistic overviews. Finally, Systems Thinking in design must work not only analytically, but also as a creative tool.

This leads to a systems approach that is slightly, un-disciplinary (H. Nelson, 1994), "anarchistic" [13] and adaptive, challenging preconceptions, models, orthodoxies, and rules. Consequently, we frequently redesign techniques and methodologies, and encourage a free-styling practice. In SOD, the most central tool is the Gigamap, as mentioned above. For now, it is enough to know that gigamapping simply means very large mapping. The simple idea is that when dealing with complexity, one has to map out as much of the situation at hand as possible, mixing and integrating different kinds of data and information. The mapping should be done in ways that are suited for the people involved. Often this is done in participatory design sessions with stakeholders often non-designers. In

---

13. I use this term in the sense Feyerabend uses it, as methodology that is highly adaptive and case sensitive and freed from orthodoxies. (Feyerabend, 1975)

such cases, the mapping needs to be simple, hands-on, and accessible for all involved.

Figure 5: The first Gigamap made by a group of students in collaboration with a neurologist, learning the basics of neuroplasticity (Valeria Gaitan, Berit Killingbergtrø Havåg, Sven Håkon Voldum, 2013).

Gigamapping is based on this free-styling practice, meaning there are no given prescriptions; the process of designing the Gigamap is an integrated part of understanding the system and the challenges at hand. Since the Gigamap provides a designerly way to investigate and design for complex systems, the Gigamap has crystalized as an enduring element in SOD.

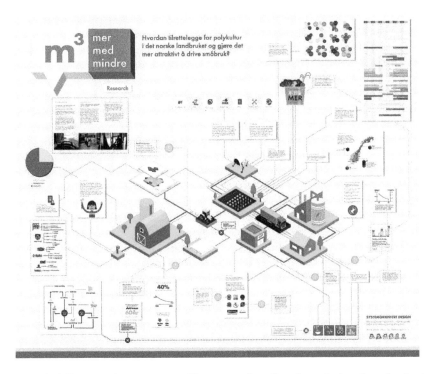

Figure 6: A Gigamap depicting a possible system of small-scale agricultural production in Norway (Group M3, GK6, Oslo School of Architecture and Design, 2018).

Integrating design with systems thinking implies the merging of an action-oriented, critical, and dialogic systems perspective with design thinking and design practice. The tension between these aspects are mapped out in *Figure 7* showing four poles between which we blend design and systems. The four poles are:

- Design practice: the activity of shaping the artefact; skills and competencies; mindset and sensibility.

- Design thinking: the reflection in design action, involvement, negotiation, and envisioning.

- Systems thinking: the reading of the world as not only entities, but also how they are related.

- Systems practice: intervening into and changing the systems; skills and competencies; mindset and sensibility.

Between these four poles, there is a field of possibilities for different versions of systemic design to flourish.

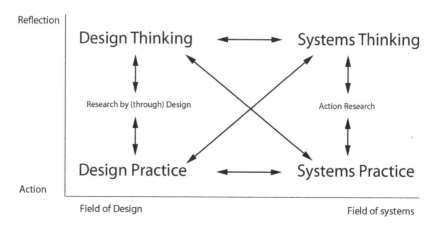

Figure 7: A field of possibilities for systemic design (Birger Sevaldson, 2013).

Systems Oriented Design: An Overview

This section establishes the necessary overview for people who want to start practising Systems Oriented Design (SOD).

What is SOD?

Systems Oriented Design is a design methodology that is geared towards complex problems. It is based on modern design methods and design thinking and underpinned with modern systems theory and systems practice. SOD seeks to offer a smooth amalgam between design and systems. SOD is mainly a mindset with a few tools. SOD is first of all a design practice, and it is defined as a methodology without fixed methods and a praxeology, describing how to practice SOD.

SOD does not provide an extensive clearly defined tool chest and prescriptions, templates, etc. on how to use these tools. The reason is that complex real-life cases vary to such a degree that standardised and hard framed processes will stand in the way of developing a deep understanding of the situation at hand. Tool chests and their use based on fixed procedures introduce a strong bias and create blind spots. Therefore, I prefer a looser framework based on a small selection of flexible adaptive tools, a mindset, and a well-developed praxeology.

In the centre is gigamapping, a powerful flexible and inclusive tool that serves as a device to explore and develop relations across fields, silos, boundaries, and disciplines, and across scales, groups of people, as well as to support dialogues in teams. Gigamapping is open to include all kinds of data representations, illustrations, models, and perspectives.

In addition, there are some supporting analytical tool, to help the thought process needed to understand and evaluate systems change.

However, since SOD is open ended and inclusive, serving as a frame for the implementation of multiple perspectives, it can be combined with other approaches, for example, systems models from Systems Dynamics or Cybernetics, or, for example, the Systemic Design Tool Kit. (Nahman & ShiftN, n.d.)

SOD in the Field of Possibilities

SOD is one suggested approach in the larger pluralistic field of Systemic Design. It might be one of the most "designerly" approaches, and it is based on, but not limited to advanced design, or Design with a capital "D," meaning the design profession as developed and nurtured over the years at the different types of design schools. Therefore, the professional designer, who possesses a set of skills and competencies developed over time, is central to discussions on design within the framework of SOD. However, this does not exclude participatory design, and non-designers doing design work (general design) in a collaborative project. Also, it does not exclude non-designers from practicing SOD fully or in parts. In particular, this book might be useful for those professional designers emerging from other educational programs and fields, and with backgrounds other than design education. Emphasising Design with a capital "D" simply means that designers skills and mindsets, like form-giving and designerly reflection in action are central to the development of SOD, and have been important aspects of the core of SOD. This places SOD near the design practice pole in the field of possibilities (*Figure 8*). We will elaborate on this in Part Two and Three.

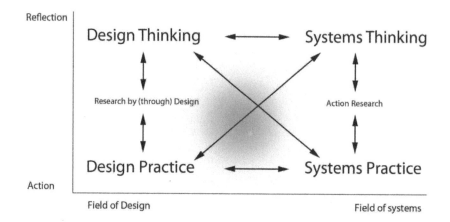

Figure 8: Here is the Field of Possibilities again, but this time with the placement of SOD in that field. SOD is positioned a little bit off centre towards the corner of Design Practice. Its boundaries are blurry and could be stretched even more into the other fields (Birger Sevaldson, 2013).

SOD emerged through a meta-design-process that has been running for years. This process has not, and hopefully never will be, concluded. It emerged from experimental design practice and was crystallised through its main concept of gigamapping. This means that things might change after this book.

To document and disseminate this we have an extensive website at: www.systemsorienteddesign.net, which functions as a living document where new ideas and concepts are continually presented.

SOD is Open Source

From its very beginnings in 2005-2006, the techniques and methodology of SOD were never thought to be precise descriptions for defined processes. On the contrary, it was emphasized that each process needs its own variation. Process design is an integrated part of any SOD project. In that sense, SOD is a "methodology without method." This means that we eagerly discuss and describe how we do things, developing the methodology, yet we are reluctant to form fixed prescriptions or methods. A method is a prescription that would guarantee the same result each time. A recipe for baking a cake is such a prescription. This does obviously not apply when working with complex living systems that might change while we plan.

30

Another aspect is that research into SOD has always been shared within the academic design research community and made accessible on the web for others to build on. This means that this methodology is a living body of knowledge and that it will develop and change over time. As an open-sourced methodology, you are welcome to use and change any part of it as you see fit. We ask that you reference the SOD page with a "based on SOD" note and respect what we call the "kernel" of SOD, as presented below.

The Kernel of SOD

The core of SOD represents the values and perspectives that determine if a project can be deemed a SOD project. These are mere guidelines and will not be policed in any way. However, we ask that you respect and consider them as the kernel of SOD.

If your project corresponds to all or most of the kernel parameters, we welcome you to reference it as a SOD project, and we would appreciate you sending us a reference to the project and / or related material to publish on the website. If the project does not correspond to most of the kernel parameters, however, we kindly ask you not to reference it as a SOD project. If the project is within the field of Systems Thinking in design, but does not commit to the kernel of SOD, then we suggest that you refer to the project as a Systemic Design project. If your project is mostly on the systems side and does not contain substantial elements of designerly approaches, design thinking, and / or design practice, then we suggest that you refer to the project as a systems engineering project, a systemic development project, or something similar.

The "kernel" of SOD is characterized by the following attributes:

1. Practicing a designerly way of understanding and creating systems.

2. Applying central SOD techniques, including gigamapping.

3. Addressing complex problems using multiple perspectives.

4. Emphasising relations and interconnections.

5. Understanding soft, as well as hard, system approaches.

6. Applying multiple perspectives, stakeholder perspectives, micro, meso, and macro perspectives[14]. Working with problem-fields, problem-networks, and situations, rather than singular problems.

7. Taking responsibility for intended and unintended consequences of the design.

8. Representing affected bystanders, as well as non-human actors.

9. Facilitating participatory processes with stakeholders, experts, and all relevant organisations and individuals.

10. Considering ethics: SOD is about improving things.

---

14. See also the four perspectives. Bird Frog, Telescope Microscope in Part Three (*Figure 94*)

Figure 9: Very early example of Gigamap of fields, thematics, and problematiques in a conceptual project for re-forestation (Sturla Godøy, 2006).

Systems Oriented DESIGN

SOD is first and foremost, DESIGN. It is not another systems model, or yet another prescriptive design method. It is a methodology that uses design as the main approach to thinking about systems. SOD is first of all based on practice and skills. It suggests a development of designer skills and designerly ways of thinking that enables one to be better prepared to work with super-complexity. A central principle in SOD is the use of multiple information sets, models, theories, and approaches. Complex issues are often never fully understood, but we might have a

33

chance to understand them sufficiently if we dare to intervene, to learn from how the system reacts to our interventions, and continue to iterate based on those learnings. Of course, complex issues are never sufficiently understood through just one singular perspective or model. Even a multi perspective model rarely provides definitive answers, but it does allow for assumptions to be triangulated, balanced, and negotiated between the different explanatory models and world views. Although uncertainty can never be overcome, this rich approach based on multiple perspectives harnesses skills that allow us to navigate and design *within* a state of uncertainty. Central to the development of these skills is the need to train our systemic sensibility the skill to perceive the world as systems composed of relations, flows, and dynamic forces, rather than as static objects. Design skills and systemic sensibility are related to the changes in mindset described above, but we are now going to dive deeper into what is needed for a professional practice in systemic design. I will briefly highlight some of these key skills and sensibilities:

Cope with More: Visualize!

Training SOD as a set of skills begins with developing the ability to cope with much larger amounts of information. The practicing designer has an inherent ability to work with complexity, but this ability can be pushed much further through training. The best means to achieve this is through our visualisation skills. Visualization is simply the best way to understand complex issues, and there is no doubt that visualizations play a central role to any planning process. It is not necessary to be a trained designer to do this; however, designers have an advantage in visual reasoning and thinking.

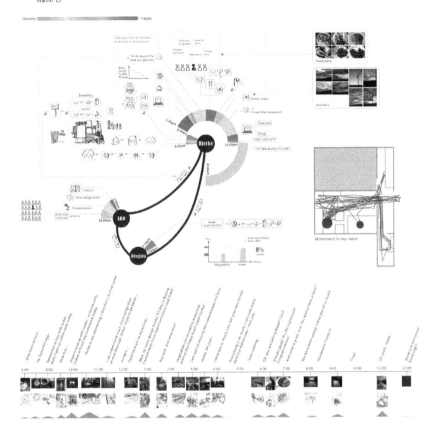

Figure 10: To train systemic sensibility and mapping skills, as well as the sense for details and looking beyond what is obvious, we use an exercise called "Mapping Me". The task is to map out the course of one day in great detail (Wanxi Li, Oslo School of Architecture and Design, SOD, 2011).

Design Relations

The systemic designer needs to train his or her ability to uncover, register, understand, and design with the interconnections between entities, rather than with the entities themselves. This implies the need to understand the dynamics of the system, to find bottlenecks, and to design solutions that could better the flow between entities, but only to such a degree that it does not cause problems elsewhere in the system (see *Figure 11*).

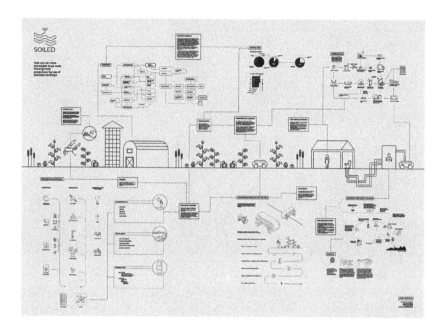

Figure 11: Production system of a Norwegian large-scale farm, involving different sub-systems like information technology for precision farming and supra systems of politically induced subsidies and delivering and refinement systems. The elements in the system can to a large degree be understood as stock and flows of materials like grain, milk, vegetables, fertiliser etc. (Group: Large Scale Farming, GK6, AHO 2020).

Imagine designing a new product with a circular economy in mind. This implies that the designer takes responsibility for the whole process, all material systems, the life cycle and the recycling. Such a complex product life can be understood as flows of materials, energy, and application of processes in a system where there are flows and buffers, often called stocks. In such systems, we find bottlenecks and missing interconnections that reduce the systems performance seen form a holistic perspective. Think of our road system to understand the systemic concepts of flows, stock and bottlenecks.

Figure 12: A traffic system consists of flows of cars and other moving elements and regulators like traffic lights and regulations. We can think of the stocks being parking lots and garages. But also congestion functions as stocks in the system (Photo David McKelvey 2012, Creative Commons[15]).

Building more roads in a traffic system does not necessarily solve the problem of congestion, since congestions are central regulators in the system. Alternatively, the designer can regulate flows by reducing or increasing them through design interventions.

Perhaps more importantly, the designer can also design new relations. Many of our problems are caused by a lack of relations. We are organized in detached silos, departments, sciences, and professions. Very often problems are left to grow because of a lack of communication between silos. However, communication is only one base level where there is potential for new links to be designed. In fact, there is great potential in designing a society where consequences are interlinked. A toll road system, for example, is already an example of such designed systems where consequences are at least partly distributed directly; if you choose to drive your car to the city, you will have to pay for your contribution to pollution. This kind of linkage between different actions and consequences can be applied to limitless occasions.

---

15. https://www.flickr.com/photos/dgmckelvey/6907752302

Look Ahead

As systemic designers, we need to look ahead to take responsibility for potential future implications of our actions. This is similar to how a chess player must look ahead to anticipate the consequences of his or her moves and the opponent's reactions. When complex positions are being evaluated, advanced chess players generally tend to look for patterns, and act intuitively based on their vast experience. A quote by British astrophysicist, Martin Reece, explains this in the context of science and its limitations:

> The physicist is like someone who's watching people playing chess and, after watching a few games, he may have worked out what the moves in the game are. But understanding the rules is just a trivial preliminary on the long route from being a novice to being a grand master. So even if we understand all the laws of physics, then exploring their consequences in the everyday world where complex structures can exist is a far more daunting task, and that's an inexhaustible one I'm sure. (Wolpert & Richards, 1988, 37).

This skill to playing the chess game of systemic design is especially important if we want to be able to search for and identify unwanted effects of the systems we design.

Design Synergies

Furthermore, we also need to train our ability to design for synergies. This means that we need to take good care of our client's interest, as well as the interest of users, customers, stakeholders, environment, and the society at large. If diverging interests cannot be coupled by finding the synergies between them, any sort of attempt at alignment will be an exhausting act that is likely doomed to fail. It is the ultimate task of SOD to hunt down the synergies between different interests to create new strategic opportunities, and design systems interventions that benefit different receivers. One example of aligning the need for ecologically sound solutions is found in the strategy of Product Service Systems (Manzini, Vezzoli, & Clark, 2001; Morelli, 2002; Vezzoli & Manzini, 2008). By turning products into services, the objective interests are aligned. For example, a company's objective interests in planning for obsolescence[16] is removed when the product is leased out as a service instead a printer made for the home market is planned to last only a limited amount of time to guarantee sale of ever new models of printers; a leased out printer, however, should last as long as possible.

---

16. Planned Obsolescence is an industrial design strategy to artificially limit a products' lifetime. The most famous example is the set 1000-hour life span of incandescence light bulbs, which is a result of an agreement between manufacturers worldwide.

Design for Unfinishedness

Traditionally, designers tend to focus on the result, or the object. New trends in design, like software design and service design, have shifted the attention from objects to experiences, interactions, narratives and versioning, or development over time. Although our most stable designs, such as roads and buildings, are designed as finished products, most of them are actually still going through processes of redesign. Buildings are renovated, their interior much more frequently than their exterior. The systems theorist, Stewart Brand, wrote about this process of change in our built environment. *Figure 13* shows his famous diagram of building's shearing layers explaining the different pace of the change taking place when buildings are renovated to adjust them to new use (Brand, 1994).

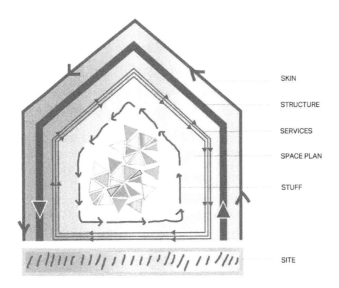

SKIN

STRUCTURE

SERVICES

SPACE PLAN

STUFF

SITE

Figure 13: Stuart Brand describes the changes taking place in buildings over time as shearing layers. The line font indicates degrees of stability, thick lines indicating more stable material subsystems than thin lines (Diagram interpreted by Palak Dudani, 2021).

Less Models, More Fields

The sciences dealing with the complex interconnections in the world are called systems sciences, Systems Thinking, and systems practices. There are a number of different approaches, all with their own theories, worldviews, and models.

Typically, SOD is less concerned with formalisms of systems models like System Dynamics, where defining causalities, positive and negative feedback loops, hierarchies, and boundaries are central. Instead, SOD is more concerned with looking at the big picture, the landscape, the fields, and the environment of the system, as well as the relations and patterns of interactions where design practice is more activated. Following strict rules for building models of systems has a clear limitation. SOD is concerned with looking beyond what the models can grasp, yet including them where they make sense not only to describe systems but for systems change. It is geared towards looking at as many interrelations as possible, working with a "field-feel" or "field-intuition". SOD looks "beyond the object," and perceives the object as a "symptom" or "outcrop" of big interwoven fields of systemic interrelations. SOD is a free designerly approach to systems which allows for finding or constructing interrelations between seemingly disconnected categories.

Learn Very Fast

Each design project is to a certain degree unique, more so the more complex it is. Therefore, for each design case, the phenomena at hand is deeply and widely researched. It often starts with a learning process that has a steep learning curve, deemed as the Very Fast Learning Process. Instead of starting with reading up on the theme, this process begins with visualisation: large Gigamaps are used for mapping out and externalize the pre-existing knowledge and assumptions of the designer and the team. When working alone, this process clarifies and makes explicit what you already know. When working in teams, you share and learn from each other to identify where different expertise lie in the team, uncovering strengths and weaknesses. This needs to be done as in-depth as time allows. The map helps to guide the first round of reading up and increasing knowledge about the case. Next, the maps are reinterpreted and fleshed out together with stakeholders. This approach helps to find the gaps on the map where further research is needed. This could include secondary research or interviews with experts. The accumulation of knowledge is guided by the overall picture generated by the first mapping. This is what makes the learning process very efficient. The gaps are zoomed in on for further research, for building up expert networks, and for defining potential interventions points[17]. All findings and insights in the rapid learning process are mapped and visualized, and it is meant to be shared and kept in play during the process. This helps to internalize large amounts of information. Guiding research by gigamapping, externalizing pre-existing knowledge, and

17. The tool we use for this is called ZIP-analyses. We will return to this later.

internalizing new knowledge are the principles of the Very Rapid Learning Process.

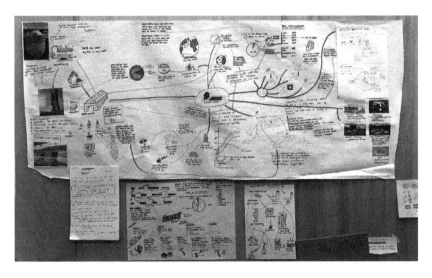

Figure 14: Early-process Gigamap of large-scale farming. This map resulted on a later stage in the Gigamap in Figure 11 (Large Scale Farming group, GK6, AHO, 2020).

Use Your Power

Designers are in a creative profession that involves products and services, normally putting them in an especially good position in the systems they are working within. This means that designers have the power to influence decision-making. Although other organisational roles might have greater decision-making power, and a design process normally involves many different experts and stakeholders, designers, together with engineers, belong to a relative small group that specializes in innovation and change. This gives us a voice we can use to induce change. The skills of visualization are especially valuable to communicate proposals for change. This power is obviously limited and often results in seemingly small changes. However, even small changes might count. If we can make a mass-produced product slightly more sustainable, we might have achieved more to reduce the CO_2 footprint than a private person, sorting garbage throughout a whole life time.

Worldview

For the designer, a systems approach implies a shift in positions and self-perception. The old worldview that was common amongst designers was having as much control as possible when creating ideal solutions solving fairly well-defined problems: the Ideal Design [18]. However, in their work as professionals, all designers are confronted with the need to interact, collaborate, and negotiate. Compromises have to be made and changes will be made to the Ideal Design, making it not so ideal anymore. This creates a disharmony between the idea of the Ideal Design, and what is possible when coping with the system. Although many designers have partly left this ideal, it still plays a defining role. The ideal design solution is perfect, complete, and finite; any change would violate this completeness. As an example, the dream of many young designers is to create a "classic," an artefact that would survive changes in fashion and cultures over time. The idea of the Ideal Design is based on an elitist view of aesthetics. This implies that one needs a certain type of training and sense of refinement to understand and appreciate a high-quality design object. It is obviously true that training can sharpen our senses and that additional knowledge can increase our appreciation of artefacts. Recognizing subtle references to historical predecessors in a piece of art is enjoyable. However, this joy is not solely just because one discovered some hidden rules in the game, but also because of self-confirmation as a knowledgeable individual. Not everybody knows their art history. This sets the observer apart from the "uneducated masses". But these are merely social systems playing out through design objects. Most art and design lovers fail to understand the systems they are part of and how they work economically, socially, and psychologically. The value of the design objects is the cultural agreements, which are partly based on the fit with cultural context and the rareness of the objects rather than some ideal quality. Though the products might be mass-produced, the reinforcements of the designer are economic compensation and eventual recognition in the design world. The ideal design objects have the role of separation objects, objects that demarcate between the accepted and the non-accepted. These objects are therefore tools of exclusiveness playing a role in social systems. Ironically, this idea of exclusivity and individuality has migrated even into mainstream mass production. In that realm, when analysed systemically, there appears to be a false theatre of uniform mass consumption portrayed as individualism.

In contrast to these ideal worlds of design, understanding the social systems open up a way to involve and engage that might bridge the gap between desire and sustainability, between refinement and solidarity, between individual needs and

---

18. The idea of the ideal design or form is discussed by Peter Bloch in a more advanced manner than presented here. The questioning of this idea is still relevant (Bloch, 1995).

the social, as well as between doing the right thing and making profits. The interesting thing is that this way may open up new possibilities. By recreating and reconnecting these contradictions, new ways of acting within and changing the social system might appear.

It is important to emphasise that engagement implies interaction with both individuals and larger socio-technological systems. This causes the challenges in design to explode. Singular problems become problem fields or problematiques. Knowledge fields, as well as cross and interdisciplinarity increase dramatically. There is no easy way to negotiate and navigate taking on such levels of complexity, but it has a lot of potential and it can be done gradually. Becoming a Systems Oriented Designer implies a shift away from the Ideal Design as separation objects towards using design as a way of linking the world together, as dialogic tools, as tools for organisations, democracy and liberation towards the design of engagement objects.

This shift implies moving from the ideas of the complete, perfect, and finite design output to a dynamic idea of design as imperfect redesign and versioning; from an elitist design culture that grants full control to the designer towards the idea of shared control and co-design within a multi-social and systemic design culture. It also implies agency for beings that cannot represent themselves, and for our planet at large. It forces us to move from elitist separation to empathetic involvement.

While the above can be seen as general criteria for good design and design ethics, their realization is not enough. Inescapably, they lead away from singular design problems towards a higher degree of complexity. This implies a need to recognise that many if not most design problems are wicked problems (Buchanan, 1992; Rittel & Webber, 1973). Seemingly simple problems are only simple because they are seen in isolation. We ignore the systems beyond and behind them, and we ignore the life cycles they are part of. Wicked problems are escaping problem descriptions; they are messy, and there is no way to understand them fully before trying to solve them. We will return to this theme later. One could question if they are problems in the normal sense of the word at all. They escape the problem definition because they are about envisioning new states that were not imagined before. It involves recognising that the ground or starting point of a process is constantly changing. While we plan, the reality we plan for changes rapidly. In addition, what seems to be the problem at first glance might not be the real issue. It might just be a symptom of deeper systemic processes. Solving the symptom could make things worse. In addition, when investigating and involving, our perspectives change. Involvement implies one becoming part of the system that is at stake. This means that the system has changed through our involvement and will change again when the involvement ends. Checkland uses this difference between an old static way of defining problems and a new dynamic way of coping with issues to distinguish between hard and soft Systems Thinking (Checkland, 2000 p.189; Lane, 2000). Denis Loveridge goes further to suggest that these be called situations rather than problems (2009). While the notion of a problem implies that it can be solved with a singular response, a situation moves away from solutioning to imply a state of change, one that can change again in the future. Using the term situation resists the reductionism that lies in the notion of the problem. This challenges the role of the designer as a "problem solver."

Furthermore, the designer's control is challenged by the realization that the world is full of emergent and self-organising systems. This has become more obvious when looking at internet-based social networks, not only in terms of how they are designed, but how they develop or not, beyond the designer's control.

Self-organisation also involves issues of community, politics, and democratic development, which are necessary to address when working with complex systemic problems. The self-organising aspects of human activity systems is obvious in social internet networking, but it is also apparent in everyday life within offices, schools, politics, traffic, stock markets, and any other social constellation. The traditional intention of designers to achieve full control appears undemocratic and unrealistic when seen from these perspectives. In worst cases, implementing more control can be counterproductive towards the needs for self-organizsation, and we end up with less efficient and less agile organisations (Slavin, 2016)[19]. Instead of inducing top-down control the designers need to be responsible towards the living systems they work with. In the spirit of Donella Meadows, one needs to adapt by "dancing with the system." The designer needs to design for flexibility and adaptation to unforeseen futures and to design resilient systems that are able to resist or survive and adapt to future distortions. This implies deep knowledge, participatory processes, and ingenious innovation. Design may have a deep impact on all levels. Seemingly neutral design ideas might cater for or hinder certain social constellations. For example, the rigid organisation of a workplace with emphasis on individual work can become an obstacle of collaboration. It is sometimes baffling how little care is taken in such manners (*Figure 15*).

---

19. This is obvious in the Norwegian health sector that has been overly controlled by New Public Management principles. The development is now heavily criticized for demotivating the employees and for being un-human towards its clients.

Figure 15: The studios at the Oslo School of Architecture and Design are designed with fixed shelves and tables, which disallow students to rearrange the interior in a way that would cater to group work or other social activities. It is impossible to understand the motivation for this arrangement of learning spaces for students educated in professions that are totally dependent on collaboration (Architects Jarmund & Vigsnæs 2000). (Photo: Birger Sevaldson, 2015).

Understanding Real Life Examples

If we look at all artefacts merely as outcomes of complex systems, they can be used as gateways for understanding systemic relations. This can be done by imagining a timeline for the lifespan of the object. The timeline would describe the material, economic, technological, social, institutional, and cultural processes that are involved during this journey. This way of thinking is often conducted as a Life Cycle Analysis (LCA), but we need to add scenarios and stories of use, as well as emotional, symbolic, and cultural aspects to the life cycle. More than that, we need to unfold a much larger network of connections than what is normal in a LCA. We can use any artefact, even the simplest one, to do this exercise.

Figure 16: A simple coffee cup is an intersection point between several super complex systems (Photo: Birger Sevaldson, 2012).

For example, if we look at a simple throwaway paper cup as a symptom of bigger systems, we can start to "unfold" this object by investigating all the preconditions for its existence. To mention a few: the cup is made of paper. Hence, it was once part of a tree. From tree to cup, we find a hyper-complex chain of processes involved in paper production, including transportation, raw material exchange, and energy input and output. However, even before the tree was harvested for pulp production, we find an immensely complex system of industrialised forestry and its consequences on the biosphere. Even beyond that there is the whole biology of the natural systems that make it all possible. At the other end of the chain, we find all the systems for distribution and for recycling. Alternatively, if we look at its content, we have an equally complex production system for coffee. The coffee bean in my cup once hung on a bush, and was picked by a worker in Columbia perhaps, before going through complex processes of refinement, trade, and transportation. Coffee also represents the cultural idea of using a plant as stimulus rather than nutrition. It is historically linked to colonialism, and is produced in an unequal political and economic context within a globalized economy. Consumption is also linked to social patterns. For example, in Norway, coffee is closely linked to social interaction. Thus, the little coffee cup can be understood as a symptom of all these complex interlinked systems, not to mention the water system, international raw material trade, as well as the political dimension of fair trade.

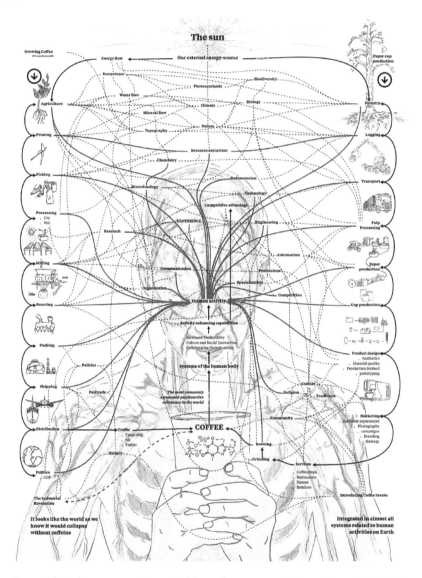

Figure 17: A diagram mapping out of the coffee cup as an intersection point (Martin Hauge, 2021).

Unfolding objects as symptoms of complex systems is a way of understanding the real world. Because this would unavoidably lead us to the rim of our knowledge, we can only do this in a limited way. However, we can take with us the realization that everything is intriguingly interlinked in similar systems like the paper cup. As a seemingly insignificant object, the paper cup becomes highly interesting when viewed through these lenses. This helps to train our sensitivity for understanding systems (see Beyond the Object).

Gigamapping

As mentioned before, in SOD, the first thing we normally do when starting a project is to draw a map of the things we already know or assume to know. By drawing the first large contours of the whole field, sketching its boundaries and positioning the project within, mapping out different stakeholders, knowledge fields, and expert networks that might be involved, and uncovering the most important white spots where additional knowledge should be sought, this initial mapping efficiently activates existing knowledge for sharing.

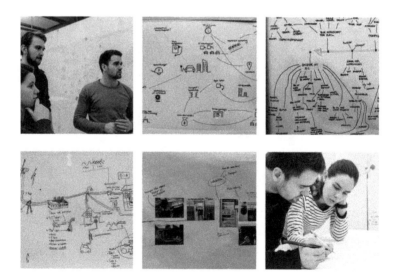

Figure 18: Early gigamapping helps make pre-existing knowledge explicit so that it can be shared with the team (Project Salto Connect, Electrical car charging system, Oslo School of Architecture and Design, Institute of Design, Oda Heier, Torgeir Hæreid, Marie Frogner, Julie Sandvoll, Trym Abrahamsen, 2017).

During this first phase, there should be absolutely no concern with the preconceptions of the case at hand. Also, one should not worry about what is relevant at this point. Too much concern with preconceived limitations will lead the process into already well-known territories, spoiling the chances of discovering new approaches and perspectives. Instead, one should map out the systems involved for their own sake, driven by curiosity and the urge to learn to understand as much as possible of the problem / situation, its environment, and the bigger landscape. Learning to understand the wider systemic context has its own value. Besides that, only later, when you have generated a deeper understanding of the system at hand, and you start to design for change, you can realize which parts of the system are important and relevant and which are not.

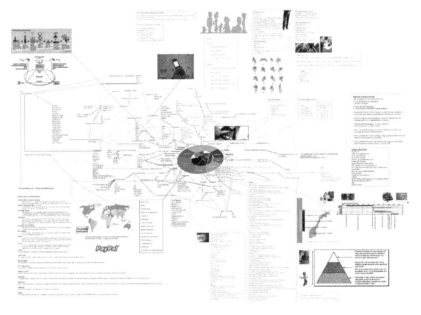

Figure 19: Example of a mixed-technique Gigamap where the core of the system is surrounded by a concept map while the outer rim is filled in with visual and textual information from research. This is a Gigamap as a process too, not intended for distribution outside of the designer and expert network. The project started with an intention to redesign the payment terminal for supermarkets, and resulted in a real-time quality comparison system that would increase consumer power (Erik L. Lindberg, 2009).

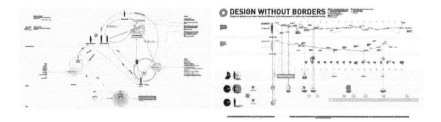

Figure 20: A Gigamap that shows both a network diagram to the left and a timeline to the right (From Design Without Borders by Mitja Sutela and Ragnhild Mjønner in collaboration with the Norwegian Design Council, 2012).

There are two mapping principles we most often apply in the beginning: network diagrams and timelines (see *Figure 1*9 and *Figure 20*)[20]. Network diagrams often start out similar to mind maps. The disadvantage of mind maps is that they have a strong focal point and a hierarchical design, like a tree structure with one origin and separate branches without connections between them. These are most often coincidental design choices rather than real systems features. Being aware of this issue helps to transform a hierarchical map into concept maps, which have a flatter, mixed-hierarchy design. Timelines are used to draw relations sequentially as they unfold. The timeline mapping technique, in particular, has proven very useful in groups with different stakeholders. It is especially suited for people in organisations to synchronise their understanding of their activities and to identify potential areas for improvements (*Figure 21*). Both these methods identify the entities within a system and the relations between them.

Figure 21: A quick and dirty Gigamap, produced by employees of a management consultancy to discuss their typical project process. In this setting, it worked as a dialogic tool and elicited both divergences in conception of the processes as well as interventions to improve them (Birger Sevaldson, 2013).

---

20. Other types of systems models might be integrated at later stages.

The maps are redrawn and developed through several versions. They can have the following functions:

- Mapping pre-existing knowledge to identify necessary research areas.

- Visualizing, organising, and making sense of knowledge gained from research (desktop research or real-life research).

- Acting as an analytical, holistic, and dialogic tool for experts to respond and comment on.

- Creating opportunity for collaborative mapping with relevant stakeholders.

- Providing a dialogic tool for open-ended and jumping yet focussed conversations.

- To elicit the "unknown unknowns"[21], the issues you don't know are issues. Providing a means to identify problems, ideas, intervention points, and potential innovations (ZIP analyses).

- A method that moves from a descriptive to generative mode, enabling the creation of new relations and entities.

- A means to visualise and communicate the final project.

Though gigamapping might seem slow and cumbersome, it actually provides an ultra-fast way of gaining a deep understanding of problems and the way that they are networked. The perceived slowness comes from the nature of unfolding super complex issues. The implementation and combination of the discussed techniques are probably the fastest ways for a designer to acquire deep and wide insights on the nature, needs, and potential of the collaborators (or clients).

The initial gigamapping has to be discussed in relation to the boundary problem, how we determine what the boundaries of a given system are. What do we include in the system itself, its environment, and in the bigger landscape? How do we know that we included the most important matters, and that we left out those that are less important? Small, seemingly peripheral issues can potentially turn out to be crucial, and what we thought was important may be less important.

---

21. This will be discussed further in Part Three.

Gigamapping helps to draw the systems boundaries in a flexible way. If we do not grasp everything in the beginning, we can constantly adjust them while the process is moving forward, and we are learning more and more.

To create a comprehensive picture of the larger landscape as early as possible, we need to forget preconceived relevance in the start, and map very widely to include seemingly irrelevant or less important issues. We cannot understand the systems sufficiently if we are only concerned with issues that seem relevant from the outset. Gigamapping is about breaking out of the preconceived frameworks that guide and determine our perceptions. When we know the big picture, we can then choose to focus on specific systems boundaries in an informed way. This ensures that we know the terrain outside the boundaries, and will be able to adjust it as needed. There are many examples of instances where important factors in the system were discovered that otherwise would not have been accounted for without this wide approach.

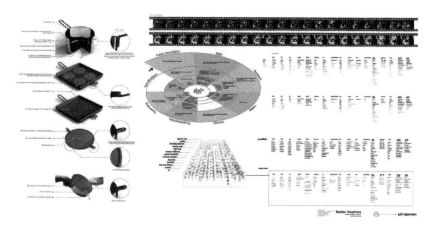

Figure 22: Cookware: The map contains a use sequence (top), A matrix of features (right) a layering of features for decision-making. (middle bottom) and a diagram of an iterative design process (centre). (Oslo School of Architecture and Design, Institute of Design, Balder Onarheim and Paal Espensen, 2008).

An example of how the boundaries of a seemingly simple system were renegotiated and developed throughout the whole process is the development of cookware (*Figure 22*)

A layered matrix-based method was developed to list, compare, and assess the different aspects (middle bottom and right). Afterwards, it underwent an iterative design process that repeatedly altered between re-describing generated ideas, researching, and developing the matrix, practicing (cooking and serving dinners) sketching, evaluating, and redefining the specifications (middle diagram). This process is illustrated in the spiral-diagram in the middle top. The project dealt with everything from production methods, material technology, economy, markets, food culture, social systems, cooking craft and traditions to sustainability. The result of this project was a set of cooking tools that were thought through from almost all thinkable perspectives.

Memory and Sharing: Externalisation and Internalisation

When starting with gigamapping we normally start with mapping out what we know. Through this we share the existing knowledge about a situation or a problem and share it across the design team and involved stakeholders. This is the externalization of knowledge.

In the Gigamap in *Figure 23*, the concept of micro distribution of energy production is mapped out and interpreted in a designed 3D diagram. This is obviously not the only way of depicting this. However, the visual richness and interesting graphic illustration together with the link to concrete projects makes the map communicative, and it is easier for the involved to relate to and discuss upon. It is also easier to on-board others with this map.

The gigamapping process is a memory tool. The visual process helps with remembering and internalising large amounts of information, models, and solutions so that this can be worked with more effortlessly in a systemic design process. This is an important point since working with systems implies training the ability to keep more information in the play throughout the design process. The gigamapping process spatializes information so that it is much easier to work with when needed. This is the process of internalising knowledge.

Figure 23: A Gigamap that has been finalised for communication purposes showing technological, social, and cultural issues regarding a concept for small-scale distributed energy harvesting. To the right, it also shows a series of suggested design products and their energy harvesting ability (Francesco Zorz1, 2009).

Observing the System

After the first Gigamap is sketched out, the areas for further research are identified. The inherent knowledge that has been mapped needs to be developed with other ways of gathering information. It is important to experience and observe the systems one works with. Real life observations are meant to help us see how things really work, which enables us to identify and challenge any preconceptions or prejudices that our assumptions are based on.

Prejudices are always obstacles to overcome in SOD. Systems often work counter-intuitively, and we need to "listen" to the systems carefully in order to better understand how they work. When conducting real life observations, framing the system is often counterproductive. A way of breaking our preconceived framing of the system is to turn our attention to details. Observing and registering the smallest details will turn attention away from ingrained framing and categorization, helping break our preconceptions of how things work.

Participant observations means acting in a system while observing it. It means to participate in the ongoing activities to learn more from an insider perspective.

The Unknown Unknowns

Gigamapping in groups, together with observations and participatory processes have a clear learning goal. When entering an unknown new field for a design process we are only able to imagine the questions we know of. These are the known unknowns. However, we also want to address the unknown unknowns[22], the questions which we do not even know are important to ask, and the problems of which we have no clue about their existence. If these unknown questions remain inside our domain of knowledge, we might still be able to find them even if they breach our own knowledge horizon. However, if we go into situations where there is little knowledge in both the individuals and the field, we work with unknown unknowns. These questions can be extremely hard to elicit or to construct. This is illustrated in the diagram in *Figure 24*, showing the "Johari Window", a framework for creating awareness of the unknown unknowns. (Luft & Ingram 1961, Ramesh & Browning, 2014). Gigamapping, with its open and flexible process, has shown to be a strong tool for eliciting the unknown unknowns in visual dialogues. This happens in dialogues with others such as users, affected bystanders, and other experts. The map works as a proposal or a complex statement that can be addressed by others by adding things you did not know were central issues. To address the hidden area one needs to carefully consider who one engages. Addressing the unknown area[23], one needs to interact with actors from outside the systems, fields, and frame-works one works within, for example, the affected bystanders (Wagenknecht, 2017).

---

22. The term "unknown unknowns" is frequently credited to American General Rumsfelt. However, the problem of the unknown unknowns has been described by others
23. I consider the Johari Window to represent a social system and not applicable to a universal scale since that renders the unknown areas meaningless.

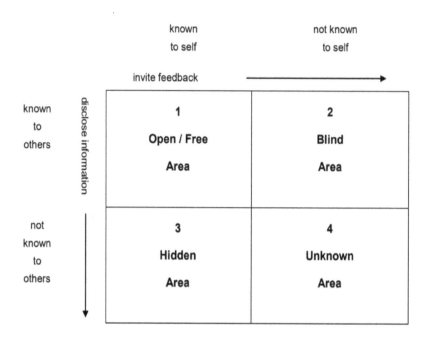

Figure 24: The Johari window shows four different knowledge-sharing situations between individuals and groups (Derived from Luft & Ingram by Birger Sevaldson, 2020).

Shortly About Creativity

Complex processes require deep knowledge and time to process this knowledge. We need to internalize large amounts of information so that we can work with and process it. To best explain this mental process, I suggest to turn to an old model of creativity. As described by mathematician Jaques Hadamard (1945), this model outlines creative work as four phases: 1. Preparation; 2. Incubation; 3. Illumination, and 4. Verification.

The preparation phase, which we have already discussed, is where complexity is brought to the table, so that we can begin to see in detail what we are up against.

The next phase, incubation, is partly the subconscious process of wrestling with complex problems over time. It requires deep engagement and dedicated time. Although it is mostly an individual process, it can be influenced by the team.

The third phase, illumination, is the moment when things fall in place and the good ideas emerge. Illumination may happen unexpectedly at odd times and places, but it can also be triggered by team work. Incubation and illumination are described as typical for highly creative people (Csikszentmihalyi, 1996, 1999).

Both incubation and illumination are elusive concepts. It is hard to understand them, therefore it is difficult to find prescriptions or methods to force them to happen. Incubation is described as the subconscious processing of problems while doing something else. To initiate and cultivate incubation, we can do a lot in the preparatory phase. The important issue is to not lock or restrict the focus too early. Open-ended investigations and information acquisition are crucial.

Switching activities to work on something else within the same project can allow ideas to simmer in the back of our heads, and help the incubation process. For example, being immersed in sketching specific items within the system can distract the mind, while still interpreting and addressing the central problems in an indirect way.

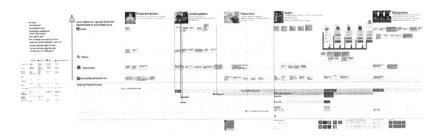

Figure 25: This image shows a timeline-based Gigamap that is both descriptive and generative. It depicts the timeline of a social networking training software based on gaming principles. Different representation techniques are used. This map became central to the software development process, and was hung in the students' workspace as a constant focal point (Student Erik Falk Petersen, 2009).

During these phases, where things are rested and one begins to work on other corners of the project or with totally different things, it is important that one continues to have direct access to process materials, including the maps, pictures, diagrams, and sketches. It is efficient to hang the materials in the design studio (*Figure 25*). Storing them on a computer is far less accessible, and one tends to forget parts of the information without the context of the larger system. This leads to the risk of selecting information at random rather than with systemic arguments.

Despite this creativity model being parted into phases that follow each other chronologically, it is almost needless to say that this is not the case when practising. One should not use this model as a tool; it is purely descriptive, as a help to interpret the creative process. Only when experiencing, for example, periods of resistance one associates it with the incubation phase. Especially preparation and incubation bleed into each other.

Control and Soft Control

As touched upon in the discussion on worldview, we tend to think of control as a negotiable issue in SOD. Very complex projects with flat hierarchies that involve many stakeholders and partners, tend to live their own lives. In such cases, it becomes even more important to drop any ideas of hard control, and to avoid design solutions that try to please everybody, i.e., "design by committee." Given the many perspectives involved, it is almost impossible to avoid conflicts, and the social dynamics need to be given attention. The project and process themselves become the system and the object of design. Being aware of these issues and approaching the project with an action research mind is important. [24] One such project was the design and production of the Deichmannske Media Stations (Menges, 2008) by a group of students at two design schools, one in Oslo, and the other in Offenbach, near Frankfurt (*Figure 26*). The project involved a systems-approach to the task of building four media stations for the library, but it also involved the challenge of applying a new material system: the use of 3D textile as distance material between vinyl ester double shells that are reinforced by glass fibre. In addition, the students faced the challenge of building the media stations at a boat builder's yard in Norway. Finally, there was a group developing the interactive electronic system, and another group programming the touch-screen interface. Guiding and managing this project produced a number of challenges to the group dynamics and learning outputs (Sevaldson, 2008). The project exemplified a process that provided situations, problems, challenges, and opportunities on multiple levels and scales. Though not everything is critically interconnected, solving them separately can only result in fragmented solutions.

---

24. This view connects with second order cybernetics and designing as dialogue. See for example Paul Pangaro's keynote lecture at RSD5 (https://vimeo.com/189864748).

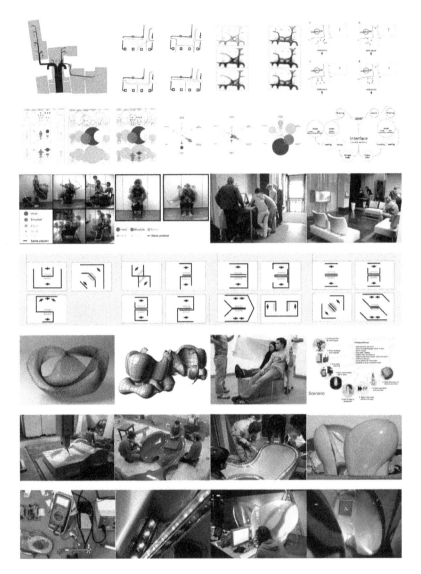

Figure 26: Images from a very complex design process – the design and construction of media stations for the Deichmanske Library in Oslo. From the top: (First row) Diagrams from the analyses of movement patterns in the library. (Second row) Diagrams that helped evaluate the many different aspects at stake. (Third row) Ergonomics and usage studies of the site. (Fourth row) Organisation principles for twin media station layouts. (Fifth row) Form studies, mock ups, and scenarios. (Sixth row) Production of moulds and shells with new material technology involving a 3D-textile. (Seventh row) Construction of interactive system and final media station to the right (Menges, 2008).

Achieving an Information Advantage

In many organisations, information does not flow freely. The makeup of shadow-systems[25], the emergence of relations across the organisation that become more important than the official line of command, and the growth of internal cultures regulate information flow. The designer in charge of researching and gigamapping the organisation often needs access to information that is not necessarily shared across different parts of the organisation. Gigamapping in groups with company employees and leaders is an efficient way to start a dialogue, to create a good starting point for collaboration, to map out stakeholders' interests, and to gain a better understanding of how the organisation works (Wettre, 2012). It is important for the designer to understand the shadow-organisation, and to get access to information that might not necessarily be deemed as relevant by the client. With a view of the organisation as a system, the designer gains an information advantage. This enables the designer to be informed of potential obstacles that the project might encounter, and also draw from the engagement of collaborators. In these situations, however, it is important for the designer to treat this information advantage with ethical respect, confidentiality, and insight.

Figure 27: Gigamapping in collaboration with the client and in exchange with education helps gain a systems picture of the organisation and their activities. It also helps uncover latent issues, prompting the right questions to ask. The company representatives should be actively engaged in the mapping process. (Photo: Halogen, 2015).

---

25. Shadow systems, defined by Stacey, are hidden structures of real power that diverge from the official organisation diagrams. All organisations develop such hidden relations and structures that are a part of the self-organisation ability of an organisation (Halpin & Hanlon, 2008).

Communication

When the project reaches its end-phase, the purpose of mapping and visualisation slowly changes from being a process tool to becoming a communication tool. A common difficulty with SOD projects is the need to be able to communicate in a split second what the project is about, while also conveying its real depth, as well as what makes it realistic and resilient.

There is no sharp divide between visualisation as a process tool and visualisation as communication. It can be challenging communicating insight to clients or decision makers who do not have intimate knowledge of the information unearthed during the mapping process. The sequence that information is accessed can be crucial. Complex system processes that are part of the solution must be communicated visually in an accessible way (*Figure 28*), which is often done better through other means like videos as opposed to large complex Gigamaps (*Figure 29*).

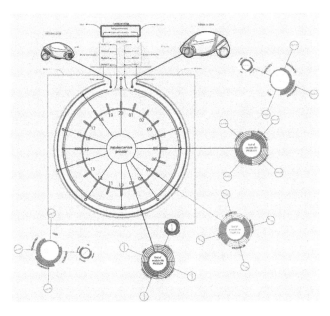

Figure 28: This visualisation explains the principles of a concept for a metabolic vehicle, an electric car that is recycled during its lifetime. Spare parts are replaced not as a response to failure, but according to a calculated plan. Parts are refurbished and recycled. During a period of some years, the entire car is replaced in this way. The car manufacturers' attention thus changes from sales to maintenance, which for many manufacturers already generates the largest profits. Large stocks of spare parts are eliminated because everything happens just in time (Recolt Metabolic Vehicle, Christopher A. Lange, 2009).

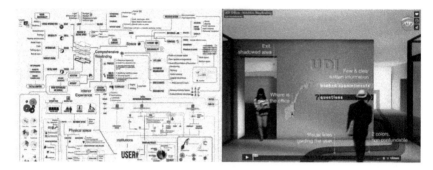

Figure 29: A Gigamap is not very normally well-suited as standalone communication tool for outsiders. One needs to be co-creator of the map or use some time to be guided to understand it. Videos, however, are an excellent means to communicate very complex projects to outsiders. (Oslo School of Architecture and Design for UDI the Norwegian Immigration Office, Lea Brochard, Nicoletta Aveni, 2012).

Uncovering New Fields for Design

An SOD approach can uncover new design fields. In a master's thesis project involving the real case of a ship accident causing large oil spills (Full City accident, 2009), the student shifted focus from improving the equipment for oil clean up to looking at accident prevention instead[26]. This shift was triggered by the wide-reaching mapping of the system and factors that caused the accident. By mapping out far more than what seemed relevant from the outset, he uncovered inconsistencies in the organisation of the system and a lack of communication between the involved stakeholders. These problems in turn became his design task. The main issue was that awareness of the situation between the actors was not coordinated. As a response to this he sketched a risk level warning and forecast system, to share the awareness of potentially dangerous situations building up. This system would work similar to a weather forecast system. It drew information from all stakeholders into a risk calculating system, which was designed as a community-building tool between official institutions like the coast guard, patrol boats, and private actors like shipping, fisheries, tug boat companies, as well as volunteer partners like leisure sailors, environmental organisations etc. In this project, his design material was no longer material systems or services, but the human activity systems themselves. And the output for the design was new

---

26. Adrian Paulsen, 2010.

systemic connections that were not imagined before bringing a long range of stakeholders together.

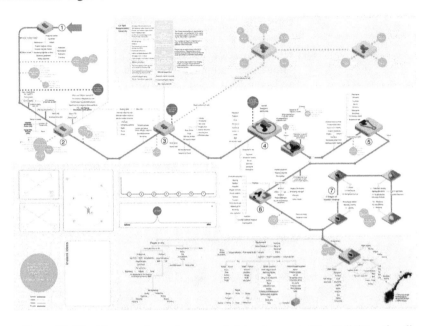

Figure 30: The Gigamap shows the sequential development of the Full City oil spill accident outside the coast of Norway. It unfolds the complexity of the process, as well as the organisations and systems involved. The Gigamap helped shift focus from the end point of spill cleanup to much earlier points where better co-ordination would have prevented the event. The project uses a real-life case as an example of an accident where this type of awareness could have made an essential difference (Adrian Paulsen, 2010).

The Hybrid Process and the Rich Design Space

Richness in the design process has been mentioned in several places so far. However, this deserves to be lifted up and discussed as a methodological concept in its own right. Richness as a required feature of a design process grappling with complexity is based on several arguments:

We can distinguish between two sorts of richness:

1. Richness that comes from the information gathered and processed. This again can be understood in the light of several different aspects.

- A complex situation by nature will contain multiple players and actors interacting within systems driven by many parameters and variables. This creates a data-rich reality to cope with.

- Multiple actors have diverse agendas and intentions, sometimes aligned but most often not. Describing, understanding, and negotiating between these agendas produces large amount of information, that needs to be handled.

- The design process addressing complexity should in one way or the other reflect the complexity. Simplification on its own does not work when we try to resolve complex situations.

- Material systems are complex when looking at the processes behind them.

- Natural systems are complex, easy to disturb and to destroy.

2. Richness from the application of numerous tools and methods in the process. There is no such thing as one universal method or one tool that can solve any design process. Especially in complex design processes numerous tools and methodologies have to be used to fully interpret the complex systems at hand. This is called the Hybrid Design Process (Sevaldson, 2005b).

The Hybrid Process brings together different modes of working and different media use. The idea is that when working with complex situations, no singular media or process is sufficient. Instead, one needs to triangulate and switch between numerous process tools and methods to fully serve the situation. The Gigamap is the central triangulation tool and environment for relating different models and perspectives. The Hybrid Process strategizes the use of different design media: digital or manual, still or video, 2D or 3D. It emphasizes the role of design media and its influence on the final design output. It also implements various methods, both figurative and diagrammatic visualization, dialogic tools, participatory methods, data gathering, interviews and queries, ethnographic methods, and so on. By simply changing design media or method, the process and its output also change. By switching between individual and teamwork, or near and distant work, the process and its output are also influenced. As such, the switch itself is considered an important driver for the process. Switching from a

1:1 mock up in the workshop to 3D digital sketch or video, or from interviews to participatory activities will create jumps in the process. The Hybrid Process demands a flexible and non-linear attitude towards the design process. Ultimately, its potential lies in the multiple perspectives and views that are generated. This creates a richness that lets new design solutions emerge. Hybridification of design processes is not restricted to initial phases only, but can be used far into the process towards its finalisation. Moreover, it is necessary that we look into the special requirements needed to run such processes; a multi-modal design needs a "Rich Design Space."

A Rich Design Space addresses both concrete spaces like the physical studio, virtual spaces like the digital realm occupied by 3D software or a blog, as well as social spaces of design collaboration. The Rich Design Space intends to help keep as much information in the game for as long as possible. This is achieved mainly by visual means with traditional visualisation techniques, but also through different electronic media. The Rich Design Space also integrates the mental space of the individuals who build it. It is therefore an individual, as well as a shared space for the limited group of people who are able to keep that holistic view.

The Rich Design Space is elaborated upon in Part Three.

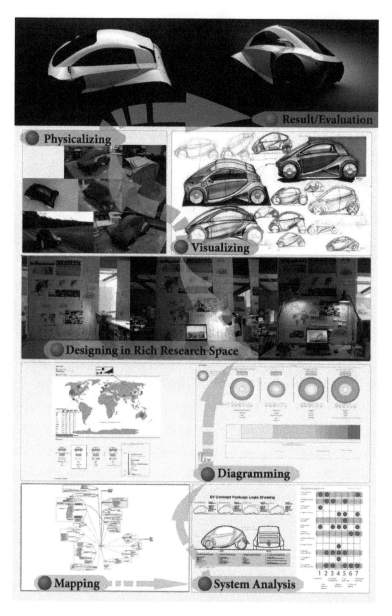

Figure 31: A poster showing the hybrid process of designing a metabolic vehicle concept. Many different modes of designing are shown and different types of data represented. The Rich Design Space depicted in the middle is central in the project (Recolt Metabolic Vehicle, Christopher A. Lange, 2009).

Additional Tool

In SOD, we have several tools and frameworks that will be treated in Part Three. Here we will only shortly mention the tool that is most often adopted by beginners, the ZIP analyses.

The Gigamap represents an inclusive holistic picture. To help identify points of intervention in the system at hand and to prioritise the actions that need to be taken, we have developed several tools and techniques for analysing and interpreting the map. This activity is not to be seen as a phase, but rather as an iterative and repetitive activity that is scattered throughout the design process, with peak function somewhere in the middle.

The most important analysis tool is ZIP analyses. This is typically conducted by searching for and identifying "ZIP points" on the Gigamap, and marking them with a letter and number. ZIP is an acronym that stands for:

Z: Zoom. This indicates an identified point or area on the map where more depth and resolution is needed.

P: Problem or Potential. This is a point or area in the system as shown on the Gigamap where there are particular problems or potentials. This could also be something that has potential in the sense that one can learn from it.

I: Intervention, Idea, and Innovation. This is where a resolution of the P-point can be found.

There are a range of other tools and techniques that help shift attention from specific entities to the relations between them. This helps evaluate, prioritize, and orchestrate systemic interventions. We will return to this in Part Three.

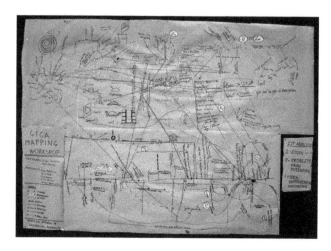

Figure 32: Zip analyses performed on a Gigamap. The ZIP points are marked in yellow (Lucie Pavlistikova, Martin Malek, Mirka Baklikova, Mariia Borisova, Georgia Papasozomenou. Supervisor Marie Davidova, 2016).

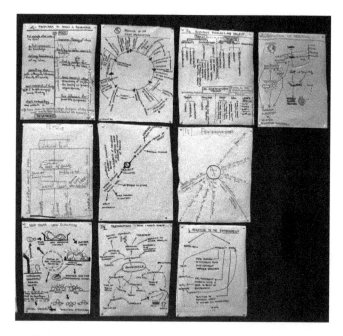

Figure 33: ZIP maps. Selected ZIP points in Figure 32 are developed in smaller sub-maps (Lucie Pavlistikova, Martin Malek, Mirka Baklikova, Mariia Borisova, Georgia Papasozomenou. Supervisor Marie Davidova, 2016).

Realisation and Implementation

Ideally, implementation in SOD is taken care of from the beginning as an integrated part of the process from the start. The deep and wide gigamapping process would have ideally uncovered the organisation's production capacities and flexibilities or lack thereof, and taken this into account from an early phase. These capacities would have been followed up on in every step towards a final design, and the thresholds for implementation would have been evaluated. It is obvious that a thorough investigation of an organisation, its markets, its technologies and production capacities, its weaknesses and strengths, as well as its possibilities and potentials will result in more robust and realistic solutions.

The example shown below is from the concept study of an aid program for disabled children in developing countries. *Figure 34* shows a mapping of the power structures and possible barriers for realising this concept while *Figure 35* shows a detailed implementation strategy. This demonstrates that gigamapping can also be useful in the implementation phases of a project (project by Charlotte Aarlan).

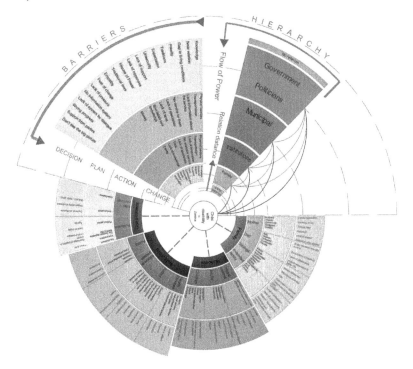

Figure 34: The mapping of power structures and barriers that are necessary to realise the project (Therese Charlotte Aarland, 2009).

Figure 35: A detailed implementation plan for establishing an international aid system catered towards disabled children, which involves Norwegian health care student exchange within a learning system in order to educate and empower local self-help processes. See also Figure 123 for another example of implementation mapping. (Therese Charlotte Aarland, 2009).

An Example: Design for Dignity in a Sexual Violence Response System

This project was the master's thesis of Manuela Aguirre Ulluoa and Jan Kristian Strømsnes at the Oslo School of Architecture and Design (Ulluoa & Strømsnes,

2012). Both students were trained in SOD. The project started off as a design-against-crime [27] project like those we have seen lately that are based on the "broken window theory" (Wilson & Kelling, 1982). It also aimed to explore the idea that good design of urban environments can prevent crime. However, through the gigamapping process the designers shifted their focus to look deeper into response systems, especially those tailored towards sexual crimes. They imagined that they could do a more concrete project there, and that they could find organisations to collaborate with. In addition, the design-against-crime project has largely been occupied with crime prevention and they saw neglected gap in design for response. They established contact with the Sexual Assault Centre (SAC) at the Legevakten emergency hospital in Oslo. This was not an easy task. Working together with the staff from SAC was like opening a new field in design to investigate how design can contribute to this case.

Figure 36: A Gigamap showing the whole landscape of sexual assault. The prevention field is to the left and the response field to the right. The image shows the final map after it was developed through many iterations to become the final design artefact shown here. Designing the map was an important reflexive thinking-through-designing process that makes it possible to organise and internalise large amounts of information, as well as crystallise and design its relations. (Manuela Aguirre & Jan Kristina Strømsnes, 2012).

SOD gave the design team the right tools to get an overview of the whole landscape of sexual violence. The Gigamap was based on expert knowledge, as well as research into qualitative and quantitative information. The research needed to be very extensive and wide-reaching. The students were entering a field where they knew very little, and it was crucial to understand the systems properly in order to suggest adequate design solutions. Through many iterations and quality checkpoints with experts, the Gigamap was made to be as precise as possible. The map also became a shared tool for the staff at SAC and the special police unit

---

27. Design against crime is developed amongst others at Central Saint Martins (CSM), University of the Arts London.

involved in the collaboration process. It created an overview of their own work and services, as well as how the whole system operated. This helped the staff to coordinate their perspectives. The map revealed the processes that victims had to go through at SAC, which initiated a user-centric baseline for the design process.

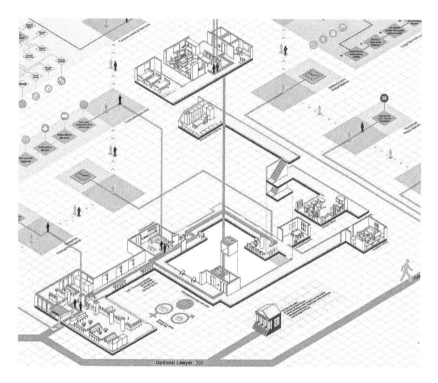

Figure 37: A cut-out of the Gigamap that shows the whole sexual assault response system, including the services of the SAC and the special police unit. This map was developed partly together with the staff from both places, and became a very useful tool for them to gain a shared picture of their operations (Manuela Aguirre & Jan Kristina Strømsnes, 2012).

SOD helped the students gain control of and systematise all of the ideas that emerged out of the mapped context and the knowledge gained from collaboration with experts. All the ideas were documented in relation to the context.

The students reported on the following benefits from gigamapping:

- It creates a shared overview that incorporates synchronized perspectives.

- It is in an understandable visual format where opportunities can be easily identified and pinpointed to the designers and stakeholders.

- It creates a common and understandable setting for dialogue and opportunities where new solutions can be placed in the existing system to result in stepwise improvement of the system.

- The Gigamap can be used in a training program for staff members, providing a common synchronized overview of the response system.

- Visualization in gigamapping creates shared images between the designers that align differences and nuances in conceptions.

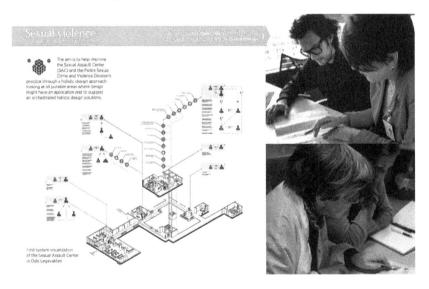

Figure 38: The map of the user journey (to the left) was constructed and co-designed with the staff from the SAC and the police. While the intention for this mapping was for students to learn in detail how the system works, it turned out to become a product of its own that was immediately adopted by the staff for their own work (Manuela Aguirre & Jan Kristina Strømsnes, 2012).

While developing the Gigamaps with the SAC staff, it became clear that this overview had great potential to be useful for stakeholders beyond the investigation phase of the project. It was therefore redesigned specifically to be used by the staff in helping them get a better overview of their own system.

Gigamapping led the students to create system intervention mappings of all their design opportunities structuring and documenting, analysing and scrutinizing their findings throughout the whole design process. From these findings, three concepts were prioritised to be taken forward.

1. Information System

The first design intervention was an information system consisting of two main parts:

- An information folder with resources that are easily accessible to the patient/victim, which includes a personal journal and additional information folders. Everything is packaged with consistent graphic design to signal clear and orderly processes.

Figure 39: Information folder showing a diagram for the victim of the system and its different steps (Manuela Aguirre & Jan Kristina Strømsnes, 2012).

- Patient's Journey Map: an overview of the different processes that the patient must go through at SAC. It functions as a tool to create dialogue between patient and staff members. It also creates an opportunity for the patient to gain more control of what is going to happen throughout the process.

The information system is about to be implemented at SAC.

2. Safety Blanket

A safety blanket is the first item or product that the victim interacts with when being taken care of by the mobile police unit after a sexual assault incident. The blanket changes the clinical and cold process of evidence collection (where paper bags, for example, are used on the hands of the victim to prevent pollution of evidence) into a more comforting and dignified situation. The blanket has pockets for protecting evidence on the victim's hands. The safety blanket can be used by victims in similar cases where collecting DNA for evidence is needed.

The safety blanket seems to be a small detail in the big system, but it is regarded as a crucial element since it is the first touch-point to the system, and it aims to initiate a dignified way of taking care of the victims.

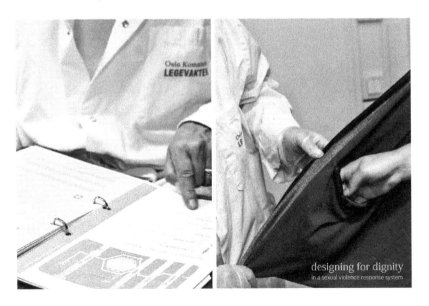

Figure 40: Information system (left) and safety blanket with built-in pockets to prevent contamination of evidence on the victim's hands (right) (Manuela Aguirre & Jan Kristina Strømsnes, 2012).

3. Guidelines for the New Sexual Assault Centre in Oslo

New facilities for SAC are going to be built in a few years. The students designed a vision for the centre's spaces, suggesting design elements that consider the dignity of the victims within changing rooms, contaminated areas, sterile areas, and other integrated areas. Information systems and other resources are also designed to be strategically placed within these areas to further put control back into the victims' hands.

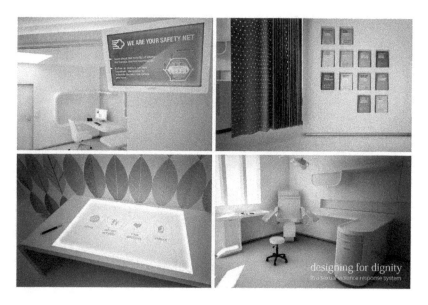

Figure 41: Suggestions for the spatial organisation and design of a new SAC. The design seeks to create a balance between the clinical environment, and a more comforting and calming atmosphere. The design of the interior and information systems are synchronized (Manuela Aguirre & Jan Kristina Strømsnes, 2012).

Typically, when designing for complex systems, there is no single design intervention or concept that is sufficient. An integration of many interventions from the object-based, to spatial, and even organisational design, might be needed. These interventions will also typically cross disciplines. In this specific case, the interventions included information design, object design, service design, architecture, and organisational design. The orchestration of these interventions and innovation is essential. This approach interestingly indicates a return of the modernist Gesamtkunstwerk, but this time, it is argued from a systems rather than composition perspective. We will return to this discussion later.

Rounding up the Short Tour of SOD

SOD represents an attempt to create a designer-centric version of Systems Thinking and systems practice. Its origin is found within design. It developed first as a designerly practice seeking to develop skills, competencies, techniques, and activities to improve the way we work with design when facing increasingly complex situations.

SOD is related to and inspired by Systems Thinking at large, such as, for example, Soft Systems Methodology[28]. The independent and designerly starting point of SOD enables the rethinking of existing perspectives in order to redefine them and construct new ones that are especially well-suited for the designer's abilities. This special approach to Systems Thinking takes into account individual as well as social creativity. It also highlights how design activity can be a genuine way of knowledge production in general and for Systems Thinking in particular. Systems Oriented Design is ultimately a deeply creative design process. The creativity comes from the systems approach; by visualising systems, one finds surprising ways forward, and creates new connections, discovering opportunities across separated domains and finding points of interventions or leverage points that have great impact on systems.

Concluding Part One

With this introduction, you can start practicing SOD right from the start. It might be a good idea to test and create your own experiences with gigamapping before moving on to the rest of the book. Feel free to read the book in a sequence of your choice. But keep in mind, the introduction only touches on ideas that will be discussed in much more detail within the ensuing chapters. The theoretical considerations of SOD are presented in Part Two of this book, which reads like a theory book, and the aspects regarding the practice of SOD are presented in Part Three of the book, which reads like a textbook.

---

28. A much deeper elaboration on the inspirations and fundaments of SOD is found in Part Two

Part Two

Contexts and Backgrounds: The Theories of SOD

Introduction to Part Two

Here we will go through the reasons and motivations for developing Systems Oriented Design, what a new merging of design and systems can provide, and the theories and background of SOD. The five chapters answer the questions: Why, What, and How of SOD.

The first chapter, **Pressing Issues**, elaborates on the need for a systemic turn in design. It describes strategies, directions, and frontiers in current design developments, as well as the breakdowns that follow the development of our society. This sums up WHY we need systemic design.

The second chapter, **What Systems Thinking Brings to Design** describes why systems thinking is needed in design, and **WHAT** it can bring to the design field.

The third chapter, **What Design Brings to Systems Thinking** describes why design and design thinking is needed in systems thinking, and **WHAT** it can bring to the systems field.

The fourth chapter, **Systemic Design: a Renaissance of Systems Thinking in Design** describes **HOW** these issues are addressed in the building up of a pluralistic and flourishing field, allowing for many diverse approaches to play out and be tested.

The fifth and last chapter, **Systems Oriented Design: Theories and Backgrounds** describes SOD as a concrete proposal for **HOW** to bring systems thinking and design together, how systemic design can look, and its theoretical and practical foundation.

This leads naturally to Part Three of this book, where the practices, praxeology, and methodology are discussed in depth.

Why Systemic Design?

The Pressing Issues: Challenges, Strategies, Directions and Frontiers

In this section, we discuss the frontier of design, the issues we meet when design migrates into more advanced and complex fields, and the pressures that design is exposed to in that process. This forms the basis for **WHY** we need a turn towards systemic design.

The Advances and the Breakdowns

We are living in the Anthropocene (Crutzen, 2006) the current geological age in which human activities dominate the climate and environment. Global entanglement is increasing through the exchange of goods, services, information, money, and travel. Our economies are interdependent, heading towards unsustainable growth, and we lack powerful alternatives [29] . While formal democracy has been spreading until recently, we see increasingly serious threats to democratic principles. Globalization has led to an increased concentration of power by global corporations operating beyond national control. The distribution of wealth is becoming increasingly unbalanced while the welfare states are running out of resources. Big data offers new possibilities, but also poses threats to individual privacy and democracy. The recent Covid-19 pandemic demonstrated the vulnerability of modern globalized societies. Decision making is put under pressure by an overwhelming amount of information and the complexity of the issues that must be decided on. The democratic systems are not designed to cope with these changes. It is very difficult to plan for resilience within systems that function only on the basis of a four-year horizon, combined with superficial voting campaigns that address singular issues rather than communicate interlinked problematiques. How can we, as voters, engage with complex, long-term issues?

Meanwhile consumerism dominates our cultures, which seems to serve commercial needs in such a way that overshadows the ideal of the informed and engaged citizen.

Such entanglement, coupled with the degree and complexity of information, climate and environment changes, social and political issues, as well as the effects of globalization all confront the field of design with ever-growing challenges. There are two sides to this:

On one side, design professions are forced to change because of increased complexity, globalization, and the need for sustainable production. We need to change the way we design in order to address complexity and to better imagine the consequences of our actions further ahead than ever before.

On the other side, design is developing as a general approach to meet the challenges we just mentioned. For example, design thinking is migrating into management as a component that can contribute handling very complex organisational issues (Boland & Collopy, 2004; Liedtka, 2018; Liedtka & Ogilvie, 2011; Martin, 2009b). But a good portion of humility and caution is needed to not make things worse while trying to make things better (Slavin, 2016). These challenges are all produced by us and in that sense, they are all result of planned human actions. One could say they are unintended effects of our design decisions.

---

29. One interesting and promising alternative is the Rethinking Economics Network
http://www.rethinkeconomics.org/

Designers might be humble when we are now suggesting that design can fix the errors of past designs. There are two reasons for such effects to emerge: we just did not care or we were not able to foresee them. Disregarding the ones who don't care, how can we know that solving a problem does not generate new ones that future generations have to deal with? We can never know for certain, but we can become better at this. Avoiding unintended and counterintuitive results requires imagination and systems insights. It requires the ability to see several moves forward, like a chess player. It requires phantasy and storytelling, like a movie maker. Acquiring and developing these skills mean that design itself as a profession, knowledge field, and practice, needs to change.

Here I mean not design in its generic sense, but as a profession and academic research field that is based on intensive training of aesthetic practice, integrating thinking and action, as well as reflection and production. This requires years of creative skills training, which ultimately includes training in systemic approaches. In that sense, I think design can be valuable in numerous situations. However, we need to change and expand what professional design is about: what are the skills, competencies, and mindsets needed for the future?

While emphasising the designerly skills and competencies, this does not exclude the designers with a different training and background than the ones from the design schools. There is a move towards inter- and transdisciplinarity in design that is exciting and promising. However, it is important to clarify these particular designerly skills also in the immigration and migration of design into and with other professions and knowledges. Realising this is the fundament for gaining from the diversification of the field of design.

The Problem of the Problem

The challenges mentioned above require us to rethink design beyond simple problem solving. The situations we confront are far too complex, and the potential consequences of getting it wrong are too serious. The act of problem solving requires that it is possible to isolate a problem, and moreover that it is possible to determine and isolate the cause of the problem and the effect of the solution. Isolation of singular problems is not only increasingly impossible, but increasingly irresponsible.

Problems do not live alone. They are always part of systems and involve other problems that interact as systems. Russell Ackoff calls these systems of problems a "mess" (1981). Rittel defined them as Wicked Problems (Rittel & Webber, 1973). Lindblom describes the limitation of planning confronted with the mess of the real world. He stated that we are generally quite good at handling the issues when being in the middle of the situation. He called this the science of muddling through (Lindblom, 1959, 1979). Weick talks of being thrown into a situation

(Weick, 2004). We do not know the consequences of our decisions. Not acting will also have its consequences. It is important to realize that no method, including systemic design, will remove the mess and help us to carry though "clean" and controlled design processes. In some periods, the feeling of being lost and muddling through will be dominant when dealing with overwhelming "messes."

In addition, there comes the problem of framing. Bela Banathy ties the systems of problems to the difficulties of defining boundaries for social systems:

> Social systems are unbounded. Factors assumed to be part of a problem are inseparably linked to other factors. A technical problem of transportation becomes a land-use problem, linked with economic, environmental, conservation, and political considerations. Can we really draw a boundary? When we seek to improve a situation, particularly if it is a public one, we find ourselves facing not a problem but a cluster of problems often called a "problematique" (Banathy, 1997, 29).

We can also imagine problematiques as fields of problems (derived from the Norwegian word, "problemfelt"), or networks of interlinked problems or systems of problems. These are themes of interrelated or similar problems that define a field of investigation. Solving singular problems in such a field can make other problems worse, or cause new ones to emerge.

The problem of problems is one of the major challenges to contemporary design. We need to develop efficient design techniques, skills, and competencies that enable the designer to bypass his or her inherent object orientation and cope with multiple interlinked issues simultaneously. The larger part of this book addresses this issue.

Professional Design and General Design

Talking of systems change through design seen from a perspective of a trained designer, it becomes essential to discuss what kind of design we talk about, and at the same time, to address who is designing when. It is clear that the core competencies of professional designers, and some of the design professions have something very valuable to contribute when it comes to developing practices for systemic design. At the same time, design is not limited to design professionals. Other professions also design, at least when we consider a wider definition of design. Obviously, engineers, city planners, and organisation managers design. Researchers design experiments. Politicians design laws that shape societies. This book, though firstly addressing designers is not excluding these other shapers of our world. On the contrary, I hope this contributes to all. Nevertheless, it is necessary to be specific when it comes to the notion of design.

Given how rich the theme of design is, it can be very blurry in its boundaries and core. The word design is used in many different ways, from demarcating a profession based on an established field and comprehensive global education systems, to being used as a general term that widely describes any activity remotely similar to those of the established professions within defined fields, such as product design, interaction design, and service design. The situation can be fairly confusing.

For example, "Design Thinking" has made it into all sorts of advanced managerial practices, while "design" is also used widely to describe activities spanning from polishing nails to arranging flowers, as well as from engineering to policymaking. At the same time, design professions and research are moving into ever new areas, and the traditional disciplines of design seem to have been watered down as we embrace greater levels of transdisciplinary work and co-design. Consequently, Herbert Simon defines design in the following way:

> Everyone designs who devise courses of action aimed at changing existing situations into preferred ones. The intellectual activity that produces material artefacts is no different fundamentally from the one that prescribes remedies for a sick patient or the one that devises a new sales plan for a company or a social welfare policy for a state (1969, p. 30).

This definition is not very useful for our purposes, as it essentially connotes that if you tell somebody who is feeling hot to take off his or her sweater, you are designing. One should be able to distinguish such everyday acts from more intentional acts such as designing shading that affords protection from the sun, for example. In addition, one should be able to distinguish between engineering, economic planning, war strategies, etc. and design. Although the boundaries between these fields overlap, there are still distinct differences. These differences are not easily recognised by non-designers, which is also something that contributes to the confusion. At the same time, not everybody who designs is suited to contribute to the type of design practice that might help us meet the challenges ahead. Large groups of designers in the consumer goods, furniture design, and fashion industries do not care much about the consequences of their actions. This might be changing; however, their main concern and starting point is not carefully considered systems change but fulfilling consumers' desires. Designing with such a starting point, there is a big risk that situations will get worse. As Russel Ackoff aptly states, "the righter we do the wrong thing, the wronger we become" (Ackoff & Sheldon, 2003).

There is a need to clarify the core competencies in design, and to further build on them. In this situation, I suggest that it is a good strategy to demarcate the design profession and academia from the other uses of the term "design." We have previously adapted the use of "Design" with a capital D as a term for professional design. I suggest using the term "general design" to distinguish all other design-like activities that are not related to the established design professions, and their supporting academic and educational strands. Let me emphasise that this distinction is not for building a discipline. On the contrary, it is for opening up the discipline for others without the core competencies of design who practice design to better understand what these core abilities are. In the same way, being clear about these abilities it makes it easier for professionally educated designers to share them with others.

The distinction between Design and general design, however, does not necessarily help or guarantee anything when it comes to ethics or responsibility, or in doing the "right thing." In fact, even holistic, and in a sense systemic Design can actually be used to do the wrong thing in a much more intentional and powerful way than general design. The work of architect Albert Speer, who was the Minister of Armaments and War Production in Nazi Germany during World War II, can be seen as a prime example of this.

Figure 42: Cathedral of Light, Nürnberg, Reichsparteitag, Lichtdom, 8th September 1936, Albert Speer. An example of doing the wrong thing extremely well. Real design, where the core competencies of the designer are playing out at their full potential can be immensely powerful, even if they are used in the service of evil, or irresponsible acts against humanity (Photo: unknown, German Federal Archive, distributed under Wikimedia Commons).

Speer was a master in staging epic sceneries, experiences, and influential symbolic architecture, street decorations, etc. that had a strong influence on the pathos of the

German people, and their feeling and identity as a nation. Imagining being there in the Cathedral of Light (*Figure 42*), no one can claim being untouched and deeply shattered by the scale, the strictness, the otherworldly intensity of the event. Speer was a genius in imposing on people a feeling of a higher cause, being part of something bigger than yourself, a cause worth dying for. Design was used to efficiently influence the emotions dominating the social system. Note that the Cathedral of Light is a holistic design, involving specially built architecture, the biggest light installation ever, an arrangement of the participants, and an event structure. It followed in the wake of Wagner's Gesamtkunstwerk (Marquard, 1983).

Forgive me for using Speer as an example. It was meant to illustrate an undisputable example of a system that was carefully designed to generate mass hysteria, as well as modify and control the human mind and behaviour in service of the Nazis' social system, something that no amateur could have achieved at the same scale. Design was integrated into Nazi propaganda to such a degree that it is justified to ask if the regime would have been possible without design? It included all aspects of industry, from artefacts to architecture, some being "un-political" in the expression (like the Volkswagen Beetle), while others were highly politicised, like the Nazi uniforms designed by Professor Karl Diebitsch. Diebitsch had a formal art and design education, and was responsible for much of the symbolic artwork that defined the Nazis movement. He is known for his design of the black SS uniform. The uniform was produced by another well-known Nazi, Hugo Ferdinand Boss, who also founded the famous fashion brand, Hugo Boss. Diebitsch became a member of the Nazi party while he was still an art student, and collaborated closely with graphic designer, Walter Heck, to design the SS uniform. He is also known for designing the then popular Allach porcelain figurines produced by imprisoned Jews under slave labour conditions.

One can argue that the Nazi artwork is bad design, and that it has a low quality as art work. However, the design is highly efficient for its purpose. And this is to say nothing of the propagandistic art of Leni Riefenstahl, one of the most talented filmmakers we have seen in the service of Nazi propaganda, especially with Triumph des Willens (Triumph of the Will), 1935, and Fest der Völker (Festival of Nations), 1938 (Loiperdinger & Culbert, 1988).

It is important to realize the systemic power of design and its potentially devastating effects in the wrong hands. Doing the wrong thing in an excellent way results in great devastation.

Nevertheless, the distinction between Design and general design is needed not only to address such highly effective and influential cases, but also to clarify an argument brought forward as a central topic in SOD, which posits that the core competencies of the designer are very valuable for working with systemic problems. It is easy to find grand examples of doing wrong, and more difficult to find ones doing the right thing. This is because doing the right thing, seen from a systems perspective of doing good, does not contain similarly unified and monolithic solutions like Speer achieved. Doing good means to take into account many issues, to negotiate between people, find balances and middle ways, and orchestrate many differently scaled interventions in the search for fair and democratic systems change.

If we accept the idea that all constructive human outputs are the result of either general design or Design, it makes sense that design at large has a universal and crucial role to play. It makes sense to propose that elevating general design to Design should, in many cases, generate more efficient outputs.

Awareness and integration of ethical considerations is crucial. Design in itself is not inherently "good." On the contrary, most design activities and industries today serve narrow purposes, and can have negative implications. Design needs to be critically examined and scrutinized, and advancements in its intellectual and practical applications are needed to fulfil its potential to serve the good. To judge if a design activity is ultimately "good," we need to understand its roles and implications across multiple levels.

Levels of Design

Now that we have established a distinction between professional design and general design, we can elaborate on these variations of design, and arrive at what is needed in systemic design in general, and in SOD particularly. I propose an argument in four parts to explain the changes that I see as necessary in order for design to be able to fulfil its potential to be a means to work with systems:

1. *Professional design is not enough:* The core of design professions is the form-giving aspect of design. Form-giving for designers is the ability to combine aesthetic considerations, composition of form, colours, and materials with functionality as well as cultural, associative, symbolic, and metaphorical signals. Central in this is the act of synthesis, the creativity to bring it all together. This sets the design professions apart from other advanced planning activities and general design. The core activities of design are visible in the production of objects, services, graphics, events, etc. that distinctly stand out in quality one way or another. This "high quality" aspect has many facets. It is expressed through appealing shapes, forms, colours, expressions, ingenious content and storytelling, original experiences, excellent functionality and use, etc. However, it also expresses internalised and unspoken cultural / political values and is often an expression of western global influence, elitist social layers, and resourcefulness. These activities

demarcate what has traditionally been seen as the designer's responsibility. Once upon a time, as designers, we dominantly fulfilled a purely aesthetic-functional role, detached from social reality and the consequences of our acts. Nowadays, designers are most often confronted with higher demands on accountability. We are more deeply entangled with social, economic, technical, and sustainability needs. We should be more concerned about the signals our designs transmit. We should engage in complex systems. But are we capable of dealing with this? The design profession and academia are currently under attack. Don Norman proposes that there should be more scientific evidence in design. He also argues that design is unsuited for social change unless designers learn more social sciences, and that the aesthetic core of design is irrelevant when facing current complex problems (Norman, 2010).

The criticism is justified; design and design education need to change in order for design to play the crucial role of addressing imminent future challenges that it seems to have potential for. This can mean solving small problems without creating new ones, or can also be as ambitious as having a part in saving the world. After all, under the generic and inclusive definition of design, all our problems are essentially designed.

The change in the responsibility of designers has challenged what we regard the core competencies of design. The emphasis on aesthetic expertise has been pushed into the background of our attention, and new kinds of competencies are competing with our attentions. This is an interesting and needed diversification of design, but it would be a cardinal error to leave the realm of aesthetics, visual thinking, and synthesis that is the core of design. The same goes for introducing extra-disciplinary studies into the education of designers, such as social sciences, on the cost of training the core abilities. Alternatively, designers should rather be trained to communicate and collaborate with, for example, social scientists. This leads to the second part of my argument.

2. *Anybody can design, but not well enough:* The loss of attention on design's aesthetic core is a mistake. The designer's aesthetic expertise consists of some very valuable skills and competencies that are needed when relating Systems Thinking and design. Most central are visualisation skills, visual thinking and the

ability to compose holistic outputs from complex, diverse, and contradictory information. In this realization, there also lies the argument for why the systems field needs design. Despite some exceptions, the systems approaches are fundamentally descriptive. Their strength is in providing a means to understand, describe, model, and simulate very complex systems. The purpose of descriptions is that they can be used as levers for change. Hence, the result is often a systems intervention or the design of new systems. We can call these systems interventions "design" in its broadest sense. They are generative activities that aim to change situations for the better. There are currently no automatic or rules-based means or methods to generate systems innovation. This cannot be solved by any scientific or evidence-based approach, nor by computational simulation. So far, the best proven, efficient, ingenious, innovative, and holistic way is through design.[30] In a way, we can turn this argument around to say that all systems outputs are designed. However, these outputs are rarely designed by systemic designers.

Distinguish professional design from general design: The above leads to the need to clarify the before-mentioned distinction between a specific use of the term design and a more general use of the word design. This is because the skills, competencies, approaches, processes, and methods developed within the design professions over decades, and recently developed into more advanced modes of operation, are seen as beneficiary to practice SOD. SOD is, as mentioned, an open and accessible format to be taken up by anybody who is interested; however, design training brings a lot to the practice of SOD. These skills and competencies take years to learn, just as with any other expertise or profession. This does not diminish general design, however. Design activities are mostly participatory, involving designers and non-designers in the same design project. This co-design process is not only necessary, but also beneficial. In addition, Design Thinking is becoming widespread as a managerial approach, and selections of design skills are increasingly taught in concentrated and simplified formats to non-designers. Moreover, many non-designers are naturally engaged in design-

---

30. This might possibly also be the reason why Design Thinking is successful in spreading to other fields.

like activities. This includes people who decorate their homes or modify cars, as well as those who design organisations, politics, and other institutional functions. In a sense, everybody is designing at times. All of these activities are mainly positive and needed. For the discussion on the role of the professional designer and the impact that design education and practice have on SOD, it is important to distinguish between professional design and general design.

3. *Distinguish design from Design:* Archer made a distinction between design and Design with a capital D (1979). Design with a Capital D is a third area of knowledge and education equal to science and the humanities, with relations to arts and technology. As Archer puts it:

> Design, in its most general educational sense, where it is equated with Science and the Humanities, is defined as the area of human experience, skill and understanding that reflects man's concern with the appreciation and adaptation of his surroundings in the light of his material and spiritual needs. In particular, though not exclusively, it relates with the configuration, composition, meaning, value and purpose in man-made phenomena (1979, p. 20).[31]

It is urgent to develop and reinforce this perspective of Design as an equal area to science and the humanities. Design should be viewed as a unique mode of knowledge production that can be used to achieve the systemic changes needed for future systemic innovations.

Design is inherently systemic. Any design must relate to users, production methods, culture, aesthetics, business economy, and technology. In that sense, it is always a result of negotiation and navigation within networks of relations between large complex systems. Without putting in the effort to understand, to the best of our abilities, these networks of relations, one will not be able to produce design outs that function well in the world.

Models, Hierarchies and Vertical Integration

When using the term design, confusion is almost unavoidable. Even after making a distinction between Design and general design, there remain many different variations in the practice of design. This becomes especially apparent when

---

31. Today, in the age of the Anthropocene, design can also be seen as an agent for non-human beings.

discussing the current and future role of design, and how design is needed in societal development of modern and egalitarian societies. Some authors have tried to address this issue. There is a need to sort the field of design, not to fragment it or categorize it, but to distinguish, for example the design of a flower vase from the design of a social transformation. Although these two extremes do indeed have some common denominators, they are also very different in essential ways.

Richard Buchanan suggests four areas (1992) or orders (2001) of design:

1. Symbolic and visual communication

2. Artefacts and material objects

3. Activities and organized services

4. Complex systems and environments

These are called placements, and are further articulated by Peter Jones (2013, p. 22). The idea is that designers can work across placements as they iterate and find places for design impact.

Meanwhile, Jones and VanPatter suggest a concept of design 1.0 to 4.0, versions of design similar to software versions, which increase in complexity with each level. (2009). See *Figure 43*.

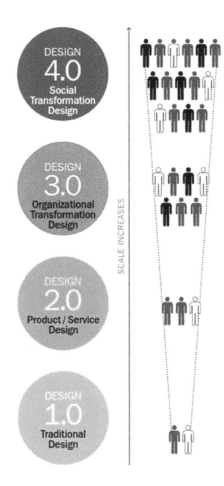

Figure 43: Four levels of design. For each level, complexity and involved stakeholders increase (P H Jones & VanPatter, 2009. Use permitted by author).

Another related categorization of design is the idea of downstream and upstream interventions. Downstream design projects deal with lower scale and more tactical interventions, while upstream projects deal with more strategic and higher scale interventions. The principal of upstream design is that the designer's strategic impact is proportionate to how high upstream the design work is placed. Such a systems hierarchy also regards downstream or lower-level activities as less complex than those of the higher-level activities *Figure 44*.

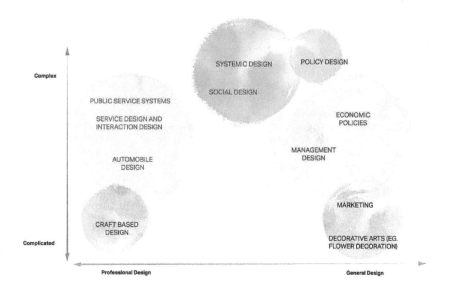

Figure 44: The design field is highly diversified and spans many types of applications, contexts, and levels of complexity. The level of design or the type of context does not determine where SOD is relevant. SOD might be involved in all corners of that diversity (Diagram by author, 2015, redrawn by Palak Dudani, 2021).

The distinction between complex high-level situations and complicated low-level problems is useful, but needs to be looked at critically. A complicated system is often defined as a system that is made out of many parts, all of them being reasonably stable, and hence it is possible to produce full descriptions of the system. Therefore, it is controllable. A car is such a complicated system. A complex system is made out of numerous parts that are unstable and that change when interacting with the environment, resulting in dynamic systems that are hard to control and to predict (Dekker, Bergström, Amer-Wåhlin, & Cilliers, 2012; Poli, 2013).

The above distinction between complicated and complex seems pretty clear. However, what is complicated and what is complex is an issue of perception. There are ample examples of complicated structures behaving unpredictably when interacting with complex environments, resulting in unexpected behaviour.

Though Systemic Design is placed by me in the upper part of *Figure 44*, being targeted towards the complex design situations, the degree of complexity is often derived from the depth of the analyses. Therefore, my claim is that systemic design, and certainly SOD, are applicable across all design levels.

As mentioned in Part One, we need, as systemic designers, to keep multiple perspectives in mind. We discuss this more in Part Three when discussing the problem of boundaries and framing. We need to maintain integration across the levels. This I call vertical integration. Low-level problems are often less complex, more because of the framing and interpretation than based on reality. Seen from a systems perspective that includes principles of bottom-up, self-organising systems, this is an insufficient model. Looking at high-level situations as having more leverage than low-level problems reflect a rather orthodox and hierarchic systems perspective where influence is rippling down through the hierarchy. Bottom-up forces, crowd sources, and public actions are counted out. This returns us to the question of who designs, and what role the systemic designer takes on. For example, systemic designers have to take into account the forces that are engaged when a systems intervention is rolled out. How the intervention is received is out of the designer's control, and hence the designer needs to take on a flexible, communicative, and responsive attitude in all systems changes. This refers to Donella Meadows' notion of dancing with systems (2002), challenging the notion of planning as such, and the concept of planning-executing. A contemporary systemic designer needs to use a more complex understanding of hierarchies in real society, where things are messier and interlinked, and acknowledging bottom up forces and the phenomenon of changes rippling upwards in systems. A systemic designer would intervene at several levels in a system in an orchestrated way.

One problem with this type of levelling is that focus on the upper levels comes at the cost of ignoring the lower levels. The upper levels are often regarded as the most advanced modes of design, where there is the biggest potential for change. It is a mistake to believe that the higher levels will automatically produce deep reaching impact. On the contrary: regarding higher levels as more important is the traditional way of organising our society. This causes all kinds of problems. Managing is seen as a profession in its own right independent from the manager's knowledge about the whole systems they manage. The breakdown of vertical integration and communication is evident in many sectors. For example, in the public sectors of the Scandinavian countries, New Public Management has caused a serious rupture in the vertical integration of the system, creating inefficiency distrust and demotivation. This is currently being attempted to be fixed by all countries introducing so-called trust reforms (Tillitsreform) (Bergh, 2019; Lavik, 2015; Vatn, 2018).

The degree of complexity is not necessarily higher in the upper levels of design as compared to the lower levels (*Figure 43*). The degree of complexity is partly dependent on the drawing of the boundary and the depth of analyses of the system at hand. Think about the before-mentioned paper cup (*Figure 16*). The trust reforms address breakdowns in social systems on the lower level, addressing the emotions and world views of individuals. Such trust is built over time and years, and reflects workplace cultures. The destruction of workplace cultures through lack of vertical systems integration takes years to fix and might be irreparable.

We have only recently, as designers, started to address these issues of culture. Enculturing is happening on all levels of organisations and more on the lower levels. At the same time, it is one of the most difficult aspects to change. A study by Manuela Aguirre promises the development of systemic design methodology for cultural change processes (Aguirre 2020).

The same need for vertical systems insight and integration is found in other sectors. If we look at industrial systems, the complexity of industrial production is immense, and the challenges to produce sustainable solutions contribute to this complexity. Small interventions on a low level can actually have big impact. For example, to reduce our dependency on fossil energy, we are now increasingly dependent on distributed power solutions, which are developed and sold as products such as solar panels on an individual user level and wind turbines on a medium level.

The systemic effects dribble down as well as filtrate up across the scales of systems and subsystems. Banathy describes an advanced role for design, and argues for building a design culture that has the "absolute prerequisite of taking change of our future and shaping our individual and collective destiny" (1997). This indicates a high-level strategic role for design across system hierarchies and scales.[32]

The Challenges in the Design Professions

In the following section, we discuss some of the big challenges the design professions are facing. These are challenges caused by the last decades of development where designers operate in an increasingly globalized world, and where the need for sustainable solutions is adding to the complexity. These challenges add up to push for a systemic change of the field of design.

Structural Challenges

I have described the increasing challenges that we are facing on a macro level (as mentioned before on p. 81), but on a micro level, the everyday life of the designer is also getting more complex. There are ever higher demands for more knowledge.

---

32. Bela Banathy was not a designer by education, but a linguist and systems scientist. However, he learned from design and design theory, and wrote extensively on the value of design. He also practiced systemic design, designing educational systems for example scout leadership programs. His work is an example of how design has made it into Systems Thinking and other fields, and how other fields learn from design. It also shows an early example of systemic design on a high level (level 4 of Jones and VanPatter).

The context that designers operate in is becoming increasingly diverse. Rules and regulations, along with an increasing focus on sustainability complicate decision making. In turn, the designer must relate to contradictory factors like manufacturing and consumption, the environment and carbon footprint, user needs, as well as client profit. A growing number of different users and other stakeholders, the civic society at large as well as non-human actors have to be consulted, both within the client's organisation, and also externally through customer surveys, focus groups, and user involvement in co-design processes. A designer today needs to acquire insights in many different fields, and the design profession is becoming increasingly watered down and spread thin. This is also a problem for design education, where the training of classic core competencies is under pressure from the need to acquire more diversified knowledge.

Ethical Challenges

In addition to the issues mentioned above, designers today are put under increasing pressure with regards to ethical consequences of their work. How can we as designers blindly continue to contribute to, and even accelerate, consumption while taking into account sustainability? How is it ethically possible to be a designer today if we continue to regard the role of the designer as (only) helping our clients gain a competitive advantage to the detriment of others? These dilemmas have caused a state of contradiction in design. How can we, when facing all the challenges mentioned above, prioritize ethical concerns?

The involvement of users and stakeholders is also an ethical challenge. Often, the designer has to represent stakeholders who may have lost their own agency. These could be people who are deprived from expressing their interests, like children, seniors with dementia, or refugees; it could also be future generations, other species, or people who are affected by the effects that are only visible to the expert. [33]

Cultural Challenges

An increase in travel and migration, the internet, a restructuring of industrial production, cultural blending and exchange, and refugee migration, etc. have led to globalization and a more multi-cultural world. Despite this multiculturalism however, there are some disturbing tendencies. Although the mix of cultures has led to a rich, diversified global culture in some areas like food, globalization also seems to result in conformism, and reducing cultural repertoire and variety. This is

---

33. Bela Banathy is known for placing an empty chair in the middle of conversations, representing future generation (Metcalf, 2014).

especially true for design fields like fashion, architecture, automobile design, etc. where Western dominance in global everyday culture is apparent.

While we live in increasingly pluralistic societies, the visual expression of mainstream design is disturbingly uniform. It is to a large degree dominated by a Western look at the cost of diversity and expression of local identity. While this is slowly changing, and for example, Asian countries are increasingly developing their own cultural expressions, the western cloth styles, architecture, and product design is still dominating. The Western style is not politically nor culturally neutral or innocent. If we think of cultural expression as a system that produces meaning, association, and symbolic expressions, it seems no longer adequate to maintain a design culture that has such a limiting effect, and that nurtures such a narrow repertoire.

There is an urgent need for design to develop a richer and more varied expression to meet diverse cultures, to enforce local identity, and to promote pluralistic expression and richness in society. More importantly, innovation and ground-breaking design work is needed to enable diversity in the design repertoire in order to fulfil and reinforce the needs of communities, neighbourhoods, and societies. This implies that designers should embrace complexity, and diversity in expression. Currently, this is not the case in mainstream design. On the contrary, there is a tendency towards increased conformity and streamlining towards limited typologies and solution spaces, leading to a general impoverishment of design.

The diversity and richness of expression in design is a cultural system of its own. It is part of our visual language and imagination. If this variety is decreasing, our imagination adaptability, identity and ability to design adequate solutions diminishes as well.

The Problem of Simplification

Unfortunately, we are trained in the simplicity paradigm. For some reason, simplicity is regarded as positive in our culture. It is partly a legacy from the modernist period in design ("less is more"), but also from managerial clichés ("KISS: Keep It Simple Stupid"), and even from science (Occam's razor)[34]. The modernist simplification was an attempt to remove all symbolism and expression from design, and reduce it to its "essence." The building should be a "machine to live in" [i.e., made famous in Le Corbusier's 1927 manifesto, *Vers Une Architecture* (Towards an Architecture)]. It is not possible to reduce human life to such simplifications, nor is it possible to rid the meaning, values, and symbols from design without losing out on the richness of our culture. Initially, the stripping of architecture of ornament as propagated by Adolf Loos, was meant to

---

34. Nelson and Stolterman criticize the same issue (H. G. Nelson & Stolterman, 2012a).

reduce it to its essence and deprive it from social and political meaning. When it comes to the modernist movement in design, a new symbolism entered immediately when it was established as a style ("Less is more"). The style expresses certain (Western) ways of living, as well as social ideals that are associated with particular values. Values like cleanliness, hygienic environment, order, and rationality reflecting an elitist social layer, and the rational life of Western reductionism, and being entrenched in Western modernism. Only interrupted by a short post-modern period, it is hard for us to comprehend how barren this expression is. However, the longing for something more is surfacing in the enormous attraction of historical cities.

So, what seems simple is in fact complexly layered with meaning. Phillip Warren Anderson brought forward the most substantial critique of the simplification paradigm in science through his famous article, "More is Different;" the title is a paraphrase of the modernist slogan (Anderson, 1972). Anderson demonstrated the principle though examples from biochemistry, attacking the reductionist hypothesis in science. On a broader level, considering "more is different" as a universal principle, this relates to a systemic approach to the issue of modernist style, reflecting Koftka's "the whole is different from its parts" (1935). We need to understand that when complexity increases in natural or social systems, new behaviour is the result. The adding up of elements changes the interplay between them so that new levels of interpretation are needed for each level of complexity. Anderson describes it this way:

> The ability to reduce everything to simple fundamental laws does not imply the ability to start from those laws and reconstruct the universe. In fact, the more the elementary particle physicists tell us about the nature of the fundamental laws, the less relevance they seem to have to the very real problems of the rest of science, much less to those of society. At each stage (of increased complexity, remark by author), entirely new laws, concepts, and generalizations are necessary, requiring inspiration and creativity to just as great a degree as in the previous one. Psychology is not applied biology, nor is biology applied chemistry (1972, p. 393).

The managerial concept of KISS is outright irresponsible in its reduction of complex organisational matters to a few issues at the cost of others. The flux of social organisational life also causes what is important and what is of priority at any moment to fluctuate which makes the application of such simplifications irresponsible and if not entirely wrong in the moment, very short-lived.

Another concept of simplification is Occam´s razor. This is a principle in science introduced by William Occam[35]. It postulates that the simpler explanation

---

35. William Occam (1287 – 1347) was a Franciscan friar and author of Summa Logicae, the Sum of Logics.

is the right one when looking at two explanations for a set of data, granted that all other conditions are the same (Blumer, Ehrenfeucht, Haussler, & Warmuth, 1987). This is more belief than reality, and has been both criticised and often applied wrongly (Domingos, 1999; Pecker, 2004). Yet, it still lives as a practical heuristic, and demonstrates a mindset that is not useful when working with systems. Looking at nature, it is full of phenomena that obviously are not simple. Not many people would argue that the universe is as simple as it could be. Hence, there is no reason to believe that the simplest theories are the right theories. The problem starts with defining simplicity. Domingos reviews different definitions of simplicity from the perspective of computational learning, concluding that "no fully satisfactory computable definition of simplicity exists, and perhaps none is possible" (Domingos, 1999, p. 1). In commonsensical terms, simplicity might be understood as phenomena or situations that are easy to oversee, or where there are few elements involved and there are few obvious interactions, and all you need to know springs to your eye. As demonstrated with our paper cup example, this is dependent on the interpretation. The problems continue with precisely describing the different interpretations of the razor. Domingos states that: "A critical review of the theoretical arguments for and against it shows that it is unfounded as a universal principle, and demonstrably false" (Domingos, 1999, p. 1). He states that the razor is useful in certain circumstances, but those circumstances are few. However, the idea of simplicity has come at the cost of removing attention from richness and complexity. When simplifying, we just do not deal with the same thing anymore, as indicated by the before-mentioned Anderson and Kofka. A good example of the importance of adding detail is the development of climate models wherever more parameters have been added to understand and interpret climate fluctuations through simulations. Details can have a crucial impact on how a system develops over time.

In design, the urge for simplicity has led the profession astray towards more narrow conceptions of design. Simplification has been popularized in design as an overall methodological perspective. This has been damaging and dangerous, particularly now that design is entering new domains. Simplification has almost become a main methodological approach for designers, and needs to be seriously challenged (Lissack, 2016).

There are no shortcuts when designers want to engage with complex problems. We need to work hard with training our abilities to cope with complex matters. A systemic approach to design implies that styles, fashions, and tastes are systems themselves as well as symptoms of value systems in society. As systemic designers, we must investigate and challenge those systems if they turn out to reinforce harmful behaviour like increased consumption of natural resources or increased separation of society. And unfortunately, this is what we see in many cases.

Three Problems of Time

The design brief is a central document in most design processes. It requires a fixation of factors before the design process starts. This has obvious advantages for writing contracts and to increase certainty of what is going to happen. However, the fixed design brief has several inbuilt problems that at worst increase the risk of failures. Since the design brief fixes things at the beginning of a process, no wonder the issues are about changes, flexibility and adaptation. In the following sections, we briefly discuss three interlinked problems regarding design processes related to time:

1. Starting with a narrowly framed design brief and solving emerging problems later.

2. Design is a learning process and the insight changes during the design process

3. The system we design for changes while we plan.

Previously, designers tended to begin with a reductive starting point for a design project. A typical brief from the client to a product designer would dictate the starting point and initial framing of the project. For an architect, the client would often provide the "program" or room plan. However, most designers have experienced the insufficient simplifications of such briefs, which are often erroneous and not strategically well-developed. Rarely do they take into account external factors, like considerations for society or the planet.

The second problem with fixed briefs is that insight into the issue at hand will increase during the process. The designer and the development team will learn a lot more about the problem area through their engagement, research, and design iterations. Designing is inherently a process of learning, and this will unavoidably change one's perspective.

The third problem is that the conditions around the project will change during the planning and project periods. While we plan, the systems change. We are always designing for living systems. Some are more critical, changing quickly, while others change slowly.

A dilemma is that changing things late in a design process comes at larger cost than changing them earlier. This is expressed in the cost / influence curve (*Figure 45*). So ideally, everything should be fixed as early as possible. The curve shows that design development invested in the early phases of a project are far less costly. However, the problem is that there often is too little effort and time invested in the development of design briefs. So the idea is to move more effort from later to earlier. If such investment reduces risks for errors later, it is well worth the effort. This is why I claim SOD processes are time saving and risk reducing.

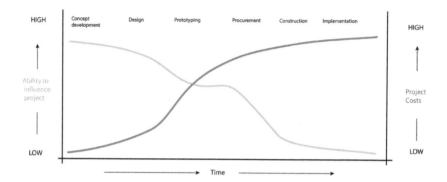

Figure 45: Cost influence curve (Birger Sevaldson, 2021).

All of these issues make the format of the classic design brief futile. To respond to this issue the Norwegian Design Council has developed the triple diamond[36] model with a particular delivery for changes in the design brief after the first diamond which concludes a "diagnosis" phase. This setup is designed for the governmental financed Stimulab projects *Figure 46*. The Stimulab project is especially geared towards solving very complex issues in public and governmental domains (Paulsen, Wildhagen, & Sevaldson, 2018; Wildhagen, 2018). SOD is a corner stone in the program.

---

36. The triple diamond model builds on the double diamond developed by the British design council. They seem to be inspired by, amongst others, Bela Banathy's divergent convergent model (Banathy, 1997). Benedicte Wildhagen from DOGA.no added the third diamond in 2018. These models are all based on the idea of analyses and synthesis first created by Pappus (290-350) (Hintikka & Remes, 1974).

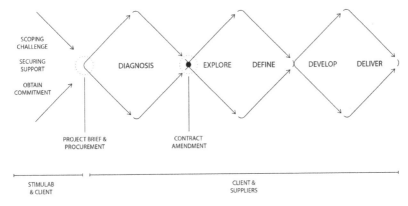

Figure 46: The triple diamond as presented by the Norwegian Design Counsil (DOGA) for the Stimulab development project for public organisations. The model puts much more effort into early phases. It also indicates a pre-process of developing an understanding for the challenges before applying for the program and a change documentation added to the contract / brief at the end of the first diamond. (StimuLab DOGA, Digdir. Permission of use by B. Wildhagen).

There is a need to change the design professions to meet the aforementioned challenges. These changes imply a change of mindset, as well as skills, competencies, techniques, and methodology, or in short: how design is practiced and which body of knowledge a designer should have. The contradiction between the need for cost framing and risk reduction and the unstable situation with learning from the process and apparent systems changes during the planning process needs to be addressed. Within the current planning paradigm, one can develop particular strategies for flexibility. Branching plans and scenarios of multiple futures can be incorporated into the design. On a higher level may be the planning – execution paradigm may need to be challenged, and different, more long-term and continuous design processes need to take over.

Ways Forward

The way forward is to change our design practice so that it is geared towards the challenges we mentioned. Design practice is a result of culture and traditions, craft, skills and competencies, mind-set, methods, and experience. All these need to be changed and trimmed towards becoming better at designing complexity. This is the main mission of SOD.

Mindset

The changes in mindset have been discussed in Part One of this book. Here, I will add some general considerations. The change in mindset implies that designers would embrace complexity and be suspicious when things look simple, realizing that apparent simplicity is a result of insufficient framing of the situation at hand. The systemic designers would act like a "scout," and search the terrain in front of them, seeking out any possible obstacle that might lie ahead. Moreover, they would enjoy this work, because they know that there is gold to be found. Understanding more of the challenges ahead is the foundation for real innovation. The mindset of the designer needs to be proactive towards complexity. Richness and complexity need to be seen as positives that contain multiple opportunities for design.

In the past, responding to conflicting interests was regarded as a compromise, a negative necessity for designers. Nowadays, we talk of negotiations as something positive, saying that design is generated in fields of tensions, interactions, and negotiations. A responsive attitude to our surroundings and to the various stakeholders can promote creativity. With this mindset, we can look at the redesign of design practice into a practice of systemic design.

Movements and Changes in Design Practices

Design culture and traditions are undergoing great change. The very nature of design is being challenged. Although the traditional notion of design still exists, there is a rupture between old and new; values of the traditional forms of design are in danger to be side-lined. We will discuss the need for new practice as well as the need to maintain some of the values and knowledge from traditional design practices later. Here, we will briefly discuss four main movements within the ongoing change of Design: convergence, divergence, migration, and immigration (*Figure 47*). In the following section, we discuss these movements in design.

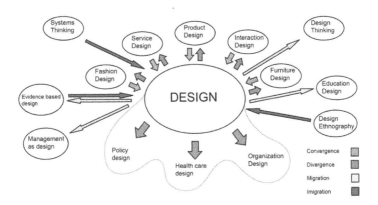

Figure 47: The design field is changing due to at least four movements. Convergence indicates that design specialities are applied together because of the need for more holistic solutions. Divergence indicates that design is specializing into sub-professions with separate knowledge bases and into new fields of application. Migration indicates that ideas and approaches are migrating from design to other fields. Immigration indicates that the application of approaches from other fields in design. This diagram shows just a few examples (Birger Sevaldson, 2018).

Design has migrated into ever-new areas with new themes and types of problems. The expanded notion of design includes almost any area, issue, problem, or field as potential projects for design. Some of these new fields have crystallized into new disciplines, e.g., interaction design and service design. There are both divergent and convergent processes at work when this forming of disciplines happens. Interaction design grows out of a need to specialize in the design of interactive experiences.[37] Service design emerged simultaneously as the western economies began to change from more traditional industries to dominantly service-based industries. The diversification of design is also apparent in the emergence of sub-specializations. Sub-specializations allow the designers' expertise to be developed in narrower frames, reaching deeper insights. These can be field specific, e.g., design for public services or typology-based specializations like hospital architecture. At the same time, parallel to this divergence, there is also a trend towards convergence, an increased generalization of design practices. This convergence is apparent in at least four ways:

---

37. Protagonists of Interaction Design regard the older field of HCI (Human Computer Interaction) to be insufficient. HCI is more based on quantitative research with intensive user testing, while interaction design is more focused on qualitative and designerly aspects of the user experience.

1. Transdisciplinarity – e.g., architects working with software development and industrial designers workings with social design.

2. Ideas, methods, techniques, and practices travelling back and forth between design specialities – e.g., product as service or the "productification" of services.

3. Designers working increasingly holistically – e.g., a product often also needs to be developed as an interaction and even in a service context.

4. The higher levels of design mentioned before are crossing disciplines naturally, with the application of generic perspectives, strategies, and principles that help to take on any challenge – e.g., adaptive expertise, participatory design, expert networks, very rapid learning etc.

Along with the divergence and convergence in design, there are two other movements in design, which we can call migration and immigration. Central ideas from design are migrating into other fields like management and general planning, where there is an increased realization that such processes are also forms of design, and that the particular mode of planning found in design is very valuable (Boland & Collopy, 2004). Another example of this is the migration of Design Thinking into business and management (Brown & Katz, 2009). At the same time, there is also a movement of other fields into the field of design. When moving into new fields, design has to be supported by additional knowledge. An example of immigration into the field of design is Design Ethnography. While designers are good at user-centric processes, they tend to fall short when designing for other cultures other than the ones they belong to. Design Ethnography helps expand the cultural landscape for design (Cranz, 2016; Wasson, 2000).

These new roles, fields, and opportunities challenge the scope of common knowledge a designer should possess. Earlier, this knowledge was more specific to the discipline, while today there is no limit to what designers need to know and should know. The demand of being informed and knowledgeable in design has long outgrown the capacity of a normal designer. However, there are other ways of dealing with this. A designer has the choice to specialize or take on a generalist role by training adaptive expertise (Smith, Ford, & Kozlowski, 1997), and working with experts. Either way, being a designer means indulging in lifelong learning processes.

All the movements in design add to the complexity of design itself. It is hard to create an orderly picture of design with all its facets, to say nothing of the many changes going on in the field. In that sense, design reflects the mess of human life and the constant struggle between order and chaos as well as control and anarchy (*Figure 50*).

Figure 48: Depicting social mess: The Fight between Carnival and Lent. (Pieter Bruegel the Elder, 1559. Public Domain).

A good way to cope with this mess of movements in design is to understand the field of design itself as a hyper complex human activity system, one that consists of interlinked and separate ideas and approaches, and one that is involved in most aspects of human life and cultures.

Exploring New Fields for Design

In the following section, we go a bit deeper into the issue of design taking on ever new challenges and entering new fields. This happens partly as the before-mentioned migration of design, and partly as divergence where design is developed into new specialities. This is the most dramatic shift of design, and the one that promises a radical change in what design can contribute to society. In this migration and diversification process, SOD can serve as a methodological framework to enter new design areas. This is exemplified in the Design for Dignity project described in the introduction. The project does not follow any established design variety, but starts with the situation the victims of sexual assaults are in. As far as we know, this was never done before. From that starting point, it crosses different design domains, resulting in a holistic design for the SAC. Another much simpler example is the Norwegian Government map in *Figure 49*.

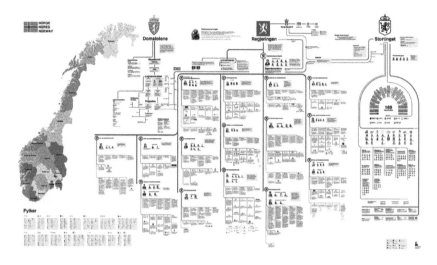

Figure 49: A map of the Norwegian state covering the three main bodies, the courts, the government, and the parliament, to the municipality level in the lower left corner (Jens Boksaspen, AHO, 2018).

The map shows a still incomplete but quite far reaching map of the system. It provides an overview and richness of information that to our knowledge has never been done before. Though this project is purely descriptive, and belongs to the genre of information visualisation, it provides a different intention. For democracy to work, citizens need to know the complexity and many of the details of our governing system. This could be a guiding aid for promoting citizen ownership to the state. One can claim that design is moving into governing, though this is only a basic example amongst many others where design processes for a while have migrated into management and organisation design (Boland & Collopy, 2004).

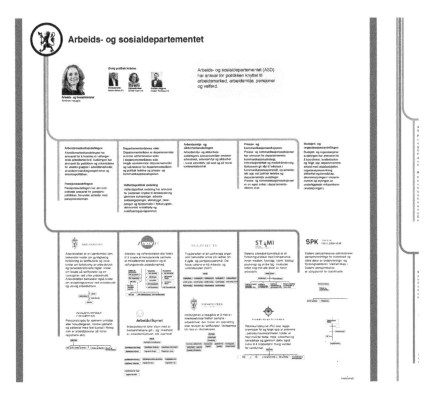

Figure 50: Detail of the Norwegian government map showing the Ministry of Labour and Social Affairs (Jens Boksaspen, AHO, 2018).

Design is constantly moving into new fields and taking on tasks that were not previously regarded as design problems. This change in the scope of the design professions is especially visible with the raising of design for health, design for public services, and design for management, organisational design, social design, and policy design. One needs to look at these changes in the design field with some care though. It is sometimes hard to distinguish general design from Design. The concept of Design Thinking has migrated into business and managerial environments, and we have already discussed the challenges of this migration into management in Part One. When it comes to diverging into new fields, there is a risk in the uncritical spread of design into these fields. There might be a gap in basic knowledge of those fields, as well as a lack of good strategies, methodologies, and practices to facilitate a successful divergence. Lack of insight, combined with little experience and overly enthusiastic beliefs in the superiority of design can lead to hubris. Diverging into new fields for design is dependent on satisfying very wide and deep learning processes, establishing networks with experts, and having good antennas and listening skills. Such projects are dependent on a good balance of courage and humbleness.

These new movements in design have raised the question, "can anything be a design task and can designers design anything?" In the following section, I dive deeper into this question.

Can Designers Design Anything?

The divergence and migration of design into new fields has been met with both resistance and enthusiasm. There is no doubt that designers can contribute substantially to many different contexts outside of what is regarded within the traditional boundaries of design. On the other hand, it is clear that a naive or exploitative use of design can do more harm than good. To answer the question, "can designers design anything?" we need to take a step back and analyse it from different perspectives. [38] Let us first look at the claim by applying the same question to another research-based profession. The comparison to doctors seems to constantly come up in our lunchtime discussions. Can doctors heal anything? The question is absurd. We all know they cannot. Designers are not doctors, so this comparison is not entirely logical, but it helps to clarify some aspects of the question. The fields are very different. Doctors are generally reactive in practice, responding to existing health problems[39]. We go to the doctor when something is wrong. Meanwhile, designers are proactive and generative, often needing to create new things. So, designers create, to a much higher degree, their criteria and conditions. At the same time, they need to involve a greater number of given dynamic parameters that inform the design. For doctors, the criteria for success are quite clear, whereas for designers, they are much more relative and discussable. Moreover, for doctors, the fundamental object of their profession, the human body, is changing slowly. There is a lot in medicine that changes fast, but human physiology is relatively stable, whereas for designers, there is no such underlying object, and the conditions we work in are changing very quickly. However, what if we put a little twist to the question: Can doctors heal anything better than non-doctors? The answer seems to be yes for most cases. What about designers? Can they design anything better than non-designers? This is much harder to answer. We have neighbouring professions, like engineers or stylists, who also seem to engage in design activities. We also have the aforementioned notion of "general design." The term "design" is used in many fields, in many ways. We do not need

---

38. The following is based on an earlier article (Sevaldson, 2013a).
39. This does obviously not apply to preventive medicine.

to entangle these definitions at the moment. For this discussion, we can simply talk about Design with a capital D.

This leads to another difference between doctors and designers. Doctors have a foundation that they share, on which they can then become specialists in clearly defined areas, or they can also choose to be generalists, which is also a well-defined role. Designers have a far less well defined foundation. There is a noticeable difference in the foundational training of an arts and craft-oriented school and an industrial design school. Specializations in design are far less well-defined, and they are in the process of convergence and divergence, as mentioned before.

This convergence and divergence is creating dynamic adaptability in the design field. Adapting to new conditions and challenges is an inherent skill and competence in design. However, is this adaptability developed enough, so that designers can jump between design specialties to design anything? Obviously, not without taking significant risks and engaging in intensive learning processes.

So, even within the boundaries of what can be regarded as professional Design, a designer cannot just design anything. Nevertheless, can they do it better than non-designers? There are some necessary skills and competencies, perspectives, and approaches that are applicable across the whole design field. For example, these include the competence and experience to run design projects, visualization skills, and the ability to integrate and synthesize solutions from tasks where there is no right or wrong answer, only better or worse solutions. The doctor's result, on the other hand, is far more easily measured. The achieved healing degree can be evaluated against a healthy state of health; even if there is a wide range of "normality" when it comes to health, it is still relatively well defined compared to the outputs of design projects, which does not have a preferred global standard. In medicine, there are grey zones too, but the goal is defined. Ideally, the patient returns to a healed state. In Design, there are no such ideals or given goals, only better or worse resolutions, and these resolutions can be very different and hard to compare. A core competence of designers is the skill to derive a result from contradicting, ill defined, complex, and fuzzy input. This is a generic ability that is especially apparent amongst designers. So, the answer is yes; designers can generally design better than non-designers within the domain of Design.

As such, we can reformulate our original question to: "Can designers take on any task, and design for any situation with relative success compared to non-designers?"

We can address this in two ways: since designers are the ones who design, they can attempt to design for any situation in the same way as doctors can attempt to heal or treat any illness. Can designers design successfully for any situation? Obviously not, just as doctors can often be unsuccessful. Nevertheless, are they more likely to succeed than non-designers? I suggest that the answer is yes.

So, the final answer is that designers are fully justified, and even to a certain degree qualified, to design for any situation. Are they successful in this? Sometimes, often not. However, designers could be much better prepared for situations where they embark on new challenges and enter new fields for design.

Designers need to be both self-confident and humble when entering new fields for design. Confident in the fact that designers can indeed do great things in areas where they traditionally have not been before, but also humble about their inherent knowledge, and being open to rapid learning and to seek out necessary expertise. Without these traits, there is risk that the work can be hilariously superficial, and in the worst case, the problem can be made worse.

The challenge with designing for new fields is the lack of information, knowledge, experience, and skills that are specific for the area. To address this, we have developed a very fast learning process, conducted in a designerly way through gigamapping. These learning processes help designers achieve an overview and single out areas where support from insiders and experts would be needed.

A Few Examples

I will start with a simple example of the need to design a porcelain lamp. Although this does not seem to involve designing in a new field, the problem here concerns the material, in this case, porcelain. The student had no prior experience with the material, so she was challenged to enter the new world of a demanding material, and to use that material in innovative ways. The ambition was to finish the lamp within a timeframe of three months. "An impossible task!" said the expert, a Professor of ceramics. Porcelain is a challenging material that takes years to master. With the rapid learning process and the expert network in place, the student succeeded within the timeframe. The learning process involved a broad investigation at the start to understand the basics, the history, technology, and material features of porcelain. The investigation was done with the help of gigamapping. This helped facilitate the dialogue with the experts and enabled the designer to ask relevant questions so that the expert discussion started on a higher level. This kick-start of the learning process was crucial to reach the deadline. The project is an example that shows how, under certain circumstances, a targeted process and a suitable approach can allow a designer to cross specialties in design.

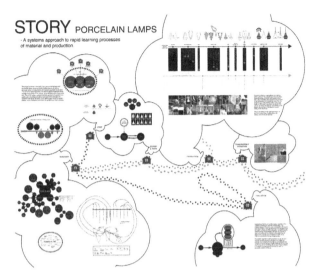

Figure 51: Final Gigamap of the very rapid learning process (VRLP) conducted in the process of making a finalized prototype for a porcelain lamp within three months. This "meta-map" shows several diagrams mappings of both qualitative and quantitative data, as well as how this was related to and used in the rapid learning process (Ida Naomi Vidal, AHO, 2010).

Figure 52: Final porcelain lamp showing the innovative use of patterning with sand blasting technology (Ida Naomi Vidal, AHO, 2010).

113

When entering new territories where the designer and sometimes even the design field at large have prior expertise, patterns, or best practices to rely on, the task becomes even more challenging. In the project "My Last Home," students worked for and in an elderly home to investigate what designers might be able to contribute (Kydland, Støylen, & Olsen, n.d.). With an open starting point and approach, the project kicked off with an intensive inquiry that included gigamapping, conversations, fieldwork, and workshops for co-designing and information mapping. At the outset, the students focused on designing for the inhabitants, the users of the elderly home. However, a deeper learning process leading to better understanding of the system (*Figure 53, Figure 54, Figure 55*) revealed that helping the staff alter their work practice could lead to much greater impact for the inhabitants. The synergy of this was that the staff got an improved working situation, and the ripple effects in the system were also significant. Given that resources were very low, the resulting solution was a simple role-defining tool that enabled the staff to take on a clearly defined social role for the inhabitants (*Figure 56*). This social role was previously taken for granted, and often dissolved in lieu of more clearly defined roles and tasks that came to the forefront. Despite the fact that such insights and discussions were nothing new in the nursing field, a simple solution was missing. The response was very positive, and the system is still in use at the elderly home today. In this case, the designers were able to contribute with their core competence. The project showed that designers could enter new ground, gain the needed knowledge and overview, the needed interaction with experts, as well as the systemic understanding to produce relevant, innovative design interventions and open up the organisation for design.

Figure 53: The Project "My Last Home," addressed the working conditions at an elderly home. The method involved extensive fieldwork and participatory design (Image: Kydland, Støylen & Olsen, AHO, 2012).

Figure 54: Different forms of information mapping used in the project (Image: Kydland, Støylen & Olsen, AHO, 2012).

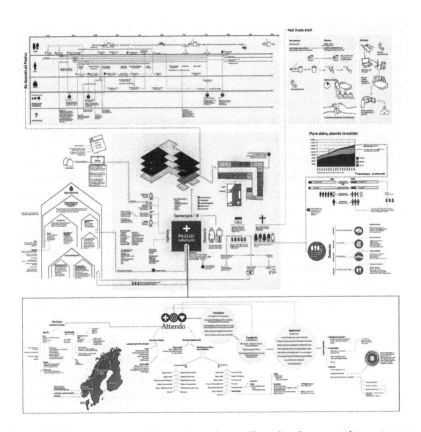

Figure 55: The many forms of observation where collected and connected in a gigamap depicting a whole system understanding (Kydland, Støylen & Olsen, AHO, 2012).

Figure 56: The working roles were divided into four main roles: Medical (blue), Environment and Hygiene (green), Nutrition and Caring (Orange), Activity and Togetherness (red). The red role was the one hardest to fulfil and used to be the one suffering in competition with the others. A button clearly communicates the roles for the inhabitants as well as for co-workers (Image: Kydland, Støylen & Olsen, AHO, 2012).

In this book, several other projects that exemplify the process of entering new territories for designers individually or for design as a field are presented. Does this establish new design fields? The answer is complex. Migration of a field into other fields always comes with some degree of adaptation and change, and sub-specialities might emerge. For a new design field to emerge, quite a lot of effort and broad application as well as methodology and theory needs to be developed. The examples shown are obviously singular cases and do not qualify for establishing a new design field. The joint effort of the systemic design movement, though, has crystalized and clarified a new field in design. Yet we need to keep in mind that this also builds on efforts years back in time.

Bruno Latour addresses this discussion in his wonderful keynote lecture, "A Cautious Prometheus? A Few Steps Toward a Philosophy of Design" for the Design History Society at the University of Falmouth in Cornwall, UK (Latour, 2008). In Greek mythology, Prometheus was a magician and inventor known for giving fire to humanity, protecting humans from the gods. He represented wisdom and foresight. In the lecture, Latour describes the humbleness and braveness that he suggests should be central to the role of the designer and which we think are central to SOD.

The important thing is to develop and demonstrate approaches, methodologies, and practices that allow the designer to enter ever-new areas for designing in both a humble and courageous way, removing the naivety that is too often demonstrated by overly-eager designers on a mission. Amongst the methodologies, approaches, and practices suggested here are the Very Rapid Learning Process, adaptive expertise, Rich Design spaces, co-inquiry and design driven by gigamapping, systemic sensibility, and systemic design at large. If we manage to develop this expertise further so that our processes become sufficiently good and flexible, we might reach a point where we can claim:

"Yes, designers can design anything."

What Systems Thinking Brings to Design

This chapter describes why systems thinking is needed in design and WHAT it can bring to the design field. It summarises the systems field and discusses particular variations in relation to design. It gives a short overview of the history of systems thinking in design and why it has not been successful in fully integrating into the design field before. This theme is obviously very complex and open for debate and interpretation. The walkthrough is therefore meandering through it, returning to issues several times to provide the insight that there are no clear cut answers nor standard positions to this discussion.

Systems At Large: A Rich and Vast Field of Thought and Practices

When looking at the field of systems thinking[40], it is a conglomerate of many different approaches and theories. This is not the place to elaborate on this, because it is far too big of a world to fully describe here. The systems literature is vast and worth a deeper study. There are several books that intend to provide an overview and discuss it as one field. Systems thinking was early theorized as a universal theory, by Betalanfy, Boulding and Weinberg and elaborated on by, for example, Skyttner. (Bertalanffy, 1969; Boulding, 1956; Skyttner, 2005; Weinberg,

---

40. The term Systems Thinking is used here as an inclusive circumscription of the large landscape of systemic approaches and related perspectives. It is also used as a term that describes a way of thinking rather than a commitment to one or the other of these theories.

1975). Systems approaches have several origins, and developed into different theories. A list of the main approaches would include Operations research, Cybernetics, Systems dynamics, Soft systems methodology, and Critical systems thinking. Besides that, there are numerous less dominant approaches and even more plentiful specific applications such as systems engineering, systems models in creativity research, and systems approaches to management, etc. One book that provides a good overview is Gerald Midgley's Systemic intervention, Philosophy, Methodology, and Practice (2000). Midgley not only provides a comprehensive overview, but also describes how the systems world has developed over time in three waves. We will return to this shortly. For now, it is important to comprehend the richness and diversity of the systems field and to keep that in mind when discussing different aspects of it in relation to design. *Figure 57* is one example of an attempt to map out the richness and diversity of the systems field and how it is related. This is but one interpretation, and one could also claim that it is far from complete.

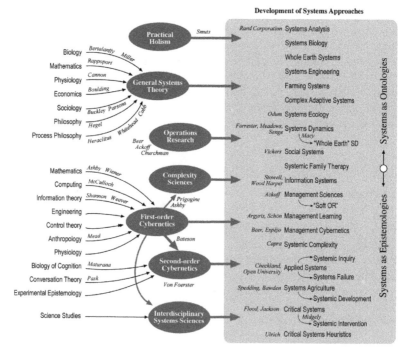

Figure 57: Map of the influences in Systems Thinking. No such mapping is complete. The main issue is that all such maps are gross simplifications of the field. For example, from the SOD perspective, it misses the relation to Gestalt theory and Soft Systems Methodology (Ison, 2008, p. 144. By permission of author).

Why Systems Models Have Failed in Design

Before the Systemic Design initiative, the implementation of Systems Thinking in design had limited effect. There may be several reasons for this. Traditionally, particular systems approaches such as Systems Dynamics or Cybernetics have mainly been academic, descriptive, and theory-heavy. This has made it challenging for designers who want to integrate systems approaches into design. While other fields developed their own adopted versions of systems approaches, this did not happen in design. One such example is Systems Engineering.

Despite the lack of success of systems perspectives in design, such ideas have been present in design theory for a long time. Early authors theorizing the role of Systems Thinking in design include the architect Christopher Alexander (Alexander, 1964) and design professor Horst Rittel (Protzen & Harris, 2010). Others like Russell Ackoff, who was trained as an architect, have referred extensively to design in their work (Ackoff & Sheldon, 2003). Bela Banathy explains systems approaches as design processes, and frequently refers to the design research field. He did great work that is still relevant when making progress in relating design and Systems Thinking (Banathy, 1997; Banathy & Jenks, 1990). Although these pioneers have contributed to Systems Thinking beyond their fields, it never really got a good foothold in common design practice. There might be many reasons for this. The systems perspectives in the "first wave of Systems Thinking"[41] were based mainly on a mechanistic worldview, a cause-and-effect perspective that could ultimately be quantified and simulated in a computer to produce predictions of how a system would behave in the future (Midgley, 2000). Such systems perspectives were predominantly descriptive and predictive. This changed with the emergence of Systems Engineering (Hall, 1962), where constructing new systems became central. However, this approach was very technical and mechanically-oriented, framing Systems Engineering as a limited approach that is useful for the construction of complex technical systems. Systems Engineering is not very applicable to other types of systems with components that behave in less predictable ways, such as social systems. This approach was insufficient for addressing the human activity-based, social, and cultural systems that are inherent in design, despite recent developments in Systems Engineering to narrow the gap towards design (Hinte & Tooren, 2008). The arrival of the so-called "second wave of Systems Thinking" with Soft Systems Methodology (SSM) changed the picture (Midgley, 2000). Not only did this break away from the mechanistic view on systems, but it also moved from description towards action. There was a growing realization that the position promulgated by the first

---

41. Midgley defines the first wave as the original, traditional systems approach as the "hard" approaches; the second wave is defined by Soft Systems Methodology, and the third wave by Critical Systems Thinking.

wave of systems theories that of an outside observer and god-like manager of systems was problematic, and that being an observer or manager implies being an integrated and inescapable part of the system. This realization was apparent in Second Order Cybernetics (Ranulph Glanville, 1994), as well as in SSM and its approach to Action Research (Checkland, 2000a). Modern systems approaches like SSM have relaxed the technical side of Systems Thinking to address social systems and human activity systems through action and Action Research (Checkland P. & Poulter, 2006)[42]. In SSM, systems are regarded as far less rigid, messier, and more flexible than in traditional systems theories. Still, there is a gap between Action Research and design. Social action as systems intervention prescribed by SSM and its approach to Action Research is different from designing. While action-oriented change processes share, for example, participation, co-creation, and a democratic foundation with contemporary design approaches, the holistic overview, visual thinking, and negotiation implied in the form-giving aspect of design are missing. We will return to this issue in the next chapter when we discuss what design brings to systems thinking.

Another reason for the failure of Systems Thinking in design might be that the design field is fragmented into many diverse approaches, which can be difficult to unify with others. In addition, the systems world is divided into camps, some of which are in disharmony with one another. None of these singular directions and models are sufficient to incorporate the multiple dimensions of the world. Because design needs to encompass an undefined and principally unlimited scope of the world, it varies according to context, setting, and agencies, leading to increased degrees of transgressions between knowledge fields and disciplines. As such, design is in many aspects undisciplined, blurry, and messy; it resists being moulded into singular, orderly models or worldviews. This might seem to be a disadvantage when it comes to solving clearly defined tasks. However, it is an advantage when grappling with complex problematiques where thinking across domains and flexibility in approaches, perspectives, and methods is needed. Design, therefore, needs to maintain an eclectic and free approach that is unrestrained from any singular orthodoxy. In design, we would prefer to triangulate between contrasting views rather than submit to singular approaches. What is required is a dialogic way of approaching the world. Such an approach to systems theories has emerged in Critical Systems Thinking, the "third wave in Systems Thinking" (Flood & Romm, 1996; M C Jackson, 1985; Ulrich, 1983). In this theoretical framework, different system perspectives are used pragmatically and critically[43]. Critical Systems Thinking solves the problem of an overly rigid

---

42. Action Research is a participatory research method used in organisations to learn how to change them through a reflective process.

43. The criticality expands beyond the critical use of different systems perspectives, to critically investigate all aspects and issues regarding the systems at hand. This includes for example issues of social exclusion (Midgley, 2000, p. 14)

application of existing system models that would squeeze the interpretation of real life into precast moulds. Inflexibility is unproductive for design, since design is fundamentally about creating something new. Nevertheless, all these explanations for the failure of Systems Thinking in design do not apply to people like Rittel, Ackof, and Banathy, who had a profound and advanced understanding of design and systems, and how they might relate to each other. What was missing, however, was the demonstration of systems approaches as design practice. It is not enough to know; one has to demonstrate how this might play out and how this might be beneficial. Which degrees of prescriptive methodology contra methodological freedom can we work with? What does systemic design look like, and how is it practiced? We need to develop design as systems intervention on its own premises. The main intention of SOD is to develop, demonstrate, and disseminate systemic design practices.

Systems Thinking Seen from the SOD Viewpoint

As mentioned, there is no place in this book for a comprehensive description of the vast field of systems theories. It also does not make sense to dive too deeply into these theories at the cost of the purpose of this text, to emphasise practice. The relevance of these theories has proven to be of limited value for the practice of SOD. This position is related to Ulrich's Critical Heuristics:

> *Critical Heuristics* (or by its full name: Critical Heuristics of Social Systems Design) is a new approach to both Systems Thinking and practical philosophy, an approach that aims to help the applied scientist in respect to this task. It does not seek to prove theoretically why and how practical reason is possible (as do all presently known 'schools' of practical philosophy) but rather concentrates on providing planners as well as affected citizens with the heuristic support they need to practice practical reason, i.e., to lay open, and reflect on, the normative implications of systems designs, problem definitions, or evaluations of social programs (Ulrich, 1983 at 277).

Despite the fact that there is limited practical value of the many systems theories for the process of designing, there are cases where they clearly play a decisive role. You would not use a Gigamap to understand the weather system. For that, other systems models would be appropriate. However, you could use gigamapping to map out the many consequences of climate change.

To understand the drivers of profit generation in the Norwegian housing market, applying a systems dynamics modelling, a causal loop diagram, with unbalanced (positive) and balanced (negative) feedback loops is preferable over other types of mapping. *Figure 58* shows a simple working draft of a causal loop diagram (leaving out stock and flows for the time). Such causal loop diagrams are used for several fields, for example in agriculture (Walters et al., 2016). Yet systems dynamics modelling has been criticised. The problem is to understand and interpret the nature of the positive and negative relations, [also called Same (S) and Opposite (O)] in a manner that correctly reflects the real life systems (Richardson, 1997). Yet in this case, it provides an overall picture of the many unbalanced loops in the system explaining why it tends to spiral out of control.

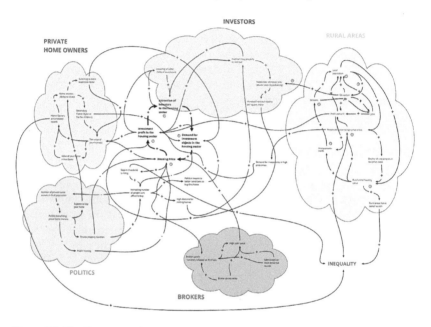

Figure 58: The Norwegian housing marked: A whirlpool of unbalanced feedback loops (Birger Sevaldson, 2020).

Other limitations of such modelling are the limitation to the amount of information one can handle, and that everything needs to be quantified. Their value is that they provide understanding of stocks and flows in systems, and they can play an important role in a larger Gigamap. The Gigamap would indicate the space for critical systems thinking where different perspectives and general criticality will come together.

Therefore, it is worth situating SOD and systemic design within the larger context of the vast systems world, and to eclectically and pragmatically draw from its achievements. We also encourage the reader to engage and read up on the literature. For now, it is sufficient to understand the contours and the richness of the field. Therefore, what follows is a short cross-section through the field of Systems Thinking and further development of the overview in Part One.

Systems Thinking is not new. Alexander A. Bogdanov (1913) is today increasingly regarded as the forerunner of systems approaches with publications dating as early as 1913. His work was largely forgotten, and Ludwig von Bertalanffy, an Austrian biologist, is often instead regarded as the father of Systems Thinking. In his famous book General Systems Theory, Bertalanffy describes the systems approach not only as something relevant for biology, but also as a general worldview to understand the interrelations between things (1969). Bertalanffy established systems theory as a principal paradigm from which theories could be developed. Since then, systems approaches have developed into many fields. According to Bertalanffy and others like Weinberg and Skyttner, General Systems Theory describes the generic validity of Systems Thinking (Skyttner, 2005; Weinberg, 2001). It spans from Cybernetics to ecology, and from applied systems approaches to new theories of the brain.

Systems Thinking developed into different branches, like Operations research (Churchman, 1970), Cybernetics (Ashby, 1956) and Systems Dynamics (Forrester, 1989, 1991). In the beginning until the post war times, systems theories were regarded as ways to explain pretty much everything in the natural and human world. The models were quite mechanistic, which worked well on natural systems while being of limited value when it came to understanding society. Ackoff was early to criticize the hard mechanistic approach to human activity systems (Ackoff & Emery, 1972), and Churchman (1979; 1970), who came from Operations Research, also contributed to softer systems approaches. Systems Dynamics was developed further into a softer version by Meadows (2008), introducing the notion of dancing with systems. This became important in understanding systems as dynamic, and that working with systems required both concrete skills and a "musicality" mindset and intuition, just as in dancing. This move towards a less rigid and mechanistic approach to Systems Thinking was concluded by Peter Checkland, introducing Soft Systems Methodology (2000b). We will return to this move a bit later.

Parallel to the emergence of different system philosophies and approaches, a great deal happened in the application of Systems Thinking. Systems perspectives find applications in the study of creativity (Gruber, 1988; Csikszentmihalyi, 1999) and in creative practice (Gruber & Wallace, 1999). People like Gharajedaghi and Christensen, among others, have described its application in management (Christensen, 2006; Gharajedaghi, 2006). This also includes writers like Majer and Rechtin, who defined Systems Architecting, a soft version of systems engineering inspired by how building architects think (Rechtin, 1999; Maier & Rechtin, 2000). Senge described systems perspectives in organisational development and management (Senge, et al., 2008). Miller and Page describe its modern application in the simulation of social life (Miller & Page, 2007), and Mariussen describes systems approaches to policy-making (Mariussen & Uhlin, 2006). Broadman et al. (Broadman & Sauser, 2008) and Gunderson et al. describe systems approaches as a crucial element for solving the large-scale problems of our times (Gunderson &

Holling, 2002). Jackson (1990), Flood (Flood. & Ulrich, 1990; Flood & Romm, 1996), Ulrich (2000a), Midgley (2000) and others have defined Critical Systems Thinking as a concept that binds the different approaches together in a pragmatic way.

With the introduction of Soft Systems Methodology, we can talk of soft and hard approaches. SSM emerged as a reaction to the insufficiency of the more cause-and-effect and mechanistic approaches applied to human activity systems, which resist an orderly model of systems and regard the human world as "messy" and disordered. Midgley describes the traditional systems theories as the first wave of systems; the emergence of SSM is the second wave of systems theories; and Critical Systems Thinking is regarded as the third wave (Midgley, 2000). There are many nuances in this picture and some of the hard approaches like Systems Dynamics or Systems Engineering have insisted that their applications include human activity systems. This is apparent in the late Donella Meadow's engaging texts (Meadows, 1999; Meadows, 2008).

Limitations

There are obviously many additional sources and discussions that could or should have made their way into the SOD ecology of knowledge. However, each approach has its limitations, and the framing of SOD is not an exception. The framing is not given nor fully argued logically. Dealing in particular with complex systems requires the honesty to admit our shortcomings. The universal limiting factor is time. Since SOD implies a systems view that breaches the given frames and that seeks connections across the gaps, one ends up with the realisation that everything is connected with everything and fully understanding a system would require a lifetime effort. This is obviously not a useful insight for action. Therefore, it makes sense to draw the limitations of SOD for now. These limitations might change in the future, and others might create a different framing for SOD or for new versions flourishing in the field of systemic design.[44]

---

44. Here I will touch upon a few obvious sources that are left out of our discussion. These are texts that obviously have something to contribute, but which I chose to leave out for now. Amongst these we can mention, for example, Niklas Luhmann's text, 'Social Systems' (1995) and his 'Ecological Communication' (1989). Gregory Bateson's 'Steps to an Ecology of Mind' (Bateson, 1975, 2000) Humberto Maturana and Francisco Varela on autopoiesis, (2002; 1980), Magnus Ramage on Systems Thinking (Ramage & Shipp, 2009), Warflield (2003) and numerous others.

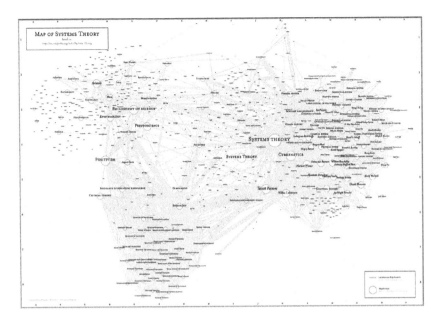

Figure 59: Map of the vast field of systems theories, generated by collecting links between articles from Wikipedia (Christopher Warnow, 2012. (Reprint permitted by author).

The judgements I made for the limitation of SOD at this stage might be easy to criticize. However, confronted with the vast complexity of the systems field itself (*Figure 59*), no recap will be complete, and some pragmatic choices have to be made.

For our purposes that is, not to suggest yet another systems perspective, but to develop a designerly approach to systems thinking and systems practice, it is sufficient to keep in mind the variety of systems approaches spanning from hard to soft and the model of the three waves, culminating with the pragmatic-eclectic approach of Critical Systems Thinking.

As argued, I want to stop diving deeper into the general field of systems theories because I doubt such a studies' relevance for developing a systemic design practice. This position seems a bit disrespectful and needs further explanation. Theories are only useful for practice in a limited way. Theories can inform certain details of practice, yet practice is based on much more than theory. Theory can inform methods, and through this, practice. However, theory is not exclusively required to change methods. Empiric experiences of what works is as important in general practice research, and much more important specifically in the field of design. Design knowledge is to a large degree built bottom up, grounded in practice.

Systems approaches have been tested and tried in design for a fair amount of time, but never made it into mainstream practices. This might be because theory-heavy systems models are top heavy, and hence disturb the main knowledge ecology of design. Traditional systems approaches required replacing central aspects of designing with prescribed systemic modelling methods that never really suited a design process. In fact, these modelling techniques seem to have a counterproductive effect on designing, reducing, and hampering generative thinking and design innovation. This was rightfully rejected by a large part of the design community because the negative implications were so obvious. This failure of Systems Thinking is described by Fred Collopy:

> Each of Systems Thinking's various manifestations demands some degree of subscription to an orthodoxy (a particular view of just what Systems Thinking is). And each requires that the user master a large number of related ideas and techniques, most of which are not particularly useful on their own (Collopy, 2009).

These requirements are at odds with how we tend to acquire new knowledge. Rather than accepting a new idea because we must, we like to try it out. A new skill is most likely to interest us if it contributes to both short-term and long-term learning objectives. And the easier it is to try out parts of a theory, the more likely we are to jump in (Collopy, 2009).

What Collopy describes is a top-down theory driven approach to developing methods. The problems of Systems Thinking are not limited to design, but they become particular obstructions to the design process. While the development of SOD was influenced by Systems Thinking, the most crucial influence is still from the design field.

From Hard to Soft

Let us meander back and dive a bit deeper into the development from hard and quantitative systems approaches towards softer approaches and an eclectic position (critical systems) that draws from multiple models and perspectives. As mentioned, Systems Thinking was predominantly understood as a rather mechanistic method to solve systems mathematically (Checkland, 2000b). The architect and writer Christopher Alexander was looking at systems in a similar way when he attempted to express the systems approach to architectural design mathematically (Alexander, 1964). As late as 1991, Jay Forrester claimed that Systems Dynamics, with the help of large computers, could accurately predict issues in company management (J. Forrester, 1991). There was an exaggerated belief in the potential of quantitative data. Relations were understood mostly in a quantitative way and from a cause-and-effect perspective. The attempt was to generate mathematical models (e.g., computer simulation) that could be used to understand and predict complex systems behaviour. Though computers and technologies for simulation have developed greatly since then, the general view today is that prediction is limited, and simulations are regarded more as learning tools and models to understand possible dynamic behaviour in the world. Let us be clear: these models are absolutely crucial for the future of the globe. Applied to climate change, they are the central tool to understand the complex interlinked processes in our global climate. It has taken years to develop them, and they have been increasingly refined and are becoming amazingly reliable.

As mentioned, the division in systems fields has in the last years become increasingly blurred, and there is a tendency towards convergence. For example, some hard approaches argue their value also lies on the soft side, adapting their approach to human activities (Lane, 2000), and others like Systems Engineering, as mentioned before, have developed variants very close to design (Hinte & Tooren, 2008), or related to ways designers are thinking, for example, Systems Architecting (Maier & Rechtin, 2000). Ranulph Glanville proposed an approach to Systemic Design very much framed by second order cybernetics (2014; 1994).

One such case of realising the shortcomings of hard systems approaches and adjusting them to meet more of the messiness typically found in human activity systems is Systems Dynamics and how it has been expanded and softened through the approach developed by Donella Meadows (D. H. Meadows, 2008). The Systems Dynamics approach is concerned with establishing and defining the elements of the system, hierarchical division, definition of feedback loops, and boundaries. In the case of boundaries, there is an admittance of the difficulties that boundaries are mental constructs (2008, p. 95). Meadows also softens the notion of hierarchy.

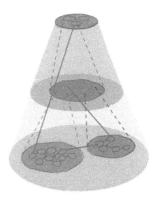

Figure 60: Diagram of systemic hierarchies where supra systems and subsystems are orderly nested. In real life situations, such clear order is hard to find. In all complexly engineered artefacts, the hierarchical order is broken as indicated by the red links. See for example Figure 66 (Redrawn and modified after Skyttner, 2005, Author and Palak Dudani).

In hard systems, the notion of hierarchy is seen as orderly, clear, and obvious. (*Figure 60*). In real-life situations, this is rarely the case, as mentioned before. For example, strictly speaking, there is hardly such a thing as a suprasystem (except the universe) that is not also a subsystem and everything vice versa. The idea common in hierarchies that subsystems are increasingly simple is not always the case. Sometimes, there are loops in the hierarchy where subsystems become supra systems upstream in the hierarchy (*Figure 68*). Meadows softens the explanation of hierarchies and explains it in terms of gradients of relations:

> In hierarchical systems, relationships within each subsystem are denser and stronger than relationships between subsystems. Everything is still connected to everything else, but not equally strongly (p.83).

This opens up for interpretation and "reading" of systems rather than regarding them as given. This implies projecting different views onto systems, using the various systems models as lenses to look at various aspects of the systems at hand.

The move towards softer versions of systems theories has been developed through critique. Jordan, for example, criticises the application of systems models as feedback systems to living organisms. His critique is that these concepts only superficially resemble the feedback idea, a diagrammatic orthodoxy originating from control engineering. He states that the description of systems should be sparse because the advanced models would bias and mislead the interpretation of living systems. He states, criticising the notion of "self-organising systems:"

> Systems is at a level of generality similar to 'phylum.' If we know the Phylum[45] to which and organism belongs and nothing else, we know very little about the organisms. Ditto for system. The only thing that needs to be common to all systems are identifiable entities and identifiable connections between them. In all other ways systems can vary unlimitedly (Jordan, 1968 at p. 64).

Jordan explains the term 'system' from a perception psychology point of view as a way we organise phenomena in our perception system and mind. He defined these core phenomena as entities and their connectivity. Since everything is connected in one or the other way, this moves the notion of systems from being something found in the world as something concrete that can be explained independently from the way we perceive it to the realm of perception, interpretation, and cognition. A similar view is expressed by Peter Checkland when describing SSM. On the other side, SSM does not mention feedback at all. However, it does not have the intentions of providing a universal theory, and Checkland is clearly aware of SSM's limitations, stating that it is basically a learning system for human

---

45. In biology, a phylum is a level of classification below kingdom and above class: https://en.wikipedia.org/wiki/Phylum

activity systems a tool to create purposeful activities rather than creating models of the real world (Checkland, 2000a).

We will return to this later.

From Order to Chaos

The emergence of chaos theory contributed to a less rigid understanding of mechanistic systems. Chaos theory demonstrated that unpredictable behaviour is not only caused by the complex interaction of systems, but was also, in relatively simple systems, inherently independent of any external influences or variations in starting conditions. A chaos system would never repeat itself. A classic example is the Lorenz attractor. The Lorenz attractor can be understood as an algorithm simulating a virtual pendulum that never would repeat the exact same path. Such chaotic pendulums are for example a pendulum with another pendulum attached to it. This describes the simplest form of a non-linear system.

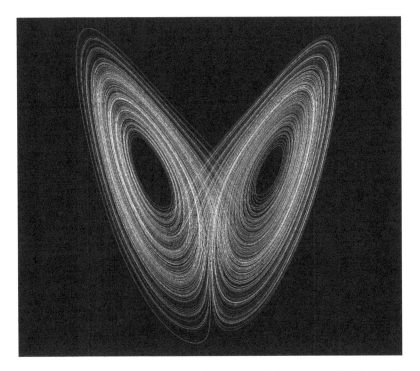

Figure 61: Lorenz attractor (Computed in Fractint by Wikimol. Public Domain).

The new insights regarding chaotic behaviour as inherent in systems changed how we understand simulations, and how much we can depend on them. The simulations are principally only able to simulate one or a few possible outcomes of an unlimited number of potential solutions. Interpretation is therefore needed to judge, critique, and validate the simulations. This adds to the argument that designed systems interpretations are to be preferred over mathematical modelling when it comes to designing for the real world. Chaos algorithms made it possible to simulate real-world systems like weather systems in a more realistic manner (Gleick, 1993). Ironically, a mathematically modelled proof was needed to demonstrate the unpredictability of very complex systems. The realization that unpredictability was built into the system without outside influence was both shocking and relieving. Shocking because it meant we were facing problems in forecasting that probably we will never totally overcome. Relieving for many, including myself, that the world is not as simplistic as regarded by the mainstream science of those days. It is a soothing thought that for millions of years waves have washed the shores of the continents but never was one wave exactly the same as another. Also, the interplay between natural and manmade systems became much more evident, further supporting the interpretation that social and cultural behaviour contributes to an even more complex, but also flexible, approach to Systems Thinking.

The emergence of chaos theory weakened the trust in hard systems and the potential of their simulations. Though the "hard" systems theories based on mathematical description of living systems have failed in their original quest to provide generic modelling principals that would allow them to simulate and predict any aspect of natural and human existence, Systems Thinking has developed further into many directions and fields. Simulations might not have lived up to the expectations when it comes to prediction, but they are more important than ever in their role as scenarios and learning devices. As mentioned, simulation models are getting better and more accurate in helping us understand the effects of climate change in these times of uncertainty. Despite this, however, the usability of hard system models in simulating human activity systems is still limited today.

The table in *Figure 62* compares central features of soft and hard systems approaches (Ison, 2008). Interesting is the realisation that soft systems approaches are more geared towards learning then goal seeking.

The 'hard' and 'soft' traditions of systems thinking compared	
The hard systems thinking tradition	**The soft systems thinking tradition**
oriented to goal seeking	oriented to learning
assumes the world contains systems that can be engineered	assumes the world is problematical but can be explored by using system models
assumes system models to be models of the world (ontologies)	assumes system models to be intellectual constructs (epistemologies)
talks the language of 'problem' and 'solutions'	talks the language of 'issues' and 'accommodations'
Advantages	**Advantages**
allows the use of powerful techniques	is available to all stakeholders including professional practitioners; keeps in touch with the human content of problem situations
Disadvantages	**Disadvantages**
may lose touch with aspects beyond the logic of the problem situation	does not produce the final answers; accepts that inquiry is never-ending

(Adapted from Checkland, 1985)

Figure 62: Comparing central features of "hard" vs "soft" systems approaches (Ison, 2008).

Complexity

Let us return to the issue of complexity. The etymology of the word "complex" is interesting. The word has Latin roots: com = together; plex = plaited (to weave, braid, entwine). Following from this, complex means woven together. It is also synonymous with surrounding and encompassing and a whole comprised of interconnected parts (Online Etymology Dictionary, n.d.). All these slightly similar yet diverse uses of the word "complex" fit well with a common-sense understanding. This is the way we have used the term in this book.

However, we need shortly to address the research that is done specifically on complexity, called complexity science or Complex Systems Science. Complexity science is a close relative of systems sciences, and one can claim that all systems theories, and methods address issues of complexity. However, Complexity science is by most sources described in a more limited manner than other systems sciences. Typically it is concerned about understanding and simulating the behaviour of large numbers of similar entities, interacting on a local scale and from this producing large scale emerging patterns or phenomena (De Dominico & Hiroki, n.d.).

There are few consistent definitions of complexity in Complexity science. Rather, complexity is defined through the features of complex systems. A renowned author in the field, Melanie Mitchel describes complex systems with the following three features:

1. Complex collective behaviour: Complex systems consist of numerous individual components following simple rules with no central control.

2. Signalling and information processing: Complex systems produce and use information from internal and external environments

3. Adaptation: The complex systems adapt through learning or evolutionary processes. (Mitchell, 2009, p. 12)

However interesting the phenomena are that complexity science is investigating, it is a rather limited approach to complexity and it does not do justice to the richness of what the word "complexity" implies nor to a common sense understanding of complexity. Rather, it addresses the particular phenomena of emergence found in the interaction of large amounts of low-level entities with strict rule sets, rather than the interaction of highly intelligent individuals following loose rulesets that might be redefined at any time. The dominant complexity theory seems limited to what suits being computerized and simulated.

When looking at complexity from field perspectives, the picture becomes richer. Christian Weber, discussing complexity in relation to product engineering and design, provides an overview of the different variations in understanding complexity related to how it is used in different fields. He states that there are many different approaches to different types of complexities, both theoretical and intuitive understanding, as well as field specific approaches (Weber, 2005).

Kolmogorov suggests that a way of measuring complexity in, for example, a text, is the length of the shortest computer program that is able to produce the text. For example, a Mandelbrot fractal is, according to that definition, not very complex, since it is produced by a rather short string of code (*Figure 63*). This resonates with an intuitive interpretation of the fractal. It is very rich and detailed, and one could intuitively say complex, but looking closer, it is a repetition of the same formations at infinite scales. There is no randomness, since all parts of the image follow the same simple rules. This limits the level of complexity of the fractal. It is rich, but not very complex at all.

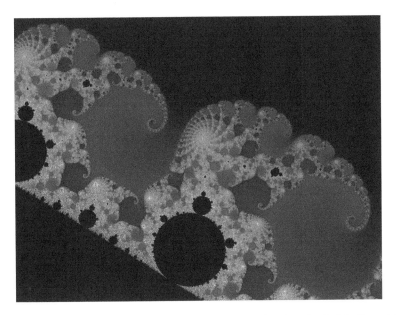

Figure 63. Mandelbrot fractal (2008 Reguiieee at English Wikipedia. Public Domain).

The higher the level of randomness, the longer it will take to compute the phenomena at hand. From that follows that, according to Komolgorov's complexity, the higher level of randomness produces the higher level of complexity and a higher level of regularity produces less complexity. This measurement is called Algorithmic Information Content (AIC). The idea that increased randomness results in a higher level of complexity is criticised by Gell-Mann;

> This property of AIC, which leads to its being called, on occasion, "algorithmic randomness," reveals the unsuitability of the quantity as a measure of complexity, since the works of Shakespeare have a lower AIC than random gibberish of the same length that would typically be typed by the proverbial roomful of monkeys (Gell-Mann, 1995, p. 16).

Though the approach in Complexity science is relevant not only for a school of fish, (*Figure 64*) but also for some human activities, such as economic systems and the internet, mentioned especially by Melanie Mitchel, it does not provide actionable models for many other human activities, such as team work, public service systems, and cultural developments and changes.

Figure 64: A school of fish operates like one organism despite that there is no top-down steering. (Anna Varona 2017, Wikimedia Commons)

Complexity sciences, seen from the perspective of SOD are framed by Information technology and the algorithms required by the computer. This is the strength of complexity science but also its limitation and weakness when confronted with the complexity of everyday life.

Gell-Mann suggest another way of measuring complexity that ties complexity science better to real life complexity than the afore mentioned AC:

> A measure that corresponds much better to what is usually meant by complexity in ordinary conversation, as well as in scientific discourse, refers not to the length of the most concise description of an entity (which is roughly what AIC is), but to the length of a concise description of a set of the entity's regularities. Thus, something almost entirely random, with practically no regularities, would have effective complexity near zero. So would something completely regular, such as a bit string consisting entirely of zeroes. Effective complexity can be high only a region intermediate between total order and complete disorder (Gell-Mann, 1995, p. 17).

This has the consequences that complexity as we understand it related to human activity systems and particularly to design as a change activity lies between the complicated and the random. Complicated meaning the accumulation of elements

134

that are not interconnected and that are not interacting, total randomness being best described as white noise, and becoming utterly uninteresting because of its lack of patterns and variations (*Figure 65*).

Figure 65: A random bit map. (Public Domain)

This leads us back to the "intuitive" conception of complexity as a term we use for systems made out of large numbers of entities that are both separate yet interconnected and interdependent. Entities may be the same and following simple rules of interaction, but they may also be highly varied and following rule sets that are differentiated and complex themselves. In addition, the rule sets and involved entities might change over time. Most everyday phenomena are of the latter category making computational approaches less useful.,

In the end, complexity is in the eye of the beholder. What seems complex to one might be rather simple to another.

Soft Systems Methodology

Let us then return once more to SSM. As mentioned, the dominant position of the hard systems approaches was finally challenged by SSM, which emerged in the 1970s, driven by the work of Peter Checkland (Checkland, 2000b, 2000a; Checkland & Poulter, 2006). He describes an evolution where Systems Thinking matures from its initial mechanistic or positivistic stage to diverse applied systems theories and practices, and finally towards SSM. In hard systems, Checkland states, it was assumed that the system and its subsystems and parts were given. They were obvious and there was not much concern beyond registering the facts, the elements, connections, and the hierarchy of the given system. This is obviously not true in vague, dynamic, and messy systems, especially human activity systems. Therefore, we need to quickly return to the notion of hierarchy. For anybody who has tried, it is evident that deriving clear hierarchies from systems is a challenge in itself. Even manmade mechanical systems are often hard to order into clear hierarchies of well-framed supra systems, systems, and subsystems. In modern engineering, many parts have multiple functions and might also act as elements in several subsystems. This principle is not new, as shown in the case of the motor bike from 1921 (*Figure 66*). In this case, the engine is part of two subsystems of the bike: the engine and the structural frame. This was a radical innovation at that time, but integrated engineering is a dominant principle today. Integrated engineering messes up the hierarchy of the mechanical systems; the system hierarchy is not obvious but is open to interpretation. This is dependent on the viewpoint: is the engine supported by the frame or is the frame supported by the engine? Or does hierarchical ordering not make sense in such a case? If it's hard to frame and draw the boundaries and understand hierarchies in technical systems, how can we expect to do this with social systems?

Figure 66: A Harley Davidson Sport 558 cc from 1921 displaying a stressed member engine where the tubes of the chassis are bolted directly to the engine, and the engine completes the structural triangle of the frame (By Lars-Göran Lindgren Sweden Wikimedia Commons).

The Soft Systems Method starts from the realization that it is utopian to determine a predefined problem definition or goal when looking at social systems. The problem definition should be derived from a certain viewpoint. In the case above, the problem field changes dramatically when the engine is regarded as a structural member.

Checkland states that systems are not features of the real world, but are mental constructs and models we use to understand the world. Checkland regards Systems Thinking as a process and a way of learning:

> [In SSM], the world is taken to be very complex, problematic, mysterious. However, our coping with it, the process of inquiry into it, it is assumed, can itself be organized as a learning system. Thus, the use of the word 'system' is no longer applied to the world, it is instead applied to the process of our dealing with the world. It is this shift of systemicity (or 'systemness') from the world to the process of inquiry into the world, which is the crucial intellectual distinction between the two fundamental forms of Systems Thinking, 'hard' and 'soft' (Checkland, 2000a, p. 17).

Another very relevant shift for design is what Checkland suggests as a move from the concept of problems to problem situations (2000a, p. 155). Arguing that time always changes the perception of problems in social systems, and that the perception of such problems is always subjective, Checkland sees this type of problem solving or response to situations as a structuring of a debate rather than goal-driven problem-solving (2000a, p. 150). Moreover, Checkland's critique of the starting conditions also resonates with design thinking. He notices that most other applied systems approaches are based on one's need to establish the end goal at the start of a study (2000a, p. 139). This is very different in SSM as well as in advanced design practice, where the process of designing is a process of goal-seeking, rather than designing with given goals. It is imperative to understand that there might be multiple interlinked goals, and that design driven by singular intentions end up with unsustainable solutions. For example, a strict focus on end user needs will easily ignore the need for sustainable action (Sevaldson, 2018; Slavin, 2016). The goals are intertwined and related, and the attention and intentions change over time so that goal-seeking is a continuous process.

The Rich Picture

The Gigamap owes a lot to the Rich Picture proposed by Checkland (Checkland P. & Poulter, 2006, p. 24). The rich picture developed in SSM is a useful way of capturing and relating the main entities structures, viewpoints, processes and issues of a situation.

Checkland describes the Rich Picture in the following way:

> The complexity of human situations is always one of multiple relationships. A picture is a good way to show relationships; in fact, it is a much better medium for that purpose than linear prose.

> In making a Rich Picture the aim is to capture, informally, the main entities, structures and viewpoints in the situation, the process going on, the current recognised issues and any potential ones (2006, p. 25).

The function of the first steps of gigamapping are quite similar to the Rich Picture. In SSM, however, the Rich Picture is seen as important but not well-developed as an integrated part of the methodology; the Rich Picture is not mentioned in SSM's seven-step methodology. Also, Rich Picture as a genre does not have a wide reach exploring the systems across scales and horizons, and does not accumulate the vast amount of data typical in Gigamaps.

It lacks all the additional stages and purposes of the Gigmap, including the mapping of the surrounding landscape, systems environment, the negotiation of boundaries, the participatory design element, the relating of categorically different data and models, as well as the generative and the creative purpose. Most of all the Gigamap engages in designing and advanced design thinking as a means of exploration. Hence the Gigamap takes on many roles throughout the process. Nevertheless, the usefulness of the Rich Picture in dialogues has been recognised.

Gigamapping shares some basic views of the Rich Picture, like the use of paper rather than a computer[46], as well as some of the limitations:

> We have to remember that however rich they are, they could be richer, and that such pictures record a snapshot of a situation that will itself not remain static for very long (2006, p. 27).

The Methodology

Checkland suggests a seven-step methodology for systemic change in human activity systems. The most interesting steps are the first two, which include the concept of the Rich Picture, as well as the concept of root definitions. A root definition is derived by asking what the system does, how it does it, and why it is done. To enrich the root definitions of a system, one can use the so-called "CATWOE" model:

C = CUSTOMERS OR CLIENTS

A = ACTORS OR AGENTS

T = TRANSFORMATION PROCESS

W = WELTANSCHAUUNG or WORLD VIEW

O = OWNERS

E = ENVIRONMENT

The function of the CATWOE model is similar to others found in design, like the AT-ONE service design model (Clatworthy, 2011), which stands for Actors, Touch-points, Offering, Need, and Experience. Such models work as frames for designers to keep what is regarded as the most important elements and factors in play in a design process. However, what are important factors might change, and the models guide the attention of the designer to focus on certain aspects and perspectives at the cost of others. Applied uncritically, such models can heavily limit how designers think. As an example, the CATWOE model divides the

---

46. Recent developments during Covid have demonstrated that these types of processes are feasible with the use of shared mapping software and video conferencing.

groups of people involved into three specific categories: customers or clients, actors or agents, and owners, while the AT-ONE model only operates with the term actors. Such differences are not trivial. They will heavily influence the designer's attention. For example, none of the models put emphasis on passive and marginalised parties of the system who are nonetheless impacted by it. These might be affected bystanders (Wagenknecht, 2017). There is also no specific attention on sustainability issues, represented by non-human beings that are also affected. The notion of agency will at its best embrace these issues, but is not treated especially in such models and risk falling out of the equation if these checkpoint models are used blindly. We therefore prefer not to use them, but to do thorough, wide-reaching systems mapping. However, such models can be used if triangulated with other framing tools and used critically.

There is much in common between SOD and SSM; the way they have been developed through practice, collaboration with industry partners and public services, and academic research is very similar. Some of the SSM methods and approaches could be useful in design, but they also have their limitations when applied in a design process. The most valuable inspiration from SSM is the mindset of seeing systems as perspectives for interpreting the world as opposed to mere de facto features. It is more challenging to apply the SSM method directly in design. These problems are similar to those of importing other methods into design. Design is a method-saturated profession, and alien methods easily end up competing, disturbing, and detracting from designing as an act of inquiry, knowledge generation, creativity, innovation, and systems change. The methodology is geared towards non-designers. The method would also work with more simple systems, but it has the same weakness as most other framed process tools. The ordering of process and result in well-sorted thought processes does not cater to very messy systems or the creative process, including the incubation phase. Also, it does not address the designerly core skills, creativity, gestalt, or visual thinking. In these ways, SSM is not fulfilling for the systemic design process.

In social systems, as stated in second-order cybernetics, the researcher cannot avoid being part of the systems investigated. The investigation will inevitably change the system. The actions of the observer might as well be well-planned, so that instead of futile attempts to minimize the observer's effect on the system, these effects can instead become a learning opportunity. When designing for human activity systems especially, given that the design team is a human activity system in its own right, where human relations are the core driver of the design process, the merging of these systems makes the distinction between the design team and the client rather meaningless. The results of such projects are dependent on the social interplay to such a degree that separating the two human activity systems is actually counterproductive. Looking at the interplay and the relations as the central change system would make discussions about participation redundant. The change team is the result of the interaction between the parts. This approach defines the concept of Action Research as the primary method in SSM for investigating human systems, and SSM regards this learning process as central.

Checkland's concept is a great contribution to systemic design, particularly his perspective of understanding Systems Thinking as a learning process where the system is found in the process rather than in the world. Checkland's starting point that the world is rather opaque and messy is more familiar to designers than other systems approaches that view the world in terms of specific systemic models that are more or less ordered and given. The realization that the concept of systems is a mental model and that "systemness" is found in the approach rather than in the world are perspectives that fit well in the designer's mind. Finally, the Action Research component in SSM is also relevant to the role of the designer, pointing towards a generative and designerly approach to systems.

Checkland takes a rather extreme position, when conceiving systems as solely mental concepts. This conclusion seems to be quite constricted to me, and I suggest a more inclusive position. There must be no doubt that entities in the world interact and influence each other. This fact is sufficient for understanding systems features as real phenomena and not only mental constructs.[47] "System" is the word we use when things interact in interdependencies, and most things do so. The word "system" is a notion that denotes a particular feature of the real world. If the more elaborated explanations and models explaining systems break down and no longer fit, this basic real-world feature remains, and we need the terminology to deal with it as a real-world phenomenon; systems are real and important to understand. In SOD, we suggest having both thoughts in play. On one hand, systems perspectives are framing and influencing the way we perceive the world and are hence mental constructs. On the other, systems perspectives describe real features of the world. Keeping both views in play helps maintain a constant critical flexibility.

Towards a Pragmatic Approach to Systems

SSM is a reaction to the shortcomings of 'hard' systems approaches that go a bit far. However, Checkland seems to be aware of the limitations of SSM, and he argues that this approach might not be suitable for certain fields like the natural sciences, for example. At the core of Checkland's critique and "relativism" lies a realization that methods are not neutral, but they mould and form the output as well as the people who conduct the methods. Hence, subscription to one particular method or model of inquiry will produce very particular and framed outputs. An

---

47. I use the term "real" here simply as opposed to abstract idea or mental model.

eclectic use of models and methods is a strategy to escape this simplistic filtering. As a pluralistic and open-ended approach, SOD embraces this (*Figure 67*).

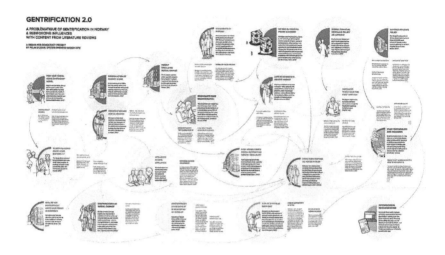

Figure 67: A content-rich causal feedback loop diagram mixed with rich textual information. The map follows the convention of systems dynamics with positive and negative connectors, visible as + and - marks on the arrows while adding visualisations and texts more common in gigamapping (Palak Dudani, Gentrification 2.0, 2018).

Design is multidisciplinary and crosses over from the cultural and social into the technological; it also relates to hard as well as soft sciences, and non-scientific "real life" human activities and practice. Therefore, an eclectic, pragmatic approach for systemic design seems to be reasonable. Fortunately, there is already a good model for such a pragmatic or critical approach to Systems Thinking— namely, Critical Systems Thinking, which will be addressed in the next sections.

Critical Systems Thinking

Systems thinkers and writers like Ulrich, Flood, Midgley, Jackson, and others (Flood & Ulrich, 1990; Flood & Romm, 1996; Jackson, 1985, 1990; Midgley, 2000; Ulrich, 1983, 2000a) defined what Midgley calls the "third wave" of Systems Thinking, following hard and soft systems approaches. Critical systems thinking is a multiple construct in itself which makes it interesting and powerful, but also harder to grasp. But realising that it contains several "criticalities" should help.

According to Midgley, Critical Systems Thinking has two major intentions or two dimensions of criticality:

1. Power relations: the second wave of soft systems approaches (SSM) was criticised for not accounting sufficiently for power relations (Ulrich, 2003) (Ulrich, 1994) (Midgley, 2000, p. 203)

2. Multi methodology: the other main pillar was formed by the notion of methodological pluralism (Michael C Jackson & Keys, 1984).

Power Relations

The issues of power relations were addressed by Ulrich through Critical Systems Heuristics (Ulrich, 1983). While SSM proposed participatory action research, it did not sufficiently address power relations. The critique stems from experiences particularly in industrial contexts where creating dialogue between managers and floor workers is influenced by the power imbalance between the groups. Ultimately, workers may experience retaliation if speaking out freely. The second wave was criticised for the lack of a theory of emancipation (Midgley, 2000).

A central aspect to discussing power relations is the discussion of the conceived boundaries of the systems, Boundary Critique (Midgley, 2000, p. 135; Midgley, Munlo, & Brown, 1998; Ulrich, 1996, 2003). While earlier systems theories regarded systems boundaries as given, Churchman introduced the notion of systems boundaries as being social constructs formed out of the perspective of the observer (Churchman, 1970). As mentioned, Churchman discusses boundaries from an industrial perspective. This is a useful opportunity to give an example. The systems perspective of an investor or owner of an industrial business is very different from that of a manager, as well as from the perspectives of a worker. While the investor would look at the wider market and competition, the manager would concentrate at the running of the business and its economy, while a worker would have deep insight into the details. So, each of them would draw the boundary differently from the others. This example is also well suited to point out the power issues that are embedded in boundary critique. We will return to this below and in Part Three, when we discuss how to design with boundary critique and how to modulate boundaries.

Multi Methodology

The concept of multi methodology seeks to bridge the many different perspectives and systems practices by promoting multi methodology (Midgley, 2000, pp. 213, 217). Each real-life case should be critically examined, and the available approaches should be evaluated regarding their suitability for the case. In addition, Midgley proposes to be creative in the development of methods and approaches suited for the case at hand (Midgley, 2000, p. 225). The best-suited systems approach is selected, or new approaches are tailored for the situation. Critical Systems Thinking is especially valuable for design because of its width and depth spanning from the crafting of objects to industrial production, services, interaction, social design, bridging culture, economy, technology, sustainability, politics, and much more. It is clear that no one single systems approach, method, or practice is sufficient for design. The criticality introduced by Critical Systems Thinking helps to judge different approaches, and to apply them where they are most suitable, as well as to critique and triangulate their output.

The Critical Systems approach is especially well suited as a backdrop and theoretical scaffold for SOD. For example, the Gigamaps produced in SOD are not clear or uniform, but multi-layered and messy in the sense that they embrace many different categories and readings into one synthesized whole, an artefact designed to understand complexity. The Gigamap might embrace, triangulate, and interrelate several different systemic perspectives and readings.

Flood and Ulrich state that a shift in interest from "systems science" to "systems rationality" is needed. This rationality binds different systems perspectives together and establishes a base for an eclectic and pragmatic approach to Systems Thinking and systems practice. Though Midgley places Checkland's SSM in the second wave, it is worth recalling the above-mentioned fact that Checkland did not look at SSM as an universal approach, but one that was suitable when working with human activity systems and less suitable when looking at systems in physics or control systems engineering, for example. Checkland's early role is acknowledged by Flood and Ulrich (Flood. & Ulrich, 1990).

The systems approach is based on a holistic view. This also implies a departure from the objectivity, neutrality, and "disinterest" in traditional science. Such objectivity is based on a separation between the observer and the observed, and a neutral position towards the subject of investigation. In contrast to this, Systems Thinking is non-reductionist in its investigations of connections and relations. This implies realizing that there is an inescapable link between subject and object, observation and intervention (Midgley, 2000). The study of a system is conducted with the intention to not only understand systemic interrelations, but to be able to intervene (Olsson & Sjöstedt, 2004). More so, it is very hard to understand the system's nature without intervening and interacting with it. Learning and intervening melt together. This is starting to sound like design.

As mentioned, in modern soft and critical systems approaches, we might choose to look at systems as mental models rather than features of real life. The "systemness" is in the observation rather than in the observed (Checkland & Poulter, 2006). Though this view is debatable, if one at least partly accepts this, it means the systems features, its structure, and boundaries are constructed and designed.

One of the central questions has been to define the boundary between the system and its environment. In traditional systems shinking, a system was defined by its boundaries, and these boundaries were taken for granted, found naturally only when one fully understood the system. When looking at systems models as part mental constructs, the concept of the boundary is destabilized and open for interpretation. Examples are everywhere: a car is part of the transportation system and inseparable from it, and there is no hard line between the trunk of a tree and its branches. Another great example is found in observing living beings within their environment; the intertwined relations between them makes it impossible to understand the living organism as separate from its environment (*Figure 68*).

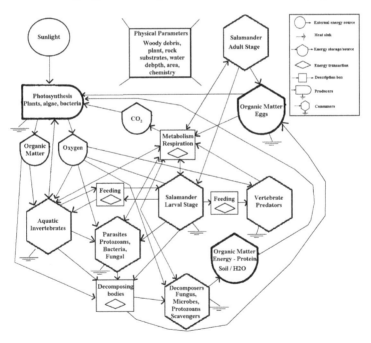

Figure 68: The food web of a salamander. The food web clearly depicts the intricate interdependencies of living organisms; there is no way to fully understand a salamander separated from its environment. It is also impossible to find given boundaries between the "salamander system" and the neighbouring systems of related living organisms (Author: Mark David Thompson. Creative Commons).

Working as a designer with a particular system, the construction of the systems boundaries should be an integrated part of the design process. They should be designed in various ways according to the perspectives, agendas, value systems, knowledge systems, and interpretations of the system. Another issue that destabilizes the boundary is that Systemic Design is always a learning process. During the learning process, the interpretation of the system changes and its boundaries need to be frequently reinvestigated and adjusted.

The "Boundary Problem" has developed into one of the central questions in Critical Systems Thinking and the methodology of addressing it is called "boundary critique" (Flood & Romm, 1996; Midgley, 2000; Ulrich, 1983, 2000b). Boundary critique implies evaluating and re-evaluating the constructed boundary when working with a system. From this follows that the boundaries need to be frequently adjusted throughout the life of a systemic design project. Boundary critique is an integrated feature of gigamapping in SOD.

This can inspire us to discuss the boundaries between the different generations of systems thinking. Despite difficulties and shortcomings of hard systems approaches, the development has not stopped. This is partly because these approaches are valuable and needed, and partly because modelling very complex systems becomes more advanced over time due to better, more complex models and increased computational power. This is paired with the necessity of continuing to understand the complexity of our living environment and predict the consequences of our actions. However, the relation between the model and its application to real-world events has changed and is cause for interpretation. Weather forecasts are an example. They are ever more accurately computed simulations, but we all maintain a sound scepticism as to their accuracy. These simulations are coupled with the growing importance of scientific visualization and the design of information. Interpretation and design has entered even the hard systems approaches.

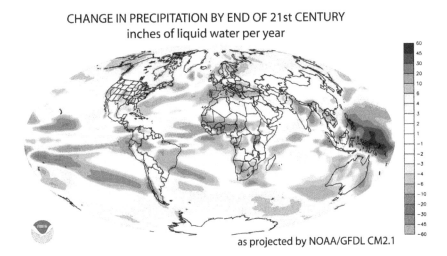

CHANGE IN PRECIPITATION BY END OF 21st CENTURY
inches of liquid water per year

as projected by NOAA/GFDL CM2.1

Figure 69: Forecast of change in precipitation. Study by the National Oceanic and Atmospheric Administration, 2005 (Image is public domain). [48]

From General Theory to Applications

Typical for general systems theory (GST) is that it applies to everything. A theory of everything is, of course, problematic. GST is useful for forming worldviews, and it is applicable in any situation, but its usefulness might be limited because it does not prescribe actions according to the local situations. Similar problems around claiming universality occur in the subfields of systems theory, such as the generic theories of Cybernetics and Systems Dynamics. The success of Systems Thinking is seen in its particular applications and adaptations to knowledge and practice domains. For example, the study of Cybernetics as an engineering field seems to have a wider spread than its generic philosophical theoretical origin [49]. Almost all knowledge fields have developed proprietary versions of Systems Thinking. As mentioned before, we find it in systems engineering, social science, finance and the stock exchange, war strategy, and theories of creativity. One exception, however, is in design, where no proprietary variant of systems has been

---

47.https://commons.wikimedia.org/wiki/File:Projected_change_in_annual_average_precipitation_for_t he_21st_century,_based_on_the_SRES_A1B_emissions_scenario,_and_simulated_by_the_GFDL_CM 2.1_model.png

49. Judged on the number of educational programs.

developed so far. We are in the midst of changing this with the systemic design movement.

Systems Architecting

One such application of systems practice that has been inspirational to SOD is Systems Architecting.

Design is a making discipline and hence closely-related to engineering sciences (Dunin-Woyseth, 2001). Systems Engineering and engineering project management in general turn out to have shortcomings when applied to human activity systems. The hardnosed approach to management has been criticized for being too inflexible, leading to narrow scopes and to less holistic approaches. The mechanistic approach to social interaction also disregarded hidden patterns of informal social networks, emergent creative cultures, and exceptional individuals. Control engineering does not work well as a model for social systems. As a supplement to the traditional Systems Engineering, Maier and Rechtin (Maier & Rechtin, 2000) suggested a new managerial profession: the systems architect.[50] Systems Architecting is described as an art and an intuitive method to keep track of the wholeness in very complex engineering projects. Systems Architecting is especially well-suited as a starting point for looking into Systems Thinking for designers. It is closely related to designing since it emerges from engineering disciplines but includes social and management thinking as well. Another interesting aspect is that it actually emphasizes the capacities of the individual or very small groups in the role of systems architects. It suggests that the systems architect is an individual with special abilities, training, and a role in close co-operation with the traditional systems engineer. This perspective is especially interesting for the creative design individual.

History and State of Systems Thinking in Design

As mentioned, Systems approaches within architecture and design are not new. It is hard to draw a line between systems thinkers that were within or outside the field of design, but the most important pioneers of Systems Thinking in architecture and design are suggestively Christopher Alexander, Buckminster Fuller, Horst Rittel, Russel Ackoff, and Bela Banathy. Ranulph Glanville, as well as Richard Buckanan and Wolfgang Jonas also contributed substantially to the emergence of Systems Thinking in design. Harold Nelson and Erik Stolterman

---

50. Not to be confused with the IT-systems architect.

were forerunners of systemic design with their book, The Design Way; Nelson, in particular, is a central figure in the emergence of systemic design.

Systems Thinkers in Design

The architect Christopher Alexander was influenced by System Thinking in his early work. His book, Notes on the Synthesis of Form (Alexander, 1964) is particularly essential and still very useful for an introduction to Systems Thinking in design. His analyses of simple objects like the teapot are easily understandable and is a forerunner for the more visual Gigamap. Towards the end of the book, he tries to fit a mathematical systems model onto human activity systems, such as an African village. This is obviously not a very successful task, and Alexander rejected its conclusion soon after the publication of the book. Trying to fit reality into a predefined method is a risk we should avoid in Systems Thinking. Rather, we need to form our actions according to the world and to a certain degree disregard methods.[51] Horst Rittel was a design teacher who came from the famous and short-lived design school in Ulm, Germany, and moved to Berkeley, California, where he became part of the "Berkeley Bubble." [52] Though his definitions of Wicked Problems are widely known, his contribution to design theory and thinking is underestimated. See for example the documentation from the Rittel Seminars (Protzen & Harris, 2010). Russell Ackoff was early to criticize the hard approach to human activity systems (Ackoff & Emery, 1972). He also had a design position, particularly in his book Redesigning Society (Ackoff & Sheldon, 2003), but the viability of the resulting design suggestions and the rather utopian solutions seem questionable.

Bela Banathy wrote extensively about design. His point of departure was education design, which is a rather general design direction, hence he did not receive the deserved attention from the mainstream design community. His conception of design is advanced, and up-to-date with the design methodology and design research discussions of the time. He addresses issues of uniqueness, boundaries, problematiques uncertainty and subjectivity, wickedness, and problem-solution interaction (Banathy, 1988, 1997; Banathy & Jenks, 1990).

Harold Nelson and Erik Stolterman are central with their seminal book, *The Design Way*, where Systems Thinking is inherent. Nelson views systemics to be

---

51. Feyerabend wrote a comprehensive critique of the concept of methods and its limitations (Feyerabend, 1975).
52. The term "Berkeley Bubble" was coined by Harold Nelson. This was a period in the 1960s and seventies with exceptional people at Berkeley who were great systems thinkers. Amongst them were Russell Ackoff, C. West Churchman, Horst Rittel, Christopher Alexander, Herbert Simon, Erik Jantsch, Sir Geoffrey Vickers, Thomas Cowan and others (H. Nelson, 2011).

the nature of design (Nelson & Stolterman, 2012). He is also one of the founders of the Systemic Design Research Network.

Gordon Rowland is a professor at Ithaca. He has written extensively on Systems Thinking in design and co-authored books, chapters, and articles with Banathy and Reigeluth (Rowland, 2015). In 1999, he published a book that has received far less attention than deserved, "The Tripartite Seed" (Rowland, 1999). The book brings together designing, learning and systems into a powerful concept that is a forerunner for systemic design.

Ranulph Glanville has several interesting proposals for thinking about the relationship between design and systems, particularly in the case of Cybernetics (Ranulph Glanville, 1994).

Richard Buchanan describes the need for Systems Thinking in his suggestion for four orders of design (Buchanan, 1992, 2001), but he does not indicate the need for a specific systemic practice.

Wolfgang Jonas wrote several papers on Systems Thinking in design. Jonas is highly developed theoretically, and contributes substantially to the bedrock of systemics in design (Jonas, 1996, 2001, 2005, 2007).

Peter H. Jones is a professor at OCADU, and a student of Alexis Christakis (Christakis & Brahms, 2003). He teaches systemic design, and is one of the founders of the Systemic Design Research Network. He is particularly known for his book Design for Care (Jones, 2013).

There are more authors who could be mentioned. However, this shows that there has been an enduring attention and discourse on Systems Thinking in design academia. This discussion has been in the forefront of Systems Thinking and has contributed to moving systems thinking towards more flexible and soft perspectives. Some of the authors are influential far beyond the field of design. It is therefore even more remarkable that the influence of Systems Thinking on mainstream design has been so marginal. I blame the divide between hand and mind, which caused the authors to ignore the practice dimension of systemic application in design. Our small revolution of systemic design is foremost about establishing and cultivating systemic design practice.

Conclusion

Modern Systems Thinking, which has moved beyond the mechanistic models of previous eras, is well-suited to support one of the central roles of the designer: synthesising complex problems by shaping objects (concrete or abstract). However, it is not sufficient to import such systems approaches into design. We need to develop new designerly systemic methodologies to meet the increasing complexity of the problems we face. I suggest using the systems world as an inspirational backdrop and a rich resource to draw from when it comes to conceptualizing and understanding how systems work. Instead of importing the particular models unchanged and submitting to a particular orthodoxy of Systems Thinking, we should keep it open, and construct new ways of practicing systemic design. Such a systemic design approach would never reach a final stage of development, but would need to adjust with increased insight, development of new technology, and as the challenges change over time. A designerly systems approach is seen more as practice, based on experience rather than theoretical knowledge. Also, the capacity to handle complex problems requires training, competencies, and skills to manoeuvre unique problematiques in real-time rather than prescribing procedures and theories. This is ideal for our project-oriented approach in design studies. How to go about doing this is also beginning to take shape. Through practice-based research and development, the foundations can be laid for educating a new generation of designers who will be given both the knowledge and practice to be able to handle the increasingly demanding challenges we will encounter in the future. This kind of research can be done in and outside the studio. This is a case of research based on teaching, and teaching based on research.

What Design Brings to Systems Thinking

In the following section, I discuss the value and importance of some core competencies of design in relation to systemic design. Many of these core competencies are high-level skills and abilities that are formed through years of training. Moreover, they are hard to describe and slightly enigmatic. For example, the ability to synthesise, to draw things together into new and innovative solutions is not fully understood and escapes prescriptions. Nevertheless, it is a core ability of the designer, and seen as implicit in the design education. Amongst these general abilities, we find such concepts as:

- Competencies in using design tools

- Composition

- Imagination of what is possible, creating visions to change the space of opportunities

- Communication through visualization

- Creating holistic resolutions through designing

- Reformulation of problematiques

- Repertoires of design approaches to different fields, cultures, economies, and technologies

- Fronesis: the ability to act from insight to determine what an unique situation requires

Through this section, we will discuss these abilities in more detail.

Examples from earlier texts on bringing together systems thinking and design are the before mentioned: *A Tripartite Seed* (Rowland, 1999) and *The Design Way* (H. G. Nelson & Stolterman, 2012a).

The Role of Design in Systemic Change

Although Systems Thinking has a long history in relation to design, it has been largely thought of by designers as separate from, and an addition to, design.

In most discussions regarding systems and design, either an unspecified connotation of the term design is used or the value of design has been under-communicated and under-demonstrated. The unspecific reference to design means that the term design is used for any planning activity, in a general sense disregarding the skills, methods, techniques, and competencies a professional designer would use. Bela Banathy compiled a vast selection of definitions or descriptions of design all relevant to systems (1997, p. 11). From the twenty-four definitions he has collected only one has a (metaphorical) reference to the act of drawing (Ackoff) and only two make a reference to creativity (Reswick and Jantsch). It is remarkable how writers in design consistently ignore the visual creativity of designers expressed in their craft, for example through drawing, building prototypes and through other types of visualisation.

Under-communicating and under-demonstrating designerly skills indicate that in the many contexts of systems in design, the core competencies of the designer have been devaluated, meaning that good design competencies and skills are seen as less important. Bruno Latour, in his discussion of the expansion of design, emphasises the central importance of designer skills and sense for details (Latour, 2008).

The emergent movement of systemic design emphasises the practice side of design. Peter Jones scrutinizes critically what design can bring to Systems Thinking (2014). Alex Ryan argues for a synthesis of Systems Thinking with design thinking (2014). Harold Nelson and Erik Stolterman argues that systemics are the logics of design, indicating the inherent need to make this core aspect of design explicit (2012b, p. 57). I argue that the designerly way of Systems Thinking must imply investigating systems through design (2013b).

I suggest changing our minds regarding how we learn to understand systems as designers. It is obviously important that a systemic design project is underpinned by descriptive data based on earlier documentation, research, and evidence from relevant fields and domains, cases, observations and field studies, ethnographies, expert consultations stakeholders, etc. However, this should be a basis for all change actions. What is particular for advanced design in general and for SOD particularly is how insight, knowledge, and visions are constructed through design. There are four important issues to be elaborated on here: the anchoring in constructivist learning, and how this separates design from other professional practices:

1. Investigations through design create pictures and visualisations about how the situation could be. It opens up a room for change and imagination. This should be closely rooted with the above mentioned information. However, such visualisations go beyond sheer data collections. They introduce new creative ways of seeing a possible output.

2. This leads to the second point: Through designing we investigate the system. When producing ideas such as "what if?" questions, it becomes easier to imagine how a system might react to such interventions. Designing is a way of exploring the nature of the systems.

3. This leads to the third point, how we learn through design: Constructivist learning theory, as introduced by Piaget and others, states that learning is indeed not like filling an empty vessel with information. On the contrary, learning is a constructive process where the individual creates her own knowledge construction. [53] The traditional design studio is a good example of a constructivist learning environment. The development of SOD and its designerly way of approaching systems and designing a picture of complex systems through Gigamaps and rich design spaces has sparked the notion of designed learning. Principally, this is not so different from constructivist learning, but just more proactive and designerly, using design techniques and methodologies actively in learning processes. See also (Rowland, 1999).

---

53. Constructivist learning theory was influenced amongst others by Lev Vygotsky, Herbert Simon and the systems thinkers Heinz von Foerster and Humberto Maturana.

4. In comparing design to other professional practices such as nursing, it is clear that design practice is dramatically different. Nursing is about establishing patterns of best practices where these patterns are to be repeated to ensure good results in situations that are fairly similar. Design on its most advanced level is an intense learning process each time where there is an engagement with breaking patterns and schemata to create unique resolutions for complex problematiques. For each systemic design project, we need to construct, or rather design, the picture of the system. Constructivist or designed learning is not a separate activity from practicing the profession, but it is the core activity of the systemic design practice.

In SOD, we regard the act of designing as the engine for understanding systems and creating systemic interventions. The way things are expressed and shaped are central to this process. Hence, the system models represented in Gigamaps, for example, are seen as design artefacts. We criticize the idea that a model can represent and mirror reality; it is merely an interpretation. The iterative design process refines this interpretation and filters it through numerous visual discourses or "graphologues," as they are called by Nelson and Stolterman (Nelson & Stolterman, 2012). The graphologues manifested in Gigamaps are possible interpretations rather than descriptions and representations of a reality. Ultimately, they are generative interpretations depicting possible interventions, ideas, and innovations regarding how things could or ought to be. Consequently, in this process, there is a smooth transition from the descriptive to the generative, from describing the system as is to re-designing it, from designing a picture of how things are to designing a vision of how things could be.

This is the powerful element design brings to the systems world, if we allow its core competencies to play out and turn our attention to skills, competencies, and practice.

An Example: The Ulstein Bridge Concept

The Ulstein Bridge Concept (UBC) research project was conducted from 2012 to 2014 as a collaboration between the Ulstein Group's subdivision, Ulstein Power and Control, and the Oslo School of Architecture and Design. The project's aim was to rethink the ship bridge (the control centre of a ship) using currently available technology.

Through this project, unforeseen systemic effects of the research, the innovation- driven design process, and its tangible output were uncovered. This means that although the assumed effect of the project output occurred, there were additional unplanned effects that went far beyond what was expected. Specifically, the output deeply influenced the shipbuilding sector in an unforeseen manner by influencing the dialogue in the ship design sector, and set new boundaries for what was possible or desirable. There were many preconditions for this unexpected impact, including:

1. Research strategy: for this project, the genre of the concept-car portraying and visualizing an idea of a near future was strategically staged.

2. Drivers: technology in that near future was becoming increasingly accessible. The consumer industry was at the forefront, with touch screens, and motion capturing, VR, and other technologies being the norm.

3. Need for better solutions: the need to address challenges within the ship bridge environment were overdue. There was a desire to find alternative ways to demonstrate holistic solutions, particularly for the potential to improve safety.

4. Presentation of the outputs: instead of communicating the concepts with reports, much effort was put into producing professional videos. This had a direct impact on the user communities, and was rapidly picked up by the industry.

5. Strategic considerations: Ulstein's decision to publicly share some parts of the project was an interesting strategic step. It was meant to position Ulstein as a innovation company. The goal was to attract innovation-oriented customers to help further develop and realize the concepts.

Mobilizing and changing the sector as a whole to set the agenda for what is possible is an ultimate task for design. Systemic approaches to this seem to be crucial.

This function of design cannot be replaced with other professions or approaches. The quality and accessibility of the design vision, the communicative professionality in the video production, the development of through-designed working demonstrators, and the high-level look and feel are all central aspects for success. This is a case for Design with a capital D. By delivering the vision about what is possible, the sector is changing its mind. The visualization, the well developed features, the video as a means to communicate the vision--all of these were necessary. They were all seen as design artefacts and design output. No written report could have the same impact.

Timing was extremely important. The vision represented a near future, demonstrating possible implementation of existing technology and a holistic design of the bridge. The radical push was in a rethinking of the bridge and challenging the regulation authorities' framework.

Although other design offices in the sector have previously shown design innovations that incrementally pushed the realm of what is possible, this project was able to demonstrate the possibility of radical innovations and big leaps. The leap was necessitated by the messy structure of sub-suppliers, each contributing their own display and interface towards a chaotic cluttering of the ship bridge's control surfaces. A systemic innovation of the whole technology and business backbone was necessary.

Overall, the output engaged the sector as a social system spanning from online fora for users (captains) to the regulatory authorities. Implementation efforts for the new ship bridge design moved as far as challenging standards for rules and regulations, putting innovation pressure on the regulation authorities. The use of design visions as change-making devices on a sector-wide strategic level is not only possible, but also very powerful. We have seen such use in car design, but transferring this into a new area like shipbuilding further demonstrates its potential and power. The systemic change is primary in the social system of the sector and its shared idea landscape or shared visions of the future. The UBC project has changed the dialogue and discussion, opening up the field for radical innovation. The project was brought forward in the establishment of an open source architecture for ship control systems, the highly successful Open Bridge Design System (Nordby, 2019) (*Figure 70*).

Next generation maritime workplaces

Figure 70: The Open Bridge Design System (AHO 2019).

The project demonstrates the immense power of design towards strategic or systemic change of a whole sector. As a mere written report, it would have never had the same impact to rapidly prepare a whole sector for a different mentality towards radical innovation. What really influenced the system was a sense of willingness and a collective vision for where the sector wants to go, the buyers' vision of what they would like to have, and the authority's insight on what is needed to reach new levels of safety. The project also demonstrates the value of open-ended and bottom-up research by design. The goals and values were not pre-defined. Instead, they were the result of a forecasting downstream design vision on an upstream strategic level. We will return to this project later in Part Three, discussing the research by design aspect.

Holistic and Dynamic Concepts in Design

In the following section, we dig deeper into what the core concepts can mean for systemic design and how they are applied in SOD.

In most, if not all works of art and design, we tend to find some central elements in one form or another. These include composition, the thoughtful arrangement and interrelation of elements, working with the creation of wholes, generating harmony (or disharmony), and synthesising ideas (content). These elements may be seen as core concepts in art, as well as design.

I propose that some of these core concepts should be central to developing the field of systemic design. The skills and competencies that are at the core of design are key to the creation of holistic solutions. These art and design practices demonstrate something unique. They demonstrate how to compose, create, plan, bring to life system components, and integrate them to produce holistic gestalts. While all other systemic approaches are dominantly descriptive, Systemic Design, especially SOD, is dominantly generative and creative. Its main role is therefore to shape, design, and compose artefacts within systems, as systems, and in systemic contexts. The artefacts at stake are material or immaterial, objects or relations, items or processes, politics or social contexts.

Current State

As mentioned, earlier attempts to integrate Systems Thinking in design have largely failed to become part of the normal mainstream profession and design education. Explanations for this failure could be that systems approaches are alien to designerly ways, or the systems approaches have been too inflexible and dogmatic to allow for a seamless integration into designing. The systems approaches have come through as elitist, alien, and inaccessible to design.

Yet, there might be other additional reasons for the sparse implementation of systems approaches in design, reasons that have so far been largely overlooked. Art and design through history has developed a series of concepts in dealing with complex issues and generating holistic resolutions. Some of these ideas and concepts are so basic and embedded in the designerly "DNA" that they have become virtually invisible. This might explain why they have not been looked at closer in this discussion. We will return to defining these core concepts and the "DNA" of design a bit later in this section.

In design, there has been, and still is, a movement away from its roots, the arts and crafts, and industrial arts. Design is becoming more academic through the field of design research, which has gone through dramatic development in the last decades. Many design researchers referred to the traditional sciences as an ideal in this process, and regard the arts and crafts as redundant and misguiding. It is not obvious that the move to a more research-based and scientific design profession naturally leads to this rather conservative position. Design is a complex theme, and diversity in research approaches should be obvious. Unfortunately, there has been a bias towards leaning too much on external scientific methods at the cost of developing field-specific research approaches. A long stream of external concepts, models, and ideas are discussed as relevant to design. Sociology, ethnography, statistics, and even natural sciences are imported into design to make it more science-based. In addition, we see an interest in other practice-based fields. Among these, we find concepts particularly drawn from the health-care sector. For example, Evidence-Based Design (EBD)[54] and Problem-Based Learning (PBL) have made their way into design. Both are problematic because of a misalignment to the designerly ways, and also because they tend to replace already existing and arguably better concepts or traditions from within design. At first sight, all these imports these imports are potentially beneficial to design research because they expand the knowledge base and horizon of design research. Such enhancement is needed since design research is partly under-developed because of its diverse range of approaches and methods. The need for methodological development in design becomes even more pressing when design is now moving into new fields. However, these imports of thought must not come at the expense of the core notions and concepts developed over years in design. It is problematic to import alien concepts into design without a process of transformation. It is even more problematic when alien concepts replace inherent ways of working and thinking that are taken for granted and partly mistrusted, but that are actually superior for design. Such examples are the replacement of generative design processes with EBD, and the distortion of the studio learning environment with less-developed PBL approaches. EBD has specific problems in the definition of the term evidence. It becomes principally problematic when creative and generative work,

---

54. EBD has recently been strongly supported on the DRS PhD list.

which mostly occur in unique situations, are based on evidence that is dependent on reliable repetition. Repetition is principally problematic in systemic design. PBL appears equally bleak and primitive when compared with the studio-based pedagogic practices developed in art and design schools since the Bauhaus, long before PBL was invented in the 1960's. The problem with the problem in PBL we already have addressed. The mistaken move away from the arts and crafts heritage of design is caused by a superficial and misinterpreted need for design to become more "scientific." In this context, scientific is misunderstood as something well-defined and restricted to the concept of evidence. This need, I argue, is false and is truly not about being more scientific, but being more commercial. The redressing of design as a science gives design an appearance of authority by disguising the inherent and truly inescapable uncertainties and risks of design. This gives customers the faulty impression that there is a lower risk.[55]

The move away from the root competencies in arts and crafts has unfortunate consequences and is arguably not a necessary move to make the discipline more "scientific." On the contrary, design research should look into the resources from arts and crafts and make them more explicit so that they can be further developed.

The contradiction between arts and science are constructed, and have their roots in an old dichotomy between those fields. In design discourse, the arts are often dismissed as being intuitive, creative, and based on metaphors, etc. But intuition, creativity, and metaphors are all part of science. This dichotomy between art and science is relatively new and should not be taken as a given. There is no logic that moving away from art will make design more scientific. John Maeda, an art and technology educator and professor puts it this way:

> Art and science. To those who practice neither, they seem like polar opposites, one data-driven, the other driven by emotion. One dominated by technical introverts, the other by expressive eccentrics. For those of us involved in either field today (and many of us have a hand in both), we know that the similarities between how artists and scientists work far outweigh their stereotypical differences. Both are dedicated to asking the big questions placed before us: "What is true? Why does it matter? How can we move society forward?" Both search deeply, and often wanderingly, for these answers. We know that the scientist's laboratory and the artist's studio are two of the last places reserved for open-ended inquiry, for failure to be a welcome part of the process, for learning to occur by a continuous feedback loop between thinking and doing (Maeda, 2013).

This discussion is old, and it is discouraging to observe how the artificial dichotomy between art, design, and science still pops up repeatedly. I will,

---

55. I have argued extensively around these misconceptions in the essay, "Discussions and Movements in Design Research" (Sevaldson, 2010).

however, turn my back on this and look forward to seeing how concepts from art and design can be integrated, particularly from the perspective of systemic design. As I will show, it is exactly these core notions of our art and design heritage that have the greatest potential for systemic design. I show that these core notions are to a large degree systemic, and that they make systemic design different and in certain ways, superior to other systems approaches.[56]

When Systems Thinking was introduced in design, the designer was implicitly asked to forget his or her training in design skills and concepts. In fact, they were replaced with hard mathematical modelling and simulations. Additionally, the new terminology was alien, and Systems Thinking in design was most often technical, theory-oriented, and presented textually rather than demonstrated and developed through good practice. Systems Thinking was conceived as prescriptions to design. It was mostly a one-way relationship. There were exceptions, however, and some systems thinkers eventually developed a good understanding for design. This became especially interesting because designing was recognised as the ultimate result of Systems Thinking by writers like Russel Ackoff, Bela Banathy, and Horst Rittel. Still, those exceptions were mostly textual and theory-oriented even when describing practice. Few real examples of resulting design projects were demonstrated. This was because most of these projects were considered general design. As in Banathy's case, for example, he was active within the field of Education Design, which references design theory, but was in part developing separately from the design cultures. Ackoff and Sheldon attempted to demonstrate designing based on systems approaches, but these demonstrations came out at best utopian, and at worst absurd (Ackoff & Sheldon, 2003). In their book, Redesigning Society, a number of faulty design solutions are shown, spanning from quadratic cities to two-seated cars (with one of the seats pointing backwards). These weird designs are argued for at length with systemic arguments. Ackoff and Sheldon demonstrate the failure of designing without design thinking and reasoning. However, things went also wrong when seen from a strict systemic perspective. There is no context, no pre-existing cities, no pre-existing car industry, etc. As well written and good as the initial parts of this book are, their demonstration of systemic design is misleading.

The radical potential of systemic design is that it deeply rethinks the relation between Systems Thinking and design. If done properly and deeply enough, the fixed relation between Systems Thinking and design can be shaken and de-stabilized in such a way that we can start to look for new answers in the amalgam of the two fields. We should create new ways of relating design and Systems Thinking. This does not mean that we as designers should read up on systems

---

56. I am using the term "systemic design" here because I think the consequences of re-relating systems and design results in this reengagement with the core notions of design. Though not everybody in the emerging field of systemic design would entirely agree with this, it is demonstrated fully in SOD.

theories first. Maybe the worst thing a young designer can do is to start with reading up on particular systems orthodoxies and learning specific systems models. Actually, when it comes to SOD, we always start with designing. This might be provocative for many cyberneticists or systems analysts, but I will argue that there is more important work ahead first if we want to avoid being stranded in the same ditches as we once were. What we need to do first of all, is to re-understand the design field as well as its heritage and potential by revisiting the designerly core concepts. Understanding the original ideas and concepts of art and design with regards to systemic design will potentially also develop both further. I propose that ability for these designerly concepts to deal with complexity and create holistic solutions are at the core of what design brings to Systems Thinking.

Making Design Explicit

Design has an inherent and tacit way of dealing with complexity and synthesis. At its best, design demonstrates a superior ability to respond to very complex and systemic problematiques. The skills that underlie this ability have hardly been made explicit, and have largely been ignored by the above-mentioned groups of writers, with the exception of Nelson and Stolterman. SOD intends to define, describe, and further develop these skills, which include the concepts of composition, orchestration, choreography, the idea of Gestalt,[57] and ultimately the idea of the Gesamtkunstwerk.

In recent debates within design research circles, this ability to design has been regarded as less important compared to the efforts to move design closer to scientific research. If this shift comes at the cost of the central design abilities mentioned above, it will be catastrophic for design on several levels. This designerly ability is truly the hallmark of design work, and it is an activity that is specific to designers. We might find seemingly similar activities in other neighbouring fields like art and engineering, but none of them has the versatile composure to address the many topics spanning from societal to technological, cultural to economic as found in design. There is danger that abandoning this root competency will destroy design. The core competence for composing holistic solutions will erode, and we will see less innovative solutions. Discussing beauty, elegance, and aesthetics in the context of Systems Thinking still seems to be problematic.[58]

---

57. Though Gestalt psychology has a systemic root.
58. When talking about beauty, elegance, etc. these are seen as neutral parameters. It could as well be ugliness or un-elegance as a conscious choice or cultural expression.

The Core Notions of Design

This list of suggested core notions of design starts with the more design-specific notions, only shared with other aesthetic practices, and ends with the general ones that are shared by several other fields or that are general for all human activity:

1. The notion of the design crafts and skills: the deep training of the needed foundation of expertise in giving shape to things. These skills include drawing (with analogue or digital tools), form-giving in all its senses, physical form, graphic form, generative, co-created, and time-based form.

2. The notion of composition: composition of space (like in a painting, object, or building) or time (like an interaction, a service, an experience). The composition of a process, a co-design workshop, an organisation, a policy etc. Composition is relating and arranging things in a way that goes far beyond sheer assembly. I suggest this to be the most important notion of design.

3. The notions of combining visual thinking, reflexive practice, and design thinking.

4. The notion of wholeness or Gestalt: to understand whole systems as figures rather than rigorous models.

5. The notion of wholeness across systems or the notion of the Gesamtkunstwerk.

6. The notion of expression or the poetic dimension of design: symbols metaphors, analogies, and semantics.

7. The notion of creativity: to imagine and envision what could be.

8. The notion of Fronesis: the experience and intellectual capacity acquired over time, how to judge, react, and practice in relation to unique real-life situations.

9. The notion of the wicked problem.

10. The notion of "Thrownness": being thrown into a situation where one cannot oversee the consequences of one's action. Not acting also has its consequences.

11. The notion of dynamics: the moving target. While we plan, things change.

12. The notion of orchestration and choreography: to arrange actors to interact and collaborate, and to time actions according to generative and emergent events over time.

13. The notion of adaptive expertise.

14. The notion of expert intuition (Dreyfus model).

15. The notions of ethics, empathy, dialogue, values, and politics.

What is truly unique to design is the composure of all these core notions of design combined with the wide reach and scope of the design fields.

I will, in the following section, elaborate on some of the notions that seem most central to SOD. The discussion touches upon composition, Gestalt, visual thinking and visualization, wholeness, orchestration, and the Gesamtkunstwerk.

Holistic Designs and the Issue of Harmony and Balance

One of the central features of the designer is the ability to create harmonic wholes. Confronted with many demands and complexities, the designer aims to synthesize a holistic response that resolve and integrate some or many of the contradictory inputs into the shape of a more or less aesthetically beautiful and elegant form. The notion of harmony and balance (or disharmony and imbalance) is not taken as given, but is constantly challenged. Harmony is a parameter rather than a goal. In many cases, disharmony is preferred. There are many ways of composing a whole, the less harmonic ways will often tell stories that are more complex. Harmony, understood as stable balance, is static compared to imbalance. Design for changing and dynamic environments requires a more advanced and nuanced notion of harmony and balance. The notion of harmony is also not congruent with the notion of the whole, despite the fact that harmony can be understood as a way of expressing an ideal type of holistic solution.

Gestalt Psychology

The "hidden" relation between design and systems surfaces when we look at Gestalt psychology. Gestalt psychology is a theory about perception. It states that we perceive patterns and whole forms rather than perceiving fragments and singular parts. We will not go deep into Gestalt psychology here, but pull out some factors that seem important for SOD.

It is no wonder that Gestalt psychology has long had a very strong position in visuals arts and design. It has been said that it is the psychological theory that resonates most with designers. The extensive work of Rudolf Arnheim has connected Gestalt psychology directly to creativity and design via visual thinking (Arnheim, 1974). The Bauhaus was already in close contact with the early Gestalt psychologists and adopted their theories (Behrens, 1998).

On the other hand, there are many links between Gestalt psychology and the systems world. Gestalt psychology is not directly related to Systems Thinking, and is normally not counted as part of but as a predecessor to Systems Thinking. Kurt Lewin is both a Gestalt theorist and systems thinker (Ramage & Shipp, 2009).

The famous statement, "the Whole is more (greater) than the sum of its parts" is often credited to Systems Thinking. But, in fact it comes from Gestalt psychology and is its central thesis. The original statement by Kurt Koffka was a little bit different:

"The whole is other than the sum of its parts".[59]

Koffka's statement was strikingly precise that the whole was not more, but different. It is not merely about addition, but rather, the whole has a different existence. This central statement proven in Gestalt psychology has been used in Systems Thinking, where it is mostly referred to as "the whole is more than the sum of its parts," and it is most often discussed in connection with emergence and synergy. An often-used example is that of a bicycle and its parts. Only when its parts are assembled can it take the role of a bicycle. It is not a very good example because Gestalt goes beyond that. Gestalt psychology is more generative. It suggests something in addition to emergence and synergy. It is the active perceptual and interpretative process of creating a whole from seemingly disconnected fragments. Unfortunately, when this slogan migrated into the systems world, it was changed and lost its real edge. The original form of the statement points to a qualitative and active perceptual difference rather than a quantitative and passive difference. Perception is seen as an act of creation, where we create the wholes we see.

When investigating the relation between Systems Thinking and design, Gestalt psychology provides several links for connecting and cross-referencing. In this discussion, it seems most useful to return to the original version of the core statement from Gestalt psychology, and turn the discussion towards the qualitative

---

59. Kurt Koffka was central in the creation of Gestalt psychology and was responsible of creating a coherent theory of Gestalt. He was propagating a holistic view on psychology.

issues. Gestalt refers to sensing as an active process where missing parts are added in perception to create wholes (*Figure 71*).

Figure 71: The images demonstrate how perception creates wholes out of patterns that actually don't provide any real information about the whole. Perception is an act of creation. (Image: Wikimedia Commons).

Central to Gestalt psychology is the idea of the whole. This means that we need to look at perception as a holistic and active or creative process. The purpose and functionality of perception is indeed to generate wholes. Perception is a creative process that interprets and adds to what is there. The mind recognises wholes (Gestalts) across many different representations. Christian von Ehrenfels explains:

> A melody is composed of singular notes. The same notes can form many different melodies. But if you do a transition of the melody to another key, the notes would be different but the melody is the same (Ehrenfels, 1890).

So, the melody generates a recognizable whole across all possible versions and intonations.

This proposes a radically different possibility than the abstract, hard, and sometimes quantitative systems models and analyses that have been predominant in large parts of Systems Thinking. Even in the softer parts of the systems world, the perception and analyses of systems remain quite abstract. All systems modelling is geared towards the understanding of interplay between many components, to generate a holistic understanding based on myriads of fragments. However, model simulations with computers frame the systems in quantitative categories and quantifiable actions. This limits the scope, flexibility, and potential creative use of the models. We therefore still need to trust our brains and our perception.

It is truly possible to train an increased capacity to cognitively embrace a greater number of entities and their relations. We have demonstrated this through gigamapping and the Rich Design Space. The process of designing plays a central role in the active internalization of big amounts of data. In the end, however, while developing extensive Gigamaps, another perspective emerges. This perspective is not about understanding each and every single component and myriads of interactions. During the mapping process, sensitivity towards a different realization emerges, leading to the creation of the Gestalt of the system.

Figure 72: The complexity of a Gigamap might reach beyond our ability to keep track of each and every detail, but can take a different role as Gestalt. It indicates the main structures, its layers and diversity, on the cost of fractional and detailed information. Another important issue is that it depicts the level of complexity at stake. As well, the creators of the map will have much greater insight and detailed knowledge than a random viewer. This insight is especially developed through the processes of visual thinking when creating the map (Chalmers School of Architecture 2015, Photo: Birger Sevaldson).

The Gestalt of the system is a construction and interpretation. It is designed. It provides us with a useful image of a mental figure that we can orient ourselves and communicate with.

In gigamapping especially, we reach the limits of the number of elements we can handle simultaneously and at the top of our heads, so that they can be brought into the forefront of our consciousness whenever needed. We manage by zooming in and out constantly and by maintaining cross-scalar thinking, such as taking a step back to reinvestigating the whole picture, or investigating details by producing zoom maps as part of a ZIP analyses (See page 275). However, most often, it is the overall feel of the system that is the most valuable result from gigamapping.[60] This means the Gestalt of the system. Through this jump, we are seamlessly drifting into a generative mode. Sensing is generative. When sensing becomes central in the interpretation of complex systems, there is the absence of any divide between sensing, thinking, and designing.

Rudolf Arnheim provides a platform for this jump through his theories on "Visual Thinking." His central argument is that there is no real divide between perception and cognition. This provides yet another connection between Gestalt and Systems Thinking, and a good argument for the constructivist or designerly gigamapping.

Now that we have established some substantial links and connection between systems and design, we have a backdrop to discuss more specific concepts from art and design in relation to systems practice, including composition, choreography, orchestration, and the notion of the Gesamtkunstwerk.

Composition

Nelson and Stolterman argue for composing as an alternative to trying to understand the world comprehensively, which they think is impossible. Designing means composing and connecting into functional assemblies, and they act as an alternative to the rational mind (2012a, p. 21). In a sense, it is justified to say we understand the world through design. This is especially the case in the age of the Anthropocene, where we tend to design the whole of the globe, either unintentionally or by plan.

Composition in design can be understood as a special way of synthesis in shape and form. In art, composition rests on its own objective, and creates its own logic. It addresses spatial organisation in painting and sculpture with the central notions of balance, imbalance, contrast, etc. Meanwhile, musical composition is concerned with the whole of a piece of music. It addresses temporal issues, rhythms, tonalities, dynamics, etc.

In design, all of these parameters may be at play. Product design may be more similar to painting and sculpture, whereas service design addresses interactions similar to those in music. Less obvious is that even products can be seen as

---

60. See the sections on sensemaking and sensesharing.

temporal objects. There is always a use that plays out over time, and often according to a certain pre-programmed scheme (*Figure 73*).

Figure 73: Japanese tea ceremony. All objects (physical products) are elements in a precisely orchestrated chain of events, almost like partakers or actors, with relations to each other playing out over time. None of the objects make sense on their own; they form a complex system together that is activated in the ceremony (1846, the later Edo Period, Copied by Kanō Osanobu and Kanō Masanobu. The original work was made in 1632. Public Domain).

Yet another aspect is that perception is bound to time. Perception in itself takes time. Perceiving an object one needs to observe it from different angles. Perceiving built environments means walking through them.

Nelson and Stolterman look at composition as a way of interrelating and connecting things. So in a way, they think of composing the relations rather than the objects themselves as the central issue in composition (2012b, p. 159)

German, Potter, and Chi from the Center for Applied Mathematics at Brown University present a view on composition that not only connects closely with Systems Thinking, but also places it in a central position in human cognition. This resonates as highly relevant to our discussion and shows how such issues migrate across sciences and knowledge fields:

> Compositionality refers to the evident ability of humans to represent entities as hierarchies of parts, with these parts themselves being meaningful entities and being reusable in a near-infinite assortment of meaningful combinations. Compositionality is generally considered to be fundamental to language

(Chomsky), but many believe, as do we, that it is fundamental to all cognition. Objects and scenes, for example, decompose naturally into hierarchy of meaningful and generic parts. Furthermore, compositions help us to identify parts unambiguously: It is often the case that components cannot be correctly interpreted in the absence of the contextual constraints imposed by their incorporation into a larger whole, i.e., a composition. Indeed, such compositions are sometimes called "higher-level constraints." (Geman, Potter, & Chi, 2002).

I do not believe fully in the natural decomposition of objects and scenes into meaningful parts. Decomposition is, to a large degree, a question of interpretation and critique the type that Ulrich and others propagated. In addition, I think they are quite object-oriented and have little emphasis on the relations between the entities. This comes as a natural consequence of their reference to language, where the relation between the words (entities) is proximal rather than a potential process or signal by its own right. Nevertheless, the quote from their paper (which later changes to become mathematical expressions with less relevance to our discussion) is interesting, because it points at systems and portrays composition as a very fundamental part of human cognition.

Figure 74: Transverse Lines, Wassily Kandinsky, 1923 (Public Domain).

So, what exactly is composition? I suggest that we look at examples where composition is isolated as the most important feature, so we can examine composition in its purest form. Kandinsky's 1923 painting in *Figure 74* is a prime example. The reason for choosing a composite pictorial composition by Kandinsky is that it represents a break from earlier rule-based compositions, which have generally adhered to the rules of symmetry and the golden ratio. It is therefore also useful to discuss issues of balance and distribution in their purest forms, undisturbed by formal orthodoxies. We will discuss seven features of the painting, with the intention to describe compositionality in "static" objects. In particular, we will pinpoint the concept of mitigating objects, which are objects that relationally bind seemingly unrelated forms together. We will then see if these principles can be used when working with systemic design composition.

1. Balance and imbalance: the painting demonstrates how dissimilar entities can balance each other. The edgy brown field to the left is balanced by the round shape to the right. Small intense objects with strong coloration for example, can balance larger objects with less intensity.

2. Relating categorically different entities: this freely-arranged composition brings together entities that are seemingly from different worlds, and resolves them into a single whole. The spline shape in the lower right corner is unique. All other curved objects are singular curves. These objects serve as translational objects that connect the unique spline to a bigger context.

3. Primitives and freeform objects: we find both primitives (triangles, trapezoids, and circular shapes) as well as freeform objects, figures, and curves in the painting. This contrast is mitigated by in-between objects that are more distorted, but recognizable primitives like oval shapes or freeform curves.

4. Composed figures: the two main shapes, the trapezoid to the left and the circular shape to the right, both have inner zones filled with figure-like forms and shapes. In addition, there are several of those "figures" in the main space, outside the inner frames of the two main objects. The "figureness" of those objects creates a relation between them. The figures in the external areas can be regarded as mitigating objects.

5. Fields and boundaries: there are several fields as mentioned the inner fields of the two main objects have more or less well-defined boundaries. Again, there are mitigating objects tying the fields together with the rest of the composition.

6. Colours: the colouring is used to distinguish, as well as blend and relate, objects to create depth in the image. The objects seem to float in front of a unified background that only very subtly influences and relates to the objects. There are many colouring approaches, but for now, it is interesting to see how the background is carefully blended around certain objects, to avoid a total detach between background and objects, such as the subtle blue "halo" around the round orange shape in the upper right corner for example.

7. Creating tension but generating a sense of a holistic resolution: this is the main experiment of the painting. Some elements, like the one in the upper-right corner, seem to almost escape the frame, but is still kept as an integral part. The richness and diversity of the painting allow the composition to almost break up, while still presenting the feeling of a holistic and complete gestalt.

The other painting that we will also briefly look at is Ucello's "Battle of San Romano" from 1432 (*Figure 75*). This painting is frequently analysed because it is an early example of the use of central perspective in a complex scene. However, the painting was chosen for our discussion because it is one of the early paintings where time plays a major role.

Figure 75: Paolo Uccello "The Battle of San Romano" 1432. Graphic analyses by 2004.

The painting is a snapshot of a decisive moment in the battle where the victorious army to the left overruns the army to the right. This is an opportunity to discuss two additional features of compositionality that might be relevant for working with systemic design.

1. The notion of past and future (time) in art: The painting has a snapshot-like quality that indicates that there is a history to the events taking place, as well as a continuation into an unknown future. The inclusion of a time dimension into a "stable" object is interesting to inspire similar approaches in the mapping of complexities, where the main weaknesses is the lack of description about dynamic development.

2. The notion of movement: in the painting, many elements contribute to the feeling of motion. The arrangements of the spears, in particular, demonstrate that they form a figure of forward motion, independent of the figurative content.[61]

Gesamtkunstwerk

Translated as total work of art, ideal work of art, universal artwork, synthesis of the arts, comprehensive artwork, all-embracing art form, or total artwork, Gesamtkunstwerk is a work of art that makes use of all or many art forms, or strives to do so. The term is a German word, which has come to be accepted in English as a term in aesthetics.

Wagner presented an idea of the Gesamtkunstwerk that was literarily boxed-in on the stage for a passive audience looking at it from the outside.[62] It combined musical composition and orchestration, spatial composition, theatrical orchestration and choreography into one holistic performance. In post-war times, the term has grown out of fashion and has been associated with fascism and an anti-modern approach to art. Koss has made an attempt to recover the original idea of the Gesamtkunstwerk by detaching it from fascism, and arguing its relations to modernity, its notion of interdisciplinary approaches, holistic composition as well as its relevance to audience engagement, co-creation, and participation (Koss, 2009). It is this conception of the term that is fundamental to the way it is used here as a concept for systemic design. However, the roots of holistic artwork are much older. The architects in the Renaissance did not see a division between their

---

61. For a more comprehensive analysis of the Ucello Painting, see Sevaldson, B. (2001). The Renaissance of Visual Thinking. In Proceedings of Konference om Arkitekturforskning og IT. Aarhus: Nordisk Forening for Arkitekturforskning.
62. Wagner sought to unify all works of art in the theatre. He was part of the 1848 revolutions, in particular the Dresden revolution, and he played a liberal role. But he also wrote the notorious essay "Das Judentum in der Musik" and his legacy, when it comes to anti-Semitism, is not the best. This, together with the heroic themes of his artwork, made him especially popular with the Nazis years later.

different tasks. They engaged in architectural structuring, interior design, exterior design, landscaping, sculpting, painting, and engineering (*Figure 76*).

Figure 76: The Ceiling of the Sistine Chapel by Michelangelo. Painting, decoration, and architectural space was seen totally integrated. (Photo: Jean-Christophe Benoist, GNU Free Document Licene)

If we look beyond the formal unity of building and art, looking at the functions, programs of use and maybe other issues like political intentions, there are many historic examples we could pick. For example, the monasteries of Europe are multifunctional complexes with societal and religious motivations, also representing economic and political power as well as being cultural hubs. However, for our case, it might be more interesting to look at two examples that were designed especially for such multi-functionality out of clear planning intentions rather than organically developed over centuries. The two examples are contemporary to their time, and from two opposing empires. The two examples have similar functions, but also clear differences. The first example is Real Sitio de San Lorenzo de El Escorial (El Escorial) built on behalf of Filip II of Spain in the years 1559-84. The second example is the Süleymaniye Camii (Suleyman Mosque) in Istanbul.

Figure 77: San Lorenzo de El Escorial. Architect Juan Bautista de Toledo, Work started in 1559 (Photo: Turismo Madrid, Wikimedia Commons)

El Escorial is a Royal Palace, a location of government functions, a monastery, , library, school, and cathedral. The combination of political and religious functions is a political statement on the unity of the royal palace with the Roman Catholic church of Spain. Therefore, this is not only purely functional organisation design, but it is also symbolic / political expression. El Escorial is a powerful statement of the Counter Reformation and an expression of the melancholic side of Spain. As a whole work of art, it is final and closed, literarily with a clearly defined outer wall marked with four corner towers. As much as it is a Gesamtkunstwerk, it is also a statement of static un-changeability. It is almost unthinkable to add or subtract from it, or that certain functions would grow at the cost of others. One might argue that the composition reflects the conservatism of the Counter Reformation.

More interestingly, we can see the development of building types towards a compositional assemblage that is interlinked with society in religious, symbolic, and functional ways. Such examples are to be found in, for example, Islamic architecture of the Ottoman Empire.

Figure 78: Süleymaniye Mosque with surrounding Külliye, Istanbul, 1558, Architect: Mimar Sinan (photo: Nevzat Yildirim, 2015)

The building complexes surrounding most imperial mosques in Istanbul are called Külliye. The term is derived from the Arabic word "kull," meaning the whole. The Külliye constitutes the holistic complex and multi-layered cultural societal organisation and a political contract between the empire and the people. Typically, the Külliye is a multi-purpose building complex for public services containing a library, soup kitchen for the poor, a birth hospital, schools, etc. In contrast to the former example, the design of the imperial mosques and their Külliye demonstrates a more complex message. While the mosques themselves are final and complete compositions, closed in the sense that it is hard to imagine anything added or subtracted, their Külliye are designed according to a much more open-ended and flexible scheme, leaving a lot of leeway to adjust to future changes and needs. The Külliye are designed according to a main scheme with their own enclosed courtyards, but with great variation in size and composition to adapt to different programs of activities.

These examples demonstrate a concept of the Gesamtkunstwerk that is politically connected to society, and that has multiple practical and symbolic functions and layers of meaning.

The idea of the Gesamtkunstwerk made its way from the stage into architecture though art nouveau, but on a smaller and more particular scale. Important names were Josef Hoffmann and Otto Wagner, Victor Horta and Paul

Hankar, Charles Rennie Mackintosh, Antoni Gaudí, Eliel Saarinen, and Henry van de Velde. However, the idea of the Gesamtkunstwerk was rather limited if we compare it to the prior historic examples, and it may be reduced to a question of style compared to the multiple meanings and connectedness we saw in the imperial mosques for example.

With the Bauhaus, a more complete vision returned, and it became more political and socially-connected. The Bauhaus looked at a new type of merged disciplinarity in the Gesamtkunstwerk. This goes beyond the interdisciplinarity we talk of today. It is a natural and necessary interdependence, rather than a planned collaboration.

A problem, or possible blind spot, is in regarding the Gesamtkunstwerk as a closed and perfect work of art. This was the case in many of the examples with the arts and crafts movement, as well as the art nouveau period, but later projects also suffer from this perspective (*Figure 79*). Achieving a formal holistic design became, in some cases, a strait jacket. A total composition needs to be static. It is a closed work of art in contrast to the richness of juxtaposition like in a home, for example. It is a collection of parts within a specific context that in-between relations can be created to tell rich and complex stories. The lack of compositional unity creates potential for open-ended and rich spaces where you can add and subtract things.

Figure 79: When the idea of the Gesamtkunstwerk gets lost in formalism. National Bank of Norway, built in 1986. Architects: Lund & Slaatto A/S (Photo: Wikimedia by user: Mahlum - Own work, Public Domain).

On the other hand, an open framework of structural and material guidelines can add to individual freedom. This is an argument for a conception of the Gesamtkunstwerk that is more freely-composed, one that is not based on perfect interrelations, but a more dynamic and open-ended approach. We will shortly go through two examples; both are from the tourist industry, one on a village scale and the other on the scale of a region. Tourism is not a bad example because of its multitude in types of intentions and attractions, its inherent dilemmas regarding local heritage and identity, and its significant impact on the economy and society.

The first example of one such open-ended, yet tightly framed approach is the village of Oia on Santorini (*Figure 80*). Local guidelines restrict the use of building materials, specific colour schemes, and building height according to the historic building tradition. The village is partly built in the rock face of the inner side of the volcano crater of Santorini. The rock is very porous and allows for digging caves that are dry and isolated. The traditional building style in the steep hillside of the crater included a cave space behind a built cement façade. The facades as well as the free standing buildings on the top of the village were dominantly white cement structures in a geometrically rich and free application, inspired from the cave geometries that were carved out of the pumice rock. The restriction of colour and material allows for a very large degree of freedom in spatial form. The result is a system that can grow organically and seamlessly without visible ruptures. After the earthquake of 1956 destroyed large parts of the village, it has been constantly (re)constructed. Since then, it has steadily grown beyond its original limitations, but the marks of growth are invisible in the structure of the village. The (re)construction is still going on. The strict schema makes seamless integration of the new buildings with the old, renovated buildings possible. The geometries support a very flexible and open-ended system with a great degree of freedom.

Figure 80: Oia, Santorini (Photo: Wikimedia Commons, User: Zde).

Our other example comes from the Canary island of Lanzarote. Lanzarote has strict building regulations that cleverly allow for modern interventions harnessed in a traditional scheme of material use and colouring. This scheme was suggested by the artist César Manrique[63]. Manrique's role in the creation of the building regulations of Lanzarote can also be seen as a more modern type of holistic and systemic intervention, and the creation of a Gesamtkunstwerk on a mega scale. It is as equally open-ended as Oia, but its influences are at a larger scale, particularly around avoiding the destructive consequences from mass tourism, preserving local identity and pride, and focusing on sustainable development (Gordillo, 2015).

---

63. César Manrique was an artist, architect, and ecologist. The reason he is not more recognised might be due to his position during the civil war as a soldier in the National Front. He also lacked formal training as an architect, which along with the fact that he was seen as a vernacular architect, made him generally disregarded by the architectural community.

Figure 81: César Manrique's architecture refers to local tradition, as well as creative expression, to reflect the dramatic landscape of Lanzarote (Casa-museo del Campesino). (Photo: Birger Sevaldson 2015)

Central to the development of Lanzarote is the Plan Insular de Ordenación del Territorio (PIOT), which is the general building plan and regulation for the island. The PIOT regulates building height, use of materials, and colour scheme. These seemingly simple regulating interventions have a major systemic impact on the society. Manrique was aware of these effects. He and his colleagues were particularly determined to avoid the destructive effects of mass tourism that have had such a vast impact on local tourism on the neighbouring islands and mainland Spain. These include the destruction of local identity, unsustainable developments, dispersion of local government and control, economic derailing, and draining of resources. Manrique was crucial in the development of the tourist industry in Lanzarote. His concern was multiple and, in some ways, contradictory. However, he was able to balance these contradictions and turn the need for development of the tourist industry into a tool for strengthening local identity. He found synergy in seemingly contradictive forces; his approach helped to frame and tame tourist developments, while also helping them thrive.

Figure 82: Contemporary tourist developments on Lanzarote by César Manrique. The building height is restricted to two stories. Material colours and the detailing of pathways, divisions, gardening, etc. are inspired and regulated by the PIOT. (Photo: Birger Sevaldson 2015).

The (re)construction of local identity occurred especially in the development and design of a number of tourist attractions. In this way, Manrique managed to bridge the contradiction between local culture and the need for economic development through mass tourism. The tourist attractions crystallized the identity of the island. These attractions, including his own home which now is open for visitors, changed the conception of beauty of Lanzarote's landscape. These projects also exemplify the creative possibilities inherent in the strict framing of the building palette. Manrique managed to merge the vernacular and historic with the modern. Concerned about originality, Manrique did not want to copy any other ideal, so he instead refined what was local (Pezzi, 2013).

Marnique's work is truly unique, and there are rarely any other comparable examples. It is local and international, concrete and systemic, economic and sustainable. His influence on the development of Lanzarote cannot be underestimated; his work exemplifies complex holistic design that cuts across scales, including aesthetics, history, identity, social design, economic development and branding, experience design, etc., and can serve as an example of a "macro-Gesamtkunstwerk." Without his designerly approach, such manifestations of visualization and social engagement it would not have happened. Maria Giulia Pezzi conducted a comprehensive analyses of Manrique's work on Lanzarote from the perspective of the tourist industry and its effects (Pezzi, 2013). Her main criticism is that the PIOT prevents a "natural" development, and that the architecture of Lanzarote is superficial, turning Lanzarote into a "theme park,"

This is a common criticism, particularly from architects who find their degree of freedom restrained. It is an inadequate and false argument. There is no such thing as a natural development. All developments are designed. Man-made systems are all designed, with some worse than others. Some develop more freely and organically, while others are more restrained, but they are all the result of strategic and detailed design choices. It is not a question of honesty, but a question of design choices. In the case of Lanzarote, the criticism is totally absurd when comparing it with the "natural" developments of mass tourism in the nearby Grand Canaria. In addition, one could claim that the contemporary architecture of Lanzarote is allowed to develop organically and gently within a guiding framework that avoids large, brutal, disruptive developments with unintended and irresponsible systemic impact.

Figure 83: César Manrique produced many unique buildings and sculptures on Lanzarote, but most importantly, he was the architect behind Lanzarote's unique building regulations that preserved the island and avoided the destructive tourism architecture. This picture shows an example of Manrique's characteristic modernist architecture and art that work well together with the vernacular building style of Lanzarote. (Photo Gernot Keller, Creative Commons).

Bringing the designerly approach that is demonstrated in the concept of the Gesamtkunstwerk into our current times of increasingly complex challenges is both promising and challenging.

The lack of depth in the interpretation of the Gesamtkunstwerk in particular and holistic design in general, developed into the degeneration of the ideal. Much of today's interdisciplinary work lacks the integration and synergy of the Gesamtkunstwerk at its best. Such work is most often more like adding layers of fragments, and conducted through the distribution of tasks rather than creating interconnected resolutions. Such fragmented solutions are typically engineering solutions designed by committees in highly regulated and standardized fields. A good example is the ship building industry, where this type of fragmented work has resulted in badly designed control environments (*Figure 84*).

Figure 84: The ship bridge of the "Norwegian Jade." A cluttered environment that is subjected to international safety regulations, but defies user friendliness and most importantly, situational awareness. (Photo: Paulo Ordoveza, Creative Commons).

The case of the ship bridge design is telling because of the obvious problems; the lack of holistic design caused, reaching from aesthetics (the environment is just ugly) to user interface clutterdness, and lack of similarities between the multiple platforms and interfaces, resulting in lesser situation awareness and endangering security.

We need to go beyond styles and formalism. Why we have not learned more from the above examples is a puzzle. What the examples teach us is that functioning designs need to engage with a myriad of issues in a flexible and adaptive way. Framing to narrowly create systems failures. We need to go down the cumbersome road where we utilize large numbers of real-life parameters (quantitative, as well as qualitative) and handle seemingly contradictory factors. Unfortunately (or fortunately?), it is not easy or even possible to quantify all these parameters and automate the generation of designs. Therefore, we need to turn to designerly ways of creating holistic solutions in very complex contexts. This implies looking at the Gestalt of complexities. This implies that the abilities of balancing, negotiating, and composing are required. These should be at the core designing for complexity today.

Approaching the concept of Gesamtkunstwerk again in a new way could clarify the merging of disciplines, the crossing of scales, and the approaches to negotiations. The New Gesamtkunstwerk is concerned more with:

- Synthesis rather than analyses.

- interplay of actors and forces rather than form.

- open design rather than complete design.

- context involvement rather than the art piece itself.

Design Thinking

Design thinking has been discussed at length since it has become a buzzword in business and management. The popularized version of Design Thinking[64] was developed by the people of the Stanford D-School (McKim, 1972), and widely spread by Tim Brown and IDEO's propagation of Design Thinking as a specific method (Brown, 2008; Brown & Katz, 2009; Brown & Wyatt, 2010). It made its way into business through the writings of Tim Brown and others (Liedtka & Ogilvie, 2011; Lockwood, 2010). This has led to a serious discussion on the role of design in management (Boland & Collopy, 2004), but also harsh critique of Design Thinking as a simplified method that can easily be learned by anyone (Kimbell, 2011, 2012).

The notion of design thinking is much older and more complex than what has been discussed in management journals. To mention a few authors, design thinking has been described early by Rowe (1987) and Buchanan (1992). It was debated by Nelson (1994), elaborated on by Nelson and Stolterman in 2002 (2012a) as well as Hegerman (2008), and was further developed in discussions by Cross (2011).

To me, the basis of design thinking is found in the relation between reflection and practice. This was described by Donald Schön through his iconic concept of the "reflective practitioner" (1982). The relation and interdependency between reflection and design practice is partly lost when we try to export design thinking to other professions like management. In this book, we think of design thinking as

---

64. I use capitalized letter for the particular version of Design Thinking that has been popularized in management, and small letters for the more generic design thinking originating from within design since the 80ties.

integrated with design practice, as reflection in action. Designing is integral with a certain type of reflection. This reflection is dependent on design activities, both in process and for visions of what might be possible. These iterations of visions are essential in widening the field of possibilities (*Figure 7*). We will not provide a comprehensive overview of this discussion. This would lead our focus astray. However, we do need to clarify a position on the question of what design thinking actually is.

Much of what this book is about is design thinking, but it is a different kind of design thinking than what is often seen in the business environment. Though design is, in a certain sense, something everybody does, it is also inseparable from the skills and competencies of designing.[65] Design thinking is the reasoning and envisioning of how things ought to be in the process of planning and making them. I see it as consisting of many different ways of thinking, all closely related to practice. Visual thinking is central. The above-mentioned core abilities of the designer are essential elements to my definition of design thinking. Systemic thinking through design and reflection in action are central components for the type of design thinking we need to nurture.

From this follows that design thinking is:

- Geared towards solving problems, changing situations, innovation, synthesis and ideation.

- Based on general and particular knowledge as well as skills, competencies and experience.

- Based on judgement and expert intuition.

- Heavily reliant on visualisation and visual thinking.

- Reliant upon testing and prototyping.

- Engaged in dialogue, shared knowledge and collaborative processes as well as individual work.

---

65. Herbert Simon's definition of design is: "Everyone designs who devise courses of action aimed at changing existing situations into preferred ones." This definition is absurd. The consequence of this is that if you tell somebody who is feeling hot to take of his or her sweater, you design. One should be able to distinguish such acts from designing shading to protect from the sun, for example. In addition, one should be able to distinguish between engineering, economic planning, war strategies, etc. and Design. The boundaries overlap, but there are also particular differences. These differences are not easily recognised by non-designers, something that contributes to the confusion (H. Simon, 1969).

- A constant learning process.

Design thinking is not entirely unique to design but is developed most clearly in the advanced design professions. Design practice is closely related and dependent on design thinking. Neither is detachable from the other, and it would be a serious mistake to think so.

Information Visualisation and Information Design

There are several fields of expertise found in the intersection of graphic design and science that are about visualising complex information. The main purpose of this field is to make information accessible. There is a direct line from diagramming to information visualization and design. Diagrams are as old as advanced human culture. One could say we draw diagrams with our hands when gesturing.

However, diagrams developed to visualize ever more complex issues. Florence Nightingale was an early user of diagrams to communicate statistics. Her diagrams are an excellent example of how quantitative date is made accessible with visualization to trigger action and change.

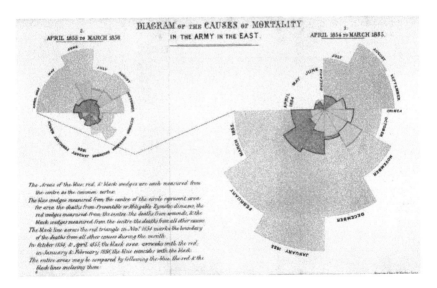

Figure 85: Florence Nightingale's diagram of causes of death during the Crimean War demonstrated that the main cause of death was infection due to lack of hygiene at the hospitals treating the wounded soldiers (blue areas in the diagram). (Public Domain)

In our times, it developed into a universe of advanced diagrams described by, for example, Tufte (Tufte, 1983). With the rise of the computer information, visualisation crystallised in several streams, one based on graphic design and the other driven by scientific visualisation. Rich quantitative information that before was impossible to interpret was now visualised in a way that made it possible to identify patterns and phenomena in the data. Information visualisation is developing its aesthetics and as a craft and, one might say, an art form (McCandless, 2009).

Information visualisation has been extremely important for science, and in many cases, the visual serves as scientific (ostensive) proof. Also, this creates a bridge between sciences and the arts. It is often aesthetic decisions that influence the interpretation of the visualisations.

However, there is a limitation to all the different threads of information visualisation. They are, with very few exemptions, descriptive. Their purpose is to make information accessible and understandable. Very often, this happens by simplification and reduction of the complexity of the material. This descriptive nature of all information visualisation is what sets it apart from the core intention of the Gigamaps and other visual tools meant for generative design processes.

Though we recognise the relation and the heritage from information visualisation, it is of less importance and less useful for the development of generative complex visualisations tools. There are other discussions on the roles of the generative diagram that seem more important and to which we will return to when discussing the concepts of SOD in Part Three.

Systemic Design: The Renaissance of Systems Thinking in Design

In the following chapter, I attempt to reconstruct the emergence of the field of systemic design. The term has been used for quite a while, but it is now used for the current emerging renaissance of Systems Thinking in design. What is unique about this renaissance is that, as mentioned, systems theories are not just imported into design, but a new realization of systemic design as a particular and strategic type of design thinking and design practice is emerging.

The use of the term, "Systemic Design" as a denotation of a method, a way of working, or an emerging mode of thinking has its roots in the late 1990's and 2000's. Previously, from the 1970's onward, the term systemic design was mostly used as an adjective (systemic) and verb (design) for pointing at particular cases (e.g., the systemic design of a computer system) or as a way of designing systems.[66] It is not mentioned as a generic method or approach, and far from being a field. When it was used in a more generic sense, it was within very specialized areas. It is therefore difficult and subjective to pinpoint the moment that the term was first coined as a design principal and potentially a methodology and a field of design theory. One of the early uses of the term as a design method related to the design field is in Bela Banathy's study of matching design methods to systems types (1988, p. 31). However, the term is read as a self-explanation in the text of Banathy and others. It is not defined or mentioned in the indices.

Reigeluth is another writer who saw the need for systemic design in a way similar to what we think of it today. Although he is an academic like Banathy and not trained as a designer in the traditional sense, he designed educational programs throughout his career. He therefore had a sense of how to compose complex artefacts and integrate them as a whole. So, both Banathy and Reigeluth did indeed have practical experience to underpin their notion of design. Reigeluth and Garfinkle proposed an early well-defined explanation of the term systemic design, and describe similarities between design and Systems Thinking in this way:

> ### *Systemic Design: A Tool for Thinking about the future.*
> Design is a complex activity. It requires both vision and an attention to detail, a variety of thinking and learning styles, creativity and persistence, and delicate interpersonal and political negotiation (Reigeluth & Garfinkle, 1994 at Preface).

Systems Thinking is also difficult. It requires keeping many aspects of the problem set in your head at one time. It is a community activity, not an individual one, with all the requisite challenges of any recoup task. Like design, Systems Thinking demands persistence, because to think systemically means to constantly reflect back to previous assumptions and to be flexible enough to change thinking that has been agreed upon previously.

Nigel Cross and Anita Clayburn Cross are among the first to use the term systemic design as a strategic mode of designing (Cross & Cross, 1996). However, their example from Formula 1 racing, where the racing team with all its functions as well as the car and the race driver himself, are proposed as an example of a systemic design, is somewhat limited compared to what we see in current systemic design practice. There is no boundary critique, or concrete systems thinking in the example, and though Cross claims the design to be a whole system design, this is hardly the case as we see it today. So, one can say Cross points to a mode of systemic designing that is only seen in an yet underdeveloped form, while others have also described much more developed concepts and ideas around systemic design without actually using the term. For example, Harold Nelson describes the

---

66. In these cases, a general use of the word design was the norm and few of these cases point at Design with capital D. Often there was an implicit reference to engineering design or IT.

need for integrating design with Systems Thinking, especially in designing for organisational change within a rapidly changing world (Nelson, 1994). Ming-fen Li discuss the relation between Systems Thinking and design thinking, and proposes to give more attention to individual development and the integration of Systems Thinking and design thinking as a collective learning process (Ming-fen, 2000). Meanwhile, Christakis uses the term closer to its current understanding as a way of designing, a design method, and attitude (Christakis & Brahms, 2003).

A central milestone in the emergence of systemic design as a special way of designing is found in Nelson and Stolterman's book The Design Way, particularly in chapter 3, "Systemics" (2012a) (First edition 2002). They regard systemics to be an integrated and important part of "the design way." It feels natural when investigating the particularities of design that some sort of Systems Thinking is central. They claim that "designers must be systemic in everything they do and make" (p. 57). They especially reinforce the argument that systemics are needed for sustainability: "Design systemic is the compound of integrative inclusive, and connected thinking aimed at taking right action doing the right thing even if not perfectly."

The first consistent version of systemic design emerged at the Politechnico of Torino in Torino, Italy around 2000. This early version was focussed on regional scale and sustainability (Barbero, 2017; Bistagnino & Campagnaro, 2014).

The new attention to systems in design was started with a seminar at AHO, Oslo in 2012. Important steps were:

- 2012-2013 the founding of the Relating Systems Thinking and Design (RSD) symposia. Since then it has been an annual conference.

- 2012 the Systemic Design Research Network was founded at a loft room of the Hotel Savoy in Oslo.

- 2014 the term systemic design was decided and established as a pluralistic and flourishing field allowing different versions and approaches to emerge.

- 2018 the network was formalised as the Systemic Design Association in Torino.

Since then, attention to Systems Thinking in design has spread and established itself as a way forward in our increasingly complex world.

This concludes a rough summary of developments and preconditions for the new development of systemic design. We will now turn our attention to SOD.

Systems-Oriented Design: Theories and Backgrounds

The main agenda of systems-oriented design is to approach systems from the particular field of design as a skill, rather than a theory. The research presented here is within the domain of applied Systems Thinking, and though it borrows from systems theories, its main goal is to argue for and demonstrate that Systems Thinking in design is better trained as a skill rather than being heavily guided by theories and prescribed methods.

Positioning SOD

The Knowledge Ecology of SOD

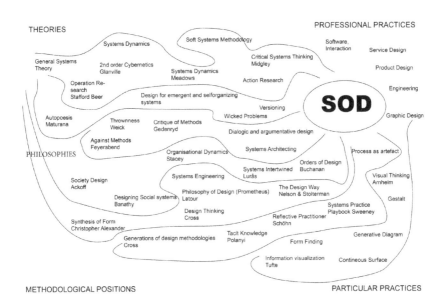

Figure 86: The knowledge ecology of SOD, simplified. (Birger Sevaldson, 2019)

The former chapters add up to a rich picture of what the sources, inspirations, and theories influencing SOD are. The chapter on what systems brings to design did touch upon the major points and aspects from the systems world that had a major influence on the crystallization of SOD, leaving out less important ones. Yet these are only forming parts of what SOD is based on. Other parts are based on the designerly ways of knowing, design theories addressed in the chapter on what design brings to systems, and practices, treated in Part Three, addressing the praxeology of SOD. SOD is composed of a rich and diverse "knowledge ecology" rather than certain directions and perspectives. This ecology is as much based on practice as theories (*Figure 86*). It is worth keeping this in mind when we discuss how SOD is positioned in this rich landscape of thoughts theories and practical philosophy.

Between Disciplines and Practices

Design has moved a long way from its start where industrial mass production, the shaping of useful consumer goods, and increasing industrial profit were at the centre of attention. Design has become more verbal and less visual and ever more information-heavy, and designing itself has become increasingly complex. The previously mentioned multiple movements (convergence, divergence, migration, immigration) create on one side a bigger and expanded design field, and on the other, new specializations. These movements include new relations to other disciplines and integration of new knowledge into design. The drivers for these developments are the ever-increasing challenges imposed upon design. The before mentioned macro trends like globalization and the need for increased sustainability pose inescapable design challenges that force us to take responsibility for the consequences of our designs. This requires dealing with other knowledge fields, and design can be torn as well as becomes squeezed between disciplines and practices. This leaves design with a problem of fragmentation resulting in partly contradictory interpretations of design. There is a need for integration and holistic approaches, methodologies, practices, and generic perspectives that bind it all together.

In SOD, designing is seen as the nucleus that integrates the design process and Systems Thinking across different design specialities and applications. SOD is seen as an umbrella that integrates layers of information and methodological approaches. By using design skills like visualization in Systems Thinking, systemic projects are turned into design projects. We use designing as a way of investigating, understanding, and changing systems. The visualizations are design artefacts, and Systems Thinking becomes totally integrated into the design process. The old design skills of shaping the object have become central again.

Integrating Systems approaches into design implies new roles for design. The systemic designers will engage more intensively, deeply, and widely with the projects in which they are involved, as well as engage in interdisciplinary ways with other fields. They will constantly search for causes and relations, always look beyond the object and beyond disciplines, and always try to think of more moves ahead. They will not fear complexity but embrace it as a source for creativity. They will proactively seek to engage in the complexity that they know is there and that they know will attack eventually if they do not take it on right from the beginning. These new roles imply that designers are intensively engaged with taking on complex challenges, whether it be for their client, the client's organisation and its environment, or for society at large. The challenges, wicked as they are, give a damn about fields and disciplines. Systems oriented designers will consequently open up new fields for design, because they will constantly redefine what should be done. They will be very creative in finding new solutions and innovations, not as a result of random brainstorming or other creativity techniques, but out of a deep understanding of context and conditions, by involving other disciplines, fields and stakeholders, and by seeing the whole, and therefore being able to design new relations and synergies. The role of SOD as a framework for bridging disconnected silos is becoming increasingly important. We will dig deeper into this in Part Three.

I suggest that in this very moment[67] when design is moving towards new levels of complexity, the designerly skills are needed more than ever. The act of designing becomes the tool for understanding systems, for creating interpretations of the systems, for refining those interpretations as design artefacts, as well as for generating and creating systems interventions. The design skills need to be balanced, though. We need to abandon some of the old urges for aestheticism, order, symmetry, and balance. These formats hardly fit for wicked problems. Further on, we need to restrain our urge for formal composition to instead compose with forces, relations, and actors. We need to give away a bit of our urge for control, and work with and for the forces at play. We need to work with the notions of negotiation, flows and parameters, and wicked problems. We need to develop tolerance towards the messiness of the real world. The original skills of the designer, skills for shaping the design artefact, are still potentially sharp tools for addressing and coping with the increasing complexity.

This implies the redefinition of the "design artefact:" What is the design artefact when I have argued that we have moved beyond the object[68] itself? Observing the object's framework, what are its relations to other objects, its history and future, its production and recycling, as well as its cultural, societal, political, and economic preconditions? The new emerging design artefact is the picture of the system, the Gigamap. It depicts the resolution, implementation, and the orchestration of many interventions. Consequently, the design artefact is now also nested inside the process. The design artefact is not the only output of the process. The design process is designed. So, the systemic design process is also a design artefact. It is the mapping and visualization of the complexity we design

---

67. Bruno Latour described this moment in his speech "A Cautious Prometheus" (Latour, 2008).
68. Recall that object is meant in an open sense as both concrete and abstract.

within. We see here the contours of another nested generative design process rather than merely gathering and visualizing descriptive information. Realizing and emphasising this nested design process opens the doors to designing for complexity in a new way. These are central concepts that lay a foundation for SOD.

Following on from the issues touched upon above, SOD combines design thinking and design practice with Systems Thinking and systems practice for imagination and communication in design processes with stakeholders and clients.

This constitutes a field of possibilities with four poles and a gradient between practice and reflection. We presented this in Part One (*Figure 8*), but here we will go a bit deeper into how SOD is positioned in the field. In the following section, I will briefly describe the four poles.

The Relation to Design Thinking

As mentioned, we should forget the notion of design thinking as something particular when it comes to certain methods and approaches. Design thinking is the thinking process that goes on in and around a design process. It is characterized by its creative components and ongoing real-time processes of thinking in action, for action and reflecting on action, along with the incubation processes for creativity. This establishes a very specific set of skills, experience, and knowledge about how to solve things, produce things, stage things, and envision what is possible.

The Relation to Design Practice

Design as practice has been discussed for a while as patterns that describe ways of working (Fry, 2008; Gedenryd, 1998; Hamilton & Jaaniste, 2009; Lawson, 1997) and as methodology (Broadbent, 2003; Cross, 1984; Jones, 1970). Design practice has fallen into somewhat fixed patterns, and certain repetitive approaches are applied by many designers to any design task. This is an obstacle when we want to change the process, so that it has the capacity to cope with a larger degree of complexity. We will therefore not pay a lot of attention to such prescriptive design methods in this book. Instead, we will look at design practice very pragmatically as the act of design. This indicates a praxiological approach rather than one based on prescriptive methodology. We will return to the discussion of praxeology in Part Three. This is related to, but not entirely dependent on, design thinking. Sometimes the doing is ahead of the thinking, and the thinking process is a form of post-rationalization. This practice is based on tacit knowledge and experience.

The Relation to Systems Thinking

Here, we should forget systems theories for a moment, and look at this very pragmatically as a way of thinking. I use the term here as a state of mind and sensibility that is defined by the ability to look beyond the object, to regard what we see immediately as symptoms of flows, process forces, and relations that are involved in dynamic interaction with a sensitivity for connections and relations. Understanding this interaction is not only a question of theory, but also a skill that can be developed towards systems practice.

The Relation to Systems Practice

Systems practice is the skill of applying Systems Thinking to real-life phenomena. It engages real life participation, the critical intuition of the expert, and a sensibility for systems and especially how they can act counter-intuitively. It includes the ability to engage and correlate complex project groups and other social systems. Systems practice has been described by Peter Checkland as an integral part of SSM (Checkland, 2000c). In SSM, systems practice is defined as a process of learning to know complex societal systems through action (i.e., Action Research). Ulrich has also described a reflexive practice as central in Critical Systems Thinking (Ulrich, 2000a). Systems practice in the form of action investigates systems though active engagement. By acting within a system and paying attention to how it reacts, we learn more about it. We learn a bit about its resilience and resistance to change and what conditions need to be fulfilled to induce change. We learn about the hidden nature of the system, the big part of the iceberg that is under the surface. We also learn how the system potentially kicks back in unexpected ways. It is hard, if not impossible, to generalize directly from such real-life experiments, since the reactions are situation dependent. However, we can carefully generalize and assume how the system could react on similar situations if we do it critically.

The Positioning Principles of SOD

SOD builds on two main principles:

1. *Design thinking is inseparable from designing.* As mentioned before, in the recent migration of design thinking to other fields like management, it has been detached from design practice. This has greatly devalued the core of design thinking. If we regard design thinking as closely related to reflection in action (Schön, 1982), it becomes clear that the value of such reflection

is closely tied to and dependent on practice. In our case, the practice is designing.

2. *We need to merge Systems Thinking and systems practice with design thinking and design practice to fully benefit from relating the two fields.* This means that it is not enough to import existing systems approaches and models into design.

Merging the two fields from the designer's perspective means redefining systems approaches to better meld with designerly skills and practices, as well as reshaping design thinking to become systemic. This indicates a full merger of the two where something slightly new transpires. This new approach to designing with and for systems is not another systems theory or a new design methodology. It is more so a way of thinking and a set of skills following a slightly new design practice.

Given these principles, it can be seen that SOD is analytical, synthetic, and generative. It is both process-oriented and solution-driven. These two principles—that design is inseparable from design thinking and that we need to merge system thinking and design thinking as well as practice—create the basis for SOD.

An Overarching Perspective

SOD does not seek to be yet another methodology to replace others. As seen in the discussion on migration and immigration, there are already a wide range of themes in design, along with corresponding methods and approaches that are valuable. SOD offers instead a higher-level approach, a praxeology composed of a loosely defined and pragmatic methodology, a methodology without methods. This sounds counter-intuitive; however, methodology is a dialogue about methods, while a method is a fixed prescription. In our case, these methods are unfixed and flexible. Instead of fixed methods, it contains a critique of methods, a library of techniques and practices, an open-ended checklist, a library of examples and relevant theories. The application of SOD includes service design, interaction design, product design, universal design, design engineering, architecture, interior architecture, and other forms of design. Amongst the approaches and theories in design, we find ergonomics, human factors, brand building theories, the concept of Product Service Systems, social design, sustainable design, and environmental design. And finally, amongst the methods, we can list participatory design, co-design, ethnography, focus groups, and service design methodologies such as the AT-ONE method, etc.

SOD does not replace any of these approaches, fields, or methodologies. Instead, SOD seeks to be an overarching umbrella that initiates an alternative way of thinking and designing for complexity. SOD draws a bigger picture—or what we call a "landscape"—in which the systems, their environments and subsystems are embedded. We use the term "landscape" because this image reaches beyond what is normally defined in systems theories as a "systems environment," which defines what is framed as relevant, and incorporates the adjacent territories that lay beyond reasonable systems boundaries. It is a kind of "world map" that shows the system and its environment. Understanding the bigger landscape beyond the systems environment is necessary for active boundary critique throughout a design process

The main technique we use for drafting, analysing, creating, and designing this very large landscape is gigamapping.

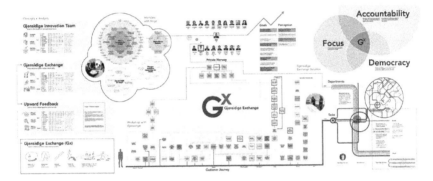

Figure 87: A Gigamap that has clear departments and structure yet relations across the structure, as well as other types of information like data, graphs, and texts. This information forms the "landscape" of the project. The case is a concept for increasing workplace democracy at Norway's biggest insurance company. The company sees workplace democracy as a way to engage human resources to their full potential. (Kevin Simmons, 2018).

Designing the system landscape in the Gigamap is the mechanism that allows SOD to be a designerly tool, a designed artefact and a design process. Most of all, SOD can be an overarching umbrella for the project to cope with super-complexity in design.

Part Three

Practices and Methodologies

Introduction to the Methodology of SOD

Before talking about methodology, let us recap what SOD is, recalling the introduction:

> Systems Oriented Design is a design methodology that is geared towards complex problems. SOD is mainly a mindset with a few tools. Its main tool is Gigamapping, an extensive genre and category breaching mapping method to grasp complexity across artificial silos and ruptures, across scales and sectors. SOD is first of all a design practice, and it is defined as a methodology without fixed methods and a praxeology, describing how to practice SOD.

SOD does not provide an extensive clearly defined tool chest, prescriptions or templates, etc. On how to use these tools. The reason is that complex real-life cases vary to such a degree that standardised and hard framed processes will stand in the way of developing deep understanding of the situation at hand. Tool chests and their use based on fixed procedures introduce a strong bias and create blind spots. Therefore, I prefer a looser framework based on a small selection of flexible adaptive tools, a mindset, and a well-developed praxeology.

In SOD, the usefulness of pre-defined methods and prescriptions is limited. To a certain degree, each project is unique, and one needs to question whether the recycling of experiences gained from similar cases might be the best approach. At the same time, it is clear that there are certain repetitive patterns, and that we recommend doing things a certain way. The very idea of gigamapping is such a methodological suggestion. The reason it stays flexible is that there is no strict prescription of how a Gigamap is produced or how it looks. It is more of a free-style approach where the design of each Gigamap is an innovative design process in its own right.

Therefore, I argue for a SOD methodology as opposed to a SOD method.[69] Methodology is an ongoing discussion about method. A method in its ultimate and finalized form is a prescription that is assumed to lead to success. Because the issues addressed in SOD are real world problematiques that are dynamic and partly unique, it is very problematic to prescribe methods. Instead, we need an ongoing methodological discussion that constantly challenges, develops, and

---

69. I find support for this position in Feyerabend, who argues there are no fixed rules that guarantee the production of knowledge (Feyerabend, 1975).

replaces our approaches. Ideally, each project demands its own method. As such, encapsulated within each project is a process for designing a bespoke method.

Gerald Midgley proposes the creative design of methods (Midgley, 2000, p. 225). He proposes that different purposes require different methods throughout a process unfolding over time. While the purposes develop and change through a process, the methods need to change and to be redesigned. At the basis for such a methodological approach lies the acceptance of multiple methods and mixing of methods. Midgley expresses this as multi-layered interventions. The methods are seen as parts in a system of its own right where the sum is different from their parts. (p. 226). This approach resonates well with the hybrid process and with Robert Yin's concept of triangulation (Yin, 1994).

Developing bespoke design processes has several advantages. The notion of design is recognised, beyond the realm of the design professions, as excellent when it comes to finding solutions for complex issues. This is reflected in the term Research Design (Creswell, 2013). In science, it is commonly recognised that experiments as well as whole research projects need to be composed in a good manner to render good results. Hence the term Research Design. There is no better term than design to describe how to make a good scientific experiment. Typically, there is more than theories at stake in designing an experiment. One needs to cope with technology, economy, robustness, materials, and procedures, etc. In addition, there is no singular answer to the design of an experiment. An experiment is judged on its theoretical fundament, its output, and repeatability, but it is also commonly recognised that an experiment can be replaced by a better, more reliable, cheaper, and simpler one at any time. The design of the experiment is ultimately tied to the design of the method. A changed experiment would require a changed method and vice versa. Others have argued that the production of knowledge should be seen as a design process, and thus follows that scientific enquiry is a form of design (Ranulph Glanville, 1994).

Another advantage in designing and redesigning methodology that depends on redesigning methods rather than on applying ready-made methods, is that the method used is bespoke and hence an integrated part of the particular design project. Feyerabend argues for a similar idea. Although he is against method, and proposes an anarchistic position towards how we do things, he is not against methodology as an ongoing discussion (1975). Horst Rittel was also critical of the effects of any design method application (1972). He argues for a mission-driven approach instead of the application of fixed methods. Inspired by NASA's systems-oriented missions, he suggests that every design problem should be seen as a mission-oriented design project.

Rittel further elaborates on what he calls the "Symmetry of Ignorance," which is relevant to the limitation of pre-conceived methods:

For practical purposes, it does not matter how something was done.

Because these problems are unique you can never demonstrate how it would have been if you would have generated the solution in some other way.

The justification of searching for systemic methods is a certain confidence or hope that they might assist in forgetting less by applying them.

People are more likely to like solutions if they have been involved in its generation; even though it might not make sense otherwise.

There is no professional expertise that is concentrated in the expert's mind.

Expertise is distributed in particular among those who are likely to become affected.

There is nobody who has the guarantee that his knowledge is superior to any other person's knowledge with regard to the problem at hand.

(Rittel, H. W. J. (1972). Son of Rittelthink.
The DMG 5th Anniversary Report, DMG Occasi, 5–10).

For Rittel, the design process should be organized as an argument or an argumentative process. This means that all the statements are systematically challenged in order to expose them to different viewpoints, because expertise and ignorance are distributed over all participants in a wicked problem. Although Rittel's notion is insightful, the Symmetry of Ignorance does not posit that there is no room for expertise, experience, skills, knowledge, and competence. I think a good interpretation is that expertise does not guarantee good decision-making, especially if one does not have a closeness to the problematique at hand. An open mind, open dialogue, and respect for other kinds of expertise should be maintained. This means recognising real-life experience as expertise.

There was a considerable shift in the conception of design methods during the 70's. As described by Cross (1982, 1984, 2007b), belief in adopting a design approach inspired by scientific methods faded as trust in prescriptive methods crumbled. A new realization was growing, and alternative ways of thinking emerged accordingly.

This shift can be summarized in the following ways:

- The design process is no longer considered a fixed sequence of activities that follows a specific order.

- Understanding the "problem" is only possible through development of concepts for possible solutions. Therefore, you need to design something to interpret the "problem" through that conceptual lens. This means that designing is the main approach to get real, deep knowledge about the "problem."

- The "catch 22" of learning about the "problem:" You cannot gather relevant information about the issue at hand before you know a bit about it. However, you cannot know the issue before you have gathered relevant information.

- There is a move away from looking at design as a problem-solving activity towards an emphasis on designing for experience, emotions, and empathy, as well as to understand problems in larger contexts as problem fields, problem networks, or "problematiques."

- There is a shift towards hybrid or conglomerate applications of design methods where the first-generation design methods are not totally abandoned, but utilized within a bigger tool set of methods that are applied in a critical way.

- Abandoning the phasing of the prescriptive design methods shifts attention and focus throughout the design process. e.g., one can start with studying implementation very early. Developing implementation requirements in this way will inform the design from the start, and they will become an integrated part of the design resolution.

- The argumentative approach to design is developed further through dialogic design and participatory design methods.

From Methods to Praxeology

Instead of prescriptions, we develop practical, suggestive procedures for how to facilitate and implement an argumentative design process. Designing this design process for each case at hand has become a natural way of working, which is further supported by patterns that are made explicit through suggestive rules and guidelines. This constitutes a new praxeology for design. Praxeology is the knowledge, experience, adaptability, and competence to operate in real world contexts. Unlike methodology, praxeology does not prescribe principles of actions; rather it suggests how to act through building rich libraries of actions. Praxeology includes and embraces tacit knowledge, craft skills, and show rather than tell. We will return to the notion of praxeology, but for now the praxeology of SOD is built around some basic principles:

1. Value Constructivism "Designism" or learning as a design process.

2. Approach systems as a designer.

3. Design the understanding and interpretation of systems.

4. Integrate learning, creativity, and designing.

5. Be humble towards the experts (users etc.).

6. Don't underestimate the "critical fresh eye."

7. Don't underestimate the splint in your eye. You are always partially blind.

8. Be brave in entering new fields.

9. Embody adaptive expertise: adaptability as a skill and competence.

10. Constantly design bespoke methods.

11. Constantly deconstruct methods.

Concepts and Models in SOD

The Ecology of Design

In SOD, we look at businesses and organisations as "ecologies." Sustainability is not only a matter of being "green," but also a matter of technology, economy, management, culture, politics, and markets. By understanding these ecologies, advantages are gained in not only traditionally green or sustainability issues, but also in finding synergies for technological and economic development.

This means that as a designer, you cannot disregard any issues of importance to your client. Not only do you need to care about the client's profit and the profits of their new product or service, you are also obligated to care for the client's environment and the bigger landscape, and how the clients operation affects this landscape.

Looking Beyond the Object: Understanding and Working with Outcroppings

From the beginning, in SOD, the slogan has been: "Look beyond the object." This is one of the basic mindsets of SOD. Objects, being material or immaterial are a natural starting point of investigating a system. They are the result of our perceptions (Gestalt), and they are formed out of our schemata and preconceptions. Objects are here understood as both material and immaterial, for example, iconic activities and processes such as cooking dinner.

Designers are traditionally object-oriented, though this is about to change through service design and interaction design. On the other hand, the object-centric perspective is continuing to grow through new concepts like the "internet of things," and the objectification of services (Lindberg & Nordin, 2008). Also, non-material things like touch points and experiences are singled out as objects. Objectification is convenient because it draws seemingly clear and tight boundaries around things. However, these boundaries are disputable and hinder the emphasis on the relations and systems of systems that make out and underpin the objects.

In any case, the need for increased attention towards the implicit consequences of design products and other outputs requires that we look at the objects of design—things, services or processes—in a different and deeper way.

We need to look beyond the object, regard its origin, understand its consumption, and plan for its Life Cycle. We need to look at its effects and side effects, the intended ones as well as the unintended, the short term as well as the long term.

In SOD, we look at objects as symptoms of processes. Often many processes are brought together in one object. The objects are Intersection Points between systems.

By investigating the systems behind the paper cup mentioned before in this manner, more layers of meaning and additional questions emerge. Is there a political dimension to this simple little artefact? It becomes clear that there indeed is a relation to fair trade, as well as to the effects of fossil fuel used in transportation, the multinational economies, and raw material exchange. The political dimensions of the simple artefact thus emerge.

Though we do not know all the details in these journeys and flows of materials, money, and activities, we know the end result, and we know that there has to be a starting point to each aspect of the object in question. With that, we might be able to imagine the in-between moments, and it is often enough to have a crude scenario of these processes. I characterize this concept of understanding as an "unfolding" of complex systems through a reading of a priori given points using the strategy of "outcrops" (a term borrowed from geology). An outcrop is a rock that emerges through the layers of sediment. If several such outcrops are present in an environment, a geologist would assume that they represent underlying bedrock that spreads all the way beneath the sediment (*Figure 88*).

Figure 88: When geologists see outcrops of bedrock, they deduce that they are connected. In the same way, we can fill in interconnections that we do not know in detail, but that we know must exist (Illustration: Birger Sevaldson).

In a similar manner, we can use partial knowledge (outcrops) to interpolate what is missing in-between. We know that coffee bean is grown and picked in a country far from Norway, and we know it is packaged and sold in the grocery store. From that, we can therefore conclude that there are transportation, trade, and refinery systems involved, even without knowing the particularities. Used in this way, the concept of outcrops as an analogy can help us to prioritize our investigations. An example of such an investigation is shown in *Figure 89*. The wonderful hand painted porcelain set of sixteen parts, packaged in the traditional handmade bamboo packaging system for export of porcelain to Europe was stamped IKEA, made in Vietnam, and sold for five euros. The case is loaded with issues from cultural aspects, globalisation, exploitation, and unequal distribution of resources. The set was so cheap that I bought one for each of my twelve students as a gift, for them to analyse and contemplate over the system that lies behind this example. The map in *Figure 90* is an attempt of unfold the systems that lie behind the phenomena.

Figure 89: A porcelain set with sixteen parts handmade in Vietnam, stamped by IKEA, and sold for 50 NOK at IKEA Norway. The patterns are hand painted. Note the beautiful handmade bamboo packaging. This is a traditional packaging for the historic porcelain trade to Europe (Photo: Birger Sevaldson).

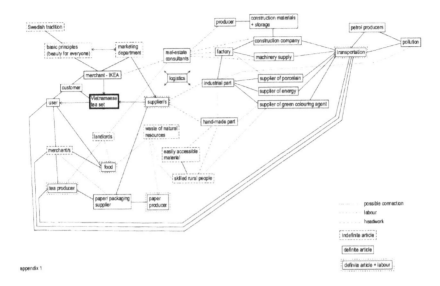

Figure 90: This Outcropping analysis imagines all the necessary conditions and steps for the above porcelain set to be produced. One obvious condition is very low paid craft labour (AHO-students, 2012).

Re-understanding the object by looking far beyond it is ultimately a strategy for designing. To understand the object beyond its obvious appearance, it helps to view it with a different perspective, or a fresh eye. This opens up new choices and interventions beyond our original assumptions. Most importantly, a fresh view allows for interventions that are cross-scalar, spanning from high-level systemic innovations to small-scale changes and designs.

The Schemata Problem

The above example of the simple paper cup demonstrates a mental jump. It bypasses our preconceptions of the object as "simple" and redefines it as something very complex. In this way, we break our schema about the object. And breaking schemata is a precondition of achieving deep innovation. [70]

---

70. The concept of Schema was first proposed by Kant, but Piaget is mostly credited for having developed it into a modern psychological theory. Arbib has a readable introduction to the notion of

Preconceptions, schemata, and prejudices are normal parts of our life and necessities for everyday survival. We use schemata to read our environments quickly by objectifying them. For example, we can immediately recognise a car, a house, a river, etc. However, schemata also frame our conception. By breaking them, we can become more creative. For example, if we design a sofa, a common design artefact and schemata, the result is given. We sit beside each other in twos or threes. However, if we break the schema of sitting and decompose it into a device for body support, one might arrive at a totally different result (*Figure 91*).

Figure 91: The sculptural furniture piece, "Extra Terrain" is an example of how the continuous surface was developed into open designs. The object breaks the schemata of furniture in the form of chairs and sofas, by ambulating between an art sculpture and a furniture piece without providing any recognisable furniture feature such as clearly-defined seating surfaces. It is up to the user to interpret how the surface should be used. In a sense, the user programs the piece in the moment of use (Kivi Sotamaa and Markus Holmsten, 2000).

The process of looking beyond the object developed through intensive gigamapping helps to break schemata and to overcome preconception. Beginning

---

schema that also deals with schema in relation to action (Motor Schema), which is interesting in our discussion on how complex processes are also dealt with as schemata (Arbib, 1992).

with a very open agenda, the mapping should, at the start, try to disregard schemata and prejudices, as well as our conceptions of usefulness and relevance. This strategy helps to uncover some of the less obvious issues, and helps to overcome a bit of the biases from our preconceptions.

It is important at this stage to realize that the mapping should include all kinds of information. One should be like a sponge, soaking up anything, while being careful to not impose any kind of filter, preconception, or schemata (Checkland P. & Poulter, 2006). One should, in periods, try to forget the initial scope, brief, ideas, or intentions, and map everything for its own sake motivated by general curiosity and interest in the bigger picture. This will help to break through beyond schemata, clichés, and archetypical solutions in order to map out information that might at first seem irrelevant but, but later might turn out to be crucial.

The Relevance Problem

The urge for relevance is a strong filter that hinders us from seeing the system with new eyes and hence, reaching deep innovation. While we investigate the system through mapping and other inquiries like literature search, fieldwork, and conversations, (integrated parts of SOD), the urge for relevance to the assumed problem or even solution at the outset will severely bias the investigation and stand in the way of learning about the system.

This urge is strong. We want to act purposefully and we do not want to waste time. We love simple straightforward processes that are orderly and logic. This is a big obstacle to embracing complexity and to learn to understand systems. We need to realize the value of not always knowing what we are doing, to experiment with our conception of things and to play with our understanding and to nurture our curiosity. We need to know more than we need to know to resolve a problem systemically. Therefore, we not only need to map out the system and its environment (the direct interactions), but also the bigger landscape (the indirect interactions) where the system and its environment is embedded.

Seemingly small issues that are far out in the periphery of the landscape, many steps away from our starting point can stop projects or turn good intentions into bad results. To find these critical issues, we need to turn off our filters, forget our intentions for a moment, and investigate in very high detail the system, its environment, fields, and landscapes reaching as wide as our resources allow. This technique will help you find the issues that you never even thought of from the outset.

While resisting the judgement of relevance in the beginning of a mapping process, it will slowly become more crucial. You cannot know what is relevant before you know the system, its environment, and landscape. In addition, you cannot make any targeted inquiries without having a good idea of what is relevant.

By first exploring the system widely without any relevance filtering, you will be able to create a comprehensive map. This allows you to become knowledgeable beyond the particular task at hand by involving in more informed, wider, and upstream discussions. This knowledge will be used to iteratively judge and prioritize relevance.

Another benefit of this strategy is that you will know more than what you strictly need. You will gain a level of field knowledge that allows you to participate in conversations with stakeholders on a slightly more informed level, enabling you to involve the social systems that always play a crucial role in any design project.

The Boundary Problem

The downside of the above strategy is the problem of judging when to stop, and what might become relevant throughout the process; in short, how to draw the boundary of the system.

Imagine yourself standing at the edge of a vast, unexplored landscape. You do not know its boundarie--where the jungle stops, and the mountain begins. The boundaries are blurred and are more like gradients. Inside that landscape lies the problematique or the situation you are about to work with as a designer. Your client is like an entity in the landscape. It is most probably a living organisation. It could be compared to an organism that lives in the landscape. But this organism does not utilize the whole landscape. The part of the landscape that is utilized by the organism is its environment. The problem, however, is that you do not know the extent of the landscape or the boundaries of the environment. Seemingly small events happening far away from the organism might kill it. Should you consider this? Should you make the cumbersome journey up the river to find its source? How far upstream should you situate your design? Here, you face a real "Catch 22:" You do not know what is relevant for the organism's environment before you know the parts of the landscape that form and influence the environment. And you cannot explore the landscape in a rational manner before you know the extent of the environment. There is only one way to solve this problem: jump into it!

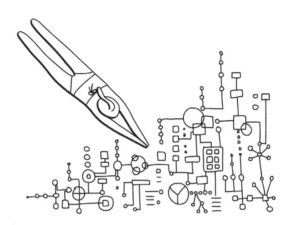

Figure 92: There is only one way to tackle the catch 22 of not being able to plan an investigation of the organisation that you serve, its environment, and the landscape: dive into it and explore. It is only when you have established a certain overview that you can then start framing the situation by drawing the boundaries of the system (Elisabeth Skjelten, 2014).

It is only when you have constructed an image of the whole landscape, the environment, and the organisation you work with or for, that you can then draw the boundaries suitable to you and the project. The boundaries will remain flexible throughout the process and beyond. Things that seemed very important will fall outside the boundaries in the future, and things that seem irrelevant now will turn out to be important and included later on. The boundaries of the system are living things that morph throughout the process as the focus develops and changes.

The boundaries change because your insights change. So, the boundaries are a mental construct. They are designed and constantly redesigned. This realization is important. At the same time, also bear in mind that what we perceive as boundaries will also change because the systems you work with are living and constantly changing. There are thus two dynamics to cope with: your own perception develops over time, and the system itself changes over time. While you plan, the system will also have inevitable changed. It is a double moving target.

In SOD, the systems' boundaries are not seen as something naturally given by the system. Although in some cases there might seem to be clear boundaries, like with an individual human being or the body of a car, these seemingly given boundaries can always be criticised and challenged. The human body is intricately interconnected with the natural world and a larger social context, and the car is part of a bigger transportation system. In SOD, the boundaries are designed and frequently redesigned according to relevance. This is not a radical idea. As mentioned before, according to SSM, the boundary is a construct. Critical Systems

Thinking suggests that the boundary is drawn out of several diverse perspectives so-called "Boundary Critique" (Midgley, 2000, p. 135; Midgley et al., 1998; Ulrich, 2000a, 2002). SOD looks at the boundary as a design object; a negotiation between what is seemingly relevant in the whole landscape, system environment, and the apparent system itself and what is realistic to cope with in the frames of the design process as it develops. In this process, we use gigamapping to identify what is relevant, and to tentatively frame the project by designing sensible systems boundaries. If the Gigamap is developed properly, it will include a far greater radius and reach than what is seemingly relevant to the project at the outset. As mentioned, this wide angled view describes the landscape of the system. [71] Meanwhile, the nearer and more directly involved surroundings is what we call the environment of the system. Generally, the systems environment is seen as the primary interaction sphere of a system. The landscape is the secondary, tertiary interactions and those beyond that. The problem with this model, however, is that it does not say anything about the importance of the interactions. Tertiary interactions might be as important as some primary interactions. It is therefore not advisable to draw the boundaries of a system according to its structural features, but rather on the bases of significance. It is easy to see that the notion of significance will produce different boundaries if the perspective changes. Boundaries are constructs and need to be value-based rather than based on structure.

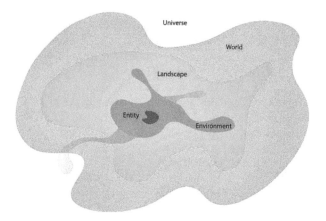

Figure 93: Diagram showing the entity (systems, situation, product, or service) we work with, its environment, landscape, world, and universe (Birger Sevaldson, 2015).

71. The term landscape is used in Transition Management, especially in the Multi-level Perspective (MLP), also sometimes called Multi-level Framework (Geels, 2002). MLP only operates with three levels, the Landscape, the Regime, and the Niche. A critique of this approach would be that it is too simplistic and applicable mostly at technological transitions.

Boundary Modulation

The central strategy regarding the construction and design of relevance is the initial expansion through gigamapping beyond what seems relevant or even reasonable at first sight. This process involves looking in any direction and with multiple perspectives. Such perspectives can be a bird's eye-view looking at the whole system and its environment from above, a frog's view looking from below and upwards, a binocular's view looking far beyond what catches the eye, and a microscopic view investigating minute details (*Figure 94*).

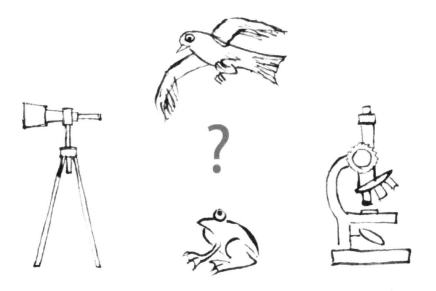

Figure 94: When investigating the system, its environment, and landscape, multiple perspectives should be at play. Besides more specific perspectives, we can distinguish four principal viewpoints that could influence the system: The bird's eye, looking down at the system to create an overview; the frog's eye, looking upwards at the system to understand power-structures and dependencies; the microscope's eye, drilling down into the details; and the telescope's eye searching for issues far out at the rim of the landscape. (Birger Sevaldson, 2018)

While the system is framed more narrowly at a later stage, it establishes an awareness of what is outside this constructed boundary. We need to know what is left out and what is included. As mentioned, some tiny issue that was initially left out might turn out to be particularly crucial as insight into the system grows. On the other hand, certain issues that we initially thought were important might turn out to play a far lesser role than anticipated. When such insights emerge, we can easily adapt and adjust the boundary of the system. This negotiation is an ongoing process that re-adjusts the boundary throughout the design process. The nature of this boundary modulation is undulating, first expanding in seemingly untargeted ways, and then periodically retracting to form intermediate conceptions of framings, and again, expanding into new directions while making it possible to settle on fairly workable and narrow boundaries towards the end (*Figure 95*). In the end, everything is designed. This goes for the Gigamap, the system itself, the boundary, and what is relevant.

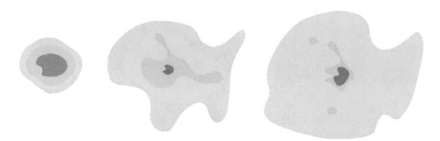

Figure 95: Boundary modulation throughout a design process. The initial conception of the problem, situation, or product is limited and is overemphasising the entity at the cost of the environment and the landscape (left). After an inquiry through gigamapping, the landscape and environment are expanded, nuanced, and given more detail (middle), and then the boundaries are constructed for operational purposes. The boundaries shrink to what is relevant and what is practically possible to include. Meanwhile, the conception of the landscape might expand further (right) (Birger Sevaldson, 2015).

Beyond the Horizon

Gigamaps are ultimately tools for drawing systems boundaries. Boundaries are needed to frame the system. They define the simplified and manageable framework for the design intervention. Simplification is also often regarded as a virtue in its own right rather than a necessity based on our brains limitations to cope with complexity. Therefore, while framing and simplifying for practical reasons, we at the same time need to train to become better at coping with complexity, which is one of the basic intentions with gigamapping and the rich design spaces we will discuss later. In any case, simplification is often done too early and too quickly. Before one can draw the boundary of a system, we need to survey and unfold the field way beyond what we assume is the horizon of relevance. Only when we have an understanding of the landscape past that horizon can we then take a step back to draw the boundary in an informed manner. With a better sense of what is left out, this overview provides the opportunity to expand and redraw the boundary to include things that might turn out to be important at a later stage. Small things at the far ends of a cause and effect chain can become crucial. We need to find those crucial triggers that are not immediately visible. Gigamapping ensures that all efforts are taken to track down what is relevant, and to include them in the design. It helps to maintain a flexible boundary that can be adjusted during a process to capture issues that may dynamically change in importance. How the role of actors and networks changes, the pace, frequency and degree of change, as well as the ripple effects of change all play a role in deciding the importance of an issue. This approach is our practice-based answer to Boundary Critique, a well-known perspective in systems thinking (Midgley, 2000).

A State of Thrownness

Here, it is appropriate to add a warning and a call for humbleness. Regardless of how intensively we register, count, measure, investigate, interpret, and map, our process is ultimately about filtering away most of the available information. Despite our efforts, it remains a reductive process. We construct and design our pictures of the system, but however rich they are, they will always be gross simplifications of reality. Therefore, we can never truly know what the effect of our interventions will be. Worse, we can never know what would have happened without our interventions or if another action had been taken. We have only one go, and each situation is unique. Weick (referring to Heidegger)[72] suggests that we are thrown into the world; we do not know exactly what to do when faced with a situation. Our actions have consequences that we cannot really oversee, but inaction also has its consequences. This state of uncertainty Weick calls "thrownness." The suggested strategy in SOD is to accept and be aware of this limitation to all our actions in the flux of the world. SOD seeks to aid in our thrownness and increase our ability to handle it. This is essentially a development of our life skills, a way to help us coping with very complex issues.

Muddling Through

Lindblom challenges the idea of global planning (Rational Comprehensive) as described in operations research and systems analyses, and compares it with the approach he finds normally used in higher level problem decision-making

---

72. Heidegger was a Nazi and anti-Semite, something that is largely forgotten when he is frequently referred to in architecture and design discourse. He deserves no further mention.

(Successive Limited Comparison). He calls this way of coping with the world "muddling through" (Lindblom, 1959). Lindblom points to the fact that rational planning breaks down because of contradiction in values and approaches. These contradictions are not solvable in a simple way; even ranking them is difficult. Lindblom's description can be likened to Rittel's wicked problems. There are no rights or wrongs when it comes to balancing conflicting values, only better or worse solutions. SOD does associate with this notion of working and planning our way through the mess of the world. We do not think that our processes will ever reach a level of orderliness or control. Such an activity is always, to a certain degree, messy and imperfect. We do not think that we will create order in our interpretation of something where order is hard to find. Moreover, we do not think that ordering will solve any complex problems. Ordering might help design a systems picture and decipher its structure. However, order needs to be regarded with suspicion. Order is a mental construct. It is always superficial and disguises other possible orders and disorders.

There will always be a degree of muddling through the complex mess that we are likely to uncover in all design projects. While Lindblom points to the fact that analyses are drastically limiting as important outcomes, alternatives, and affected values are often neglected, we think that muddling through can be combined with fairly comprehensive analyses, where as many factors as possible are taken into account. As systemic designers, we cannot completely sort out the mess, but we can help create a better understanding of it, and more critically consider the consequences of our actions. A pragmatic approach would be to muddle through the analyses. Hence SOD and gigamapping processes are always a bit messy and do have a flavour of muddling though.

Designing Complexity

Designers have some real advantages when it comes to working with and for complexity. These advantages are partly found in the position of designers and partly in their skills.

Designers are positioned ideally to achieve and influence change. We have to understand our role and position in the system we are within. We are often in an independent position, hired as consultants, and are more or less asked to initiate change, to design something new. Or as in-house designers, we often work with several branches of an organisation, such as engineering and marketing. Despite this, we might feel disempowered because we would ideally like to work more strategically, upstream, and closer to the top executive decision-makers. However, most often, we are working with decision-makers at the lower level. While the higher-level roles within an organisation are often concerned with structures and strategies rather than the look and feel of their products or services, it is this look and feel that make the difference. This goes both for reaching out to customers and citizens, as well as for communication within the organisation and to inform decision-makers. Although we might sometimes feel disempowered, we have a strong voice. Designers produce the visual and conceptual material on, by, and through which decisions are made even higher up in the organisation. Very few other professions are in the position to have a voice with decision-makers that has these particular effects. However, designers are not trained to understand the system they work within and how to play it.[73] Yet, combined with the designer's aesthetic and ethical background, their cultural compass and values, multiplicity, and interdisciplinarity, they are well-prepared to play a crucial role. This is not to say that designers will be listened to in every instance. Nevertheless, they have a position to have a voice—maybe a weak one in the beginning, but one has the potential to grow louder.

The second big advantage that designers have is their skillset. This is about their ability to visualize, to communicate, and to combine and integrate this with Design Thinking. Visual thinking (Arnheim, 1969) provides enormous advantages for accessing, internalising, communicating, and externalizing complex information. Through visualisation, designers can coordinate perspectives, tease out knowledge, and co-create with experts to produce communicable visions and ideas, prepare for interventions, and synthesise innovative resolutions.

---

73. Designers work in intertwined systems (Lurås, 2016): The systems we design within, the systems we design for, and the systems we design.

Figure 96: The Ulstein Bridge Vision design research project created a vision of the near-future ship bridge based on known technology. The vision was presented with a high-end video production that was released to the public by the Ulstein Group, and it had a big impact on the whole ship-building sector. It changed the discussion around what was possible in the design of the ships bridges. (Ulstein Group, 2011).

Another beneficial aspect of the designer's skillset is the ability and capacity to engage with fuzzy front-end problems–those that are ill-defined or undefinable problematiques and "wicked problems" (Rittel & Webber, 1973). Situations that resist clear and stable definitions pose enormous challenges to traditional planning. The designer's ability to create tentative visions in iterations, to learn through designing and co-design, and to critically reflect on the result is a particular effective way of planning, creating, and innovating for such situations.

Verbal and textual communication have value in this process, but also clear limitations. Visual representations of visions are superior to texts or words for communicating complex change processes (*Figure 96*).

Visual Thinking as Practice

As mentioned, one of the main resources for SOD is based on the designer's ability to visualise, or in other words, the designer's ability for visual thinking. We will dig a bit deeper into this aspect and relate it to the methodology of SOD.

Visualisation has a long history in design and is inherently design's main process and communication tool. The role of visualisation has been explored by people like Arnheim (1969) McCulloch (1996) and Evans (1997). Arnheim promotes the view that there is no real division between perception and thinking. Visualisation has become the designer's strongest tool for coping with complexity. The traditional techniques are still relevant, but reinforced with new media. This has implications on design thinking and on next-generation complex visualisation in the design processes (Leerberg, 2004). The importance and potential of visual thinking in design thinking has also been elaborated on by the author (Sevaldson, 2001).

When designing, we visualize the "thing"–the object we design. But there is another level to this. We often use diagrams to visualize organisational principles or abstract structures and relations. One simple example is the structural analyses proposed by Tjalve (1976). Alexander describes early-on the importance of diagramming when it comes to Systems Thinking and dealing with complex design tasks (1964, (Alexander, 1965). Tufte followed with a comprehensive overview of the diagram and its many uses (1983). The diagram was used in design for understanding, thinking, conceptualizing. In the 1990's, however, something radical happened. The role of the diagram was discussed in length by a wide range of writers in architecture (Allen, 1999; Berkel & Bos, 1999; Bettum & Michael, 2000; Hensel, Menges, & Weinstock, 2004; Massumi, 1998; Sevaldson, 1999c; Somol, 1998). In these discussions, the diagram went beyond the descriptive to take on a generative role in the design process. Eisenman describes the generative role of the diagram as being an "agent sabotaging the architect's intention" (1999a, 1999b). This refers to the schemata discussion we had before. The architects' intentions were seen as framed, and the abstract generative diagram was there to break the preconceived ideas and archetypes. An interpretation of this might be that the intentions and preconceptions of the architect were seen as obstacles to innovation. The diagrams that Eisenman and others talked about were often very abstract, with no predefined programmatic content. The OCEAN Design Research Association took on this approach and developed it further (OCEAN-NORTH, 1998; OCEAN, Bettum, Larsen, & Sevaldson, 1998). They were useful because of their formal and structural qualities, and their openness for interpretation, hence, visual thinking. They served as vehicles for early structuring and organisation of buildings and urban sites, before they were programmed with specific activities and functions. Only at later stages were these structures coded and given meaning. This seems like an absurd process where form is given, and functions grafted into it. This approach was partly related to thinking of these designs as open-ended, and that much of the "programming" was going to be done by the users who would inhabit the structures in unforeseen ways in the future, thereby "programming" these spaces themselves through their activities. The idea was that certain structural organisations would be more suited for this kind of co-programming and co-designing than others. This is an interesting approach seen from a systems perspective, as well as a creative process. It turned attention away from locked archetypes, metaphors, and categories towards abstract structures. This was a strategy to free the action space for the user. It also redefined the notion of control by the designer, and opened up strategies for co-design.

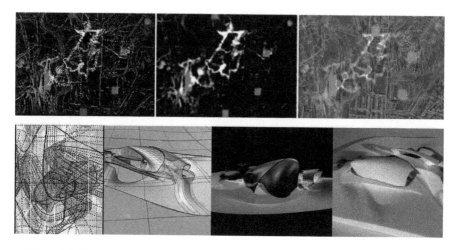

Figure 97: Experimental design with Generative diagrams: Top row, three stages from initial draft diagram generated with particle animation (top left) to the processed diagram used to inform the location of pavilions in the Tøyen Park in Oslo. Lower row: A similar generative diagramming process was used to design the pavilions. Initial diagram to the left, different stages of development ending in a physical 3d print model of one pavilion to the right (Ambient Amplifiers, Sevaldson & Duong, 2000).

New practices of visualisation developed rapidly with the spread of computer graphics. They started to address time and dynamic processes when animation was first used by architect Greg Lynn as a generative rather than representational diagramming technique (Lynn, 1999).

In OCEAN, experiments with generative diagrams and animations resulted in the concept of Dynamic Generative Diagrams (Bettum & Michael, 2000; Sevaldson, 1999a, 1999c, 2000a). The Dynamic Generative Diagram was seen as a creative means where the designer partly negotiated design control with the computer. Animation techniques were used to incorporate time in the generative diagrams. The discussion on the role of the diagram and creative visual thinking unfortunately faded, however, when the attention of architects shifted to another aspect of design computing: parametric design.

Three very important aspects of the Dynamic Generative Diagrams that were brought into SOD and gigamapping are the idea of generative diagramming, regarding the diagram as merely snapshots of dynamic systems, and acknowledging that the diagram might be more or less abstract and open for interpretation.

Systems of Systems

Designers work with complex systems, they design systems, but they are also embedded in systems. This is not something that we are always aware of. Sigrun Lurås constructed a model that helps to decode the systemic complexity that is the natural consequence of any design process. It is a tool to help make sense of the mess. It suggests three main perspectives for analysing the design project situation:

1. The system we design

2. The system(s) we design for

3. The system(s) we design within

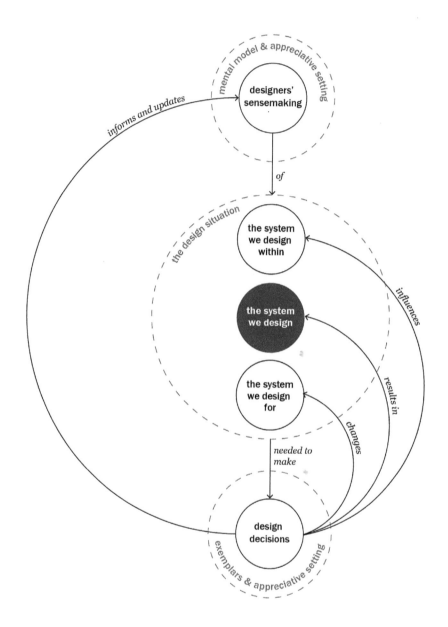

Figure 98: The systemic sensemaking model (Sigrun Lurås, 2016).

Lurås describes the model as the following:

> These systems are examples of "systems of systems" and can be further divided into subsystems in a range of ways, depending on how we choose to divide them. There are no strict boundaries among the systems; they are intertwined and form a system in themselves a system representing the full design situation, including all factors that influence the situated design work. The model emphasizes that making sense of all three systems is necessary in order to make design decisions that result in satisfactory solutions for the system we design, change the system we design for, and also influence the system we design within (2016, p. 9).

In SOD, the gigamapping process does not necessarily distinguish between the three systems of systems, but it is possible and useful to develop these perspectives also as Gigamaps. In addition, we can add a fourth level, a meta-level of designing the design inquiry. The systemic design process is a constructed system on its own. This is an important aspect of SOD. The fact that we can't escape being part of the system we try to change is addressed in second order cybernetics (Ranulph Glanville, 1994).

It is useful to negotiate the three levels of systems that designers engage with. In systemic design projects, especially when engaging in action and social change, the three levels might overlap or merge and they heavily influence and contribute to form the fourth level the design of the design process.

An example is the master theses of Niloufar Gharavi and Melina Hozhbari (2018). Two master students at AHO with Iranian backgrounds decided to work with the situation that asylum seekers find themselves in after arriving at reception centres. They described it as being stuck in a situation of waiting, and they wanted to work with this situation. Mapping out the field revealed many actors, being NGOs, companies, free-lance humanitarians, and authorities that contributed to better the situations. They discovered the fragmented ways these organisations operated and concluded that trying to coordinate their activities was needed. After unsuccessful attempts to bring a group of them around a table to map out the system to find ways of coordination, they realised that these NGOs were partly competing and did not have a driver for collaboration. Their initial plans seemed to fail. However, since they looked at the whole context from a systemic perspective from the very beginning, they found an important turn. They were from the beginning in the process of negotiating with the reception centre and on-boarding the asylum seekers, while they were doing the workshops with all the other stakeholders. They were able to "Dance with the System" and quickly change the order of priorities and strategize based on that experience.

This turned out to result in a lucky turn. Instead of helping the NGOs that formed a system of its own, they turned their attention directly to the asylum seekers as individuals. With a reception centre in Oslo as starting point, they established a dialogue. They realised that the NGOs were not very popular, and that the asylum seekers were tired of their fragmented and uncoordinated attempts.

They felt somehow exploited. So when the students approached the reception centre, a great deal of resistance had to be overcome. It helped with their background, however total engagement was needed. This included one of the students performing the Iranian drum. This was an act of creating contact and bridging gaps. It was also an act of communicating that they were similar in some important ways. They also wanted to give something to the asylum seekers group as a gesture towards building mutual interrelation.

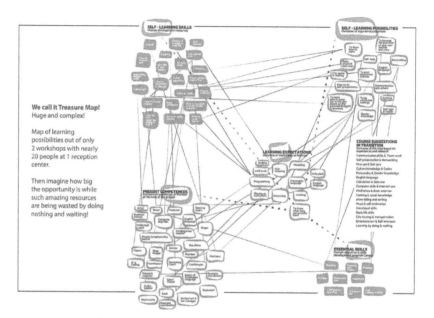

Figure 99: Mapping out the resources of a group of asylum seekers at the Refstad reception centre in Oslo (Niloufar Gharavi and Melina Hozhabri, 2018).

The students then started to work with empowering the asylum seekers by engaging their resources. They designed a package containing self-analyses, a game and tools for dialogue between them. This resulted in the asylum seekers self-organising their activities, spanning from a doctor starting up a first aid course to former boxer starting a training group etc. The system was building the asylum seekers confidence and enthusiasm and helped them out of a passive waiting time.

The system was successful and spread to other centres[74]. The project was very much alive when this was written and it was short-listed for the Red Dot award.

This shows how important it is to be aware of the systems we design for, the systems we design with, and the systems we design. Getting this wrong can lead to useless results, and in worst cases, it can even be harmful.

Intentions and Agencies

The role of the designer working within complex human activity systems involves an orientation towards inquiry. This implies a dialogic approach where experts and stakeholders are engaged in different degrees of collaboration, spanning from consulting to co-designing. Ideally, such a process would engage with all possible stakeholders and involved or affected parties. Realistically, this is not possible. Many resources will not be available for practical reasons. Other voices would be silent because of social reasons. Amongst the ones affected by our designs are future generations. There are many groups and individuals who simply do not have a voice.

The systemic designer is obliged to represent these silent voices as well as possible. The ethical argument is that we do not want our systemic interventions to cause unintended harm to groups that have been left out of the process. However, there is also a systemic argument: if you have failed to consider the relevance of including certain groups in your designed picture of the complex system, it is simply not a complete enough picture.

The designer who is trained to work within complex networks populated with many voices, who is skilful at balancing elements and forces, and who is trained to find synergies and resolve contradictions is well-suited to act as an agent for underrepresented voices.

In some cases, the designer also needs to be a counteragent. Many societies have hidden power structures and strong lobbyist forces–advocates that serve the resourceful at the cost of others or common interest. Such imbalances have a destructive effect on the systems as a whole. The long-term effects of short-sighted policies will eventually backfire. It is the system thinkers' ethical obligation to unravel and communicate the severe consequences that such imbalances in societies will have in the long term. They must also attempt to identify and expose more intelligent approaches and synergies that could better address the interests of the vast majority. The failure of societal systems might cause a spiralling effect towards decay and break down, something that we have seen often enough. A fair number of these breakdowns are caused by the fact that

---

74. See the whole report here: https://systemsorienteddesign.net/index.php/projects/master-projects/2018/home-in-transition

many of the forces in power do not recognise their own long-term interests, far from following any ethical social contract.

Figure 100: The breakdown of the "social contract" caused by short-term profit through de-regulated financial politics led to outburst of social unrest with the Occupy Wall Street movement. The decline of the movement is not an indicator that the underlying conflict has been resolved; rather, it is the result of other social dynamics likely caused by lack of sufficient understanding of the system one addresses, generates, and works within (Photo: David Shankbone. Public Domain).

SOD Toolbox

In the following section, we will go through the SOD tools starting with the most influential and generic one the Gigamap. These tools are supported by a number of additional tools, made for addressing particular issues and points in the systemic design process. Amongst these are a library for systemic relations and an analytical tool set.

Gigamapping: Visualising for Complexity

The most central concept in SOD is the Gigamap. Though this concept is discussed in many places within this book, we will discuss it as methodology in this chapter.

Gigamaps are visualizing complex systems. They are process tools more than communication tools. They are tools for visual thinking. They are the most central way for designing the pictures of the systems we work with.

One of the most important, but also underdeveloped, advantages of the designer when it comes to design for complexity is their special ability to use visualisation as a tool for thinking, analysis, process, and communication. Visualisation and visual thinking have increased in importance after design computing has become standard (Sevaldson, 2001). Visualisation in design is used for representation, drawing sketches, and rendering possible solutions. More recently, visualisation in design has been inspired by information visualisation and visualisation of dynamic actions like service design blueprints and storyboards. Most of these applications and other uses of diagramming in design have specific limitations to theme and scope. For example, service design blueprints are mostly framed by the emerging disciplinary boundaries. And information visualisation as a field is almost entirely concerned with communication, and less with processes.

Visualisation skills can also be used in more abstract phases of the design process. Fields of knowledge can be visualised so that a better overview is achieved. The complexity of a problem can be mapped out and visualised. Structures of systems and processes can be diagrammed. There is a lot of value in the tentative and iterative "not-always-knowing-what-one-is-doing" states of diagrammatic sketching and visualisation. The potential of true visual thinking emerges not only from documenting thoughts, but by visualising and dynamically forming the analyses and developing insights from the visualisation.

The Relation to Other Ways of Diagramming

Gigamapping is nothing principally new. We find similar approaches like mind mapping or concept mapping. The Rich Picture, introduced by Checkland (1981), is especially relevant as a predecessor of Gigamapping, particularly because it was introduced as a means of working with Soft Systems Methodology, e.g., human activity systems. The intentions behind the Rich Picture are partly similar to those of gigamapping. The way the Rich Picture is practised is quite limited in scope, and dependent on numbers of issues at hand. Its main aim is to create an overview through ordering and simplification. In addition, the Rich Picture is mainly practised as an illustrated network diagram. The most significant thing that distinguishes the Gigamap from the Rich Picture is the generative nature of the Gigamap and its interpretative openness.

Gigamapping breaks the barriers of information overload by separating the process tasks and the communication tasks. In its first phases, the Gigamap needs only to communicate to its creators. It is a process tool. This allows for a dramatic increase in the amount of information captured since creating the map internalizes a far larger amount of information than if it would have to communicate to an outsider. This allows the map to be much more complex than if it was to be used as a communication tool. In addition, the graphic means and the designer's ability are central. The Gigamap is regarded as a design artefact one for reflection in action. This nested design process has proven to be very efficient in getting a grip on higher levels of complexity.

Another way that Gigamaps might differ is in the fact that they should layer many types of information. Categorically separated information channels need to be interrelated.

Yet another difference is the multi-scalar approach in gigamapping, spanning from the global scale down to small details. This means that a Gigamap looks widely to the rim of the system, its environments and the landscape (horizontal reach), and at the same time looks deeply into certain details while also looking upwards to the big picture (vertical reach). This induces a special "Myriadic Quality" to the map where attention is shifted away from specific links and relations to overall patterns and figures (or the Gestalt) of the system. Patterns, structures, tendencies, and overall composition are just as important to understand as specific relations.

The Gigamap is a very powerful tool for dialogue allowing flexible discussions across fields and relations.

Some core distinctive characteristics to remember about the Gigamap are:

- A Gigamap is in the outset a process tool, and a tool for visual thinking and dialogue.

- A Gigamap must go beyond linear cause-effect diagramming.

- A Gigamap must relate and depict both quantitative and qualitative information.

- A Gigamap has both wide horizontal reach and deep vertical reach.

- A Gigamap must be high resolution and achieve the "Myriadic Quality."

- A Gigamap is connecting seemingly disconnected items, groups, categories and systems.

- A Gigamap is intentionally vague, representing an inclusive and un-dogmatic approach to large-scale mapping.

Gigamapping as Bridging

A general phenomenon that causes problems in projects dealing with high degrees of complexity is information or communication breakdowns and misaligned perspectives. These issues are what I call "ruptures." Ruptures can appear because of structural reasons (the system's information structure is insufficient), over time (things get lost in the process), or by general misconception of the implications. A central aspect of working with very complex tasks is to keep as many aspects of a problem field in play for as long as possible throughout the process. A natural progression in the design process is synthesis, when ideas emerge and interventions are designed and where there is a narrowing down of possible solutions. This occurs throughout the process, but more intensely towards the end of the design process, when the windows of opportunity are closing, resources invested are increasing, and errors would have more serious consequences than earlier in the process. However, synthesizing processes are often hampered with problems. One problem is that given the sheer amount of information, not everything is properly taken into consideration. Small issues that seem unimportant in the outset can become crucial for the process at certain later moments. If they are forgotten because of information overload, the result can be a costly rupture in the process. Another typical rupture may occur when the client organisation is not understood properly. Different sections of the organisation are not always well coordinated which can lead to ruptures in the design process. An early anchoring of the project in the relevant sections of the organisation can be crucial. Such sections would be marketing, business development, strategic management, technology, and production. Typically, implementation challenges are often underestimated. This is due to a rupture between the models that one operates accordingly and the reality that these models represent. The most common error with these models is that they are over simplified. The use of erroneous models could be caused by ignorance or biases, e.g., satisfying the need to land a sale and deferring coping with the problems later. No model is without fault, but richer, and more elaborate, inclusive models run a lower risk of excluding important issues. This implies both risk lowering but also time saving. Also, richer models that defy simplification are less fixed and stable, they are easier to adjust to changes in the process and the system.

Ruptures can be caused by:

- A lack of ability to cope with information overload causes decisions to be made only based on short-term memory.

- The client and its environment are not understood well enough.

- Misalignment within organisations causes misaligned perspectives (one's own and the client's perspectives).

- The horizon is not framed properly or is framed too narrowly.

- Implementation problems that were not foreseen.

- Having different conceptions of the system's shape, structure, extent, and connectivity.

- Having different sensitivity towards the system.

Actors

Ruptures always appear between actors in the process. The first rupture is caused by not all actors being represented in the project. Assuming one provides a complete list of actors it can be very long. However, in the proposed Matrix of Ruptures (*Figure 101*), we have simplified it to consist of the individual designers, the design team, the client, experts, users, society, and agency (stakeholders who cannot represent themselves). We can map out the relations between this simplified set of actors in a matrix to determine what the relations are, and where the most critical ruptures can emerge.

	Designer	Design team	client	experts	users	Society	Agency
Designer	?						?
Design team		?					
client	?				?	?	
experts							
users					?		
Society							
Agency							?

Figure 101: The matrix of ruptures: A matrix with the simplified set of actors can be used to identify potential ruptures before they appear. Interestingly, one can also use such a matrix to speculate if individuals are coordinated with themselves. Ruptures and hidden contradictions within one person's picture of the system are normal when it comes to working according to multiple perspectives (Birger Sevaldson, 2015).

The question marks indicate potential ruptures. Interestingly, ruptures can appear even within the worldview of an individual designer, particularly when a composed picture of a situation contains unresolved contradictions caused by insufficient information or incomplete pictures of the situation.

A central intention in SOD is to act proactively on complexity. Shying away from potential difficulties and solving them when they eventually emerge is a bad strategy. It is expensive, inefficient, and the space for responding in a good way is limited. Imagining possible problems in advance is a better strategy. The matrix of ruptures is a tool to actively seek for potential ruptures.

The function of the Gigamap is to help bridge the ruptures and to find, if possible, synergetic or balanced solutions. It is important not to be naïve about this. We cannot solve all conflicts through design and communication. There are people, organisations, and politicians that are determined to work for their own benefit at the cost of others. We find these types in the financial industries, in national and local politicians, as well as in leaders of companies, dictatorships, criminal organisations, in fact in any working place, even within families. On the other hand, many conflicts are based on a lack of shared perspectives, insufficient information, and the breakdown of communication. Before antagonizing such operators, it is important to ensure that they understand their own long-term interests, which are most often different and in conflict with their short-term actions.

Figure 102: Relativity by M.C. Escher, 1953.

The Gigamap: The Ultimate Bridging Device

The Gigamap has proven to be an ultimate bridging device. It is easy to learn and easy to apply. Within groups of collaborators in particular, the Gigamap's bridging and synchronizing effect is substantial. We have run a number of workshops with business leaders and other groups who have reported on this effect (*Figure 103 and 104*). Even for people who have worked together for years and who should be fairly synchronized, hidden ruptures are unearthed and addressed.

Figure 103: A quick draft produced by staff of The Performance Group in 2011. The timeline shows a typical process of their consultancy. A lot of problems and potentials were discovered and ideas shared. (Photo: Birger Sevaldson)

The former Performance Group leader development consultancy (now merged with Rambøll) started to include gigamapping (in the form of timelines especially) in their rich tool chest of methods and workshops. They reported a very high level of satisfaction in the feedback from the leader groups that participated in the workshops. The dynamics of such gigamapping dialogic workshops were described as following:

> Gigamapping helped them to have a "rambling" discussion that makes it possible to get an overview of a whole, relationships and consequences, and they continually worked on a proper (high) level. This demonstrates two typical problems for management groups: A) when they are decomposing a complex situation to discuss a portion at the time, it becomes impossible (difficult) to stick to the case because it has so many links to other issues (and if one does not have a Gigamap each individual in the management team will jump on the links they associate without others having a chance to follow); B) when discussing individual cases, the discussion tends to be too detailed and they dig themselves down into things and become more officers than leaders. As leaders, they should focus on the major relationships, balancing risk and burden of organisation and priorities. It slips when they go too deeply into the issues. Gigamapping helps us to stay on the right (high) level (Wettre, 2012; translation by the author).

Typical phenomena that resulted from gigamapping in workshops are:

- The capacity to have unfocussed discussion where jumps between issues are not a big problem because the map is used as a dialogic support. When jumping from one issue to another, represented in the map by jumping from one place to another, participants would typically point at the new place where they think the discussion should divert. This brings the rest of the group immediately to the new perspective.

- Synchronising or creating awareness of unequal worldviews and perspectives. Even within teams that have worked together for a long time, ruptures in perspectives are relatively normal.

- Controlling the level of discussion. The visual dialogue helps the discussion to remain on the same level or allows participants to dive into details or zoom out to helicopter views whenever needed.

- Different expertise is externalized and shared.

Figure 104: Different situations of dialogic mapping (Photos: Birger Sevaldson and Linda Blaasvær).

Needless to say, the suggested techniques will not entirely remove any ruptures, but they ensure that a proper effort is made to avoid them, to bridge them as much as possible, or to be prepared for them to occur.

A Short Case

"On the Same Page" was a project that worked with the Office for Elderly Homes in Oslo. The office was monitoring and administrating over fifty units. They were going through a major revision of their system by transitioning from a two-level model of care intensity to the introduction of a three-level model. The process was dependent on a very high level of communication between large groups of administrators and staff. To get a grip on the complexity, the students facilitated workshops with over fifty participants (*Figure 105*).

Figure 105: Example of a gigamapping process that involved a large number of participants from a public service in Oslo. They were in the middle of an organisational reforming process that had run into problems because of large amounts of ruptures. The gigamapping, together with the development of new bespoke collaborative tools helped, them to get back on track (From "On the same page," L. LeBlanc et. Al. AHO, Oslo, 2014).

The main problem was on the level of dialogue. A group of five master's students took on the project and designed bespoke tools based on the idea of Gigamapping to secure the synchronization of these dialogues. The process was originally based on traditional meeting schematics with a plan for working meetings amongst the many groups. The participants reported, and the students observed and recorded frequent communication breakdowns caused by the process' level of complexity.

Figure 106: Employees at the directorate for elderly care co-designing and prototyping a dialogic tool for bettering very complex conversations with visual dialogue. (Photo: Bogen, Jensen, LeBlanc, & Tveit)

The students worked out a dialogue tool that was developed, co-designed, and prototyped together with a group of central employees at the directorate (*Figure 106*). The effect of the tool was evaluated through observation and voice recordings that were compared with former voice recordings taken before the tool was implemented. The effect was very satisfactory and the office adopted the tools, methods, and process to further develop the tools on their own (Bogen, Jensen, LeBlanc, & Tveit, 2014).

Types of Gigamapping

There is no definite number of types of Gigamaps. I arrived at a tentative list of maps by going through a large number of gigamapping exercises. It is possible and probably beneficial sometimes to design a new type that is specifically adapted to the problem at hand. Despite this, there might be some patterns emerging, and it might be helpful to apply a diversity of approaches to understand better a complex situation. One such heuristic is presented by Ray Ison (Ison,

2008) where different diagram types are suggested to fit different purposes in action research as shown in *Figure 62*.

The main motivation in design is to reach holistic resolutions of situations that will play out and function in real life situations. This is achieved by the Gigamap. The Gigamap collects and interrelates the different types of diagrams above. Therefore, creating a strict typology of Gigamaps is difficult if not purposeless.

Instead of refining a typology of Gigamaps, which might become prescriptive and replace the work needed to think through and design the maps according to the situation, we present three ways of understanding the span and richness of gigamapping. The first is a model developed by Adrian Paulsen at Halogen AS. The second is a collection of exemplars collected through teaching and practising SOD. The third is a list of visualization components and media that might be included in the gigamapping process but would never constitute a Gigamap on their own.

The Halogen Model: Stereotypes Vs Free Modelling

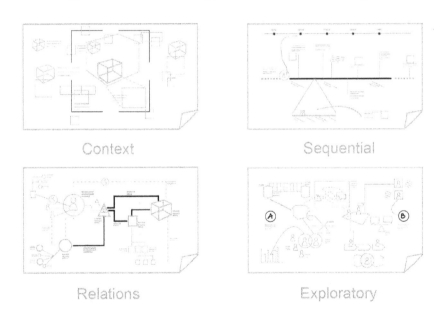

Figure 107: The Halogen model of four types of Gigamaps (Adrian Paulsen, 2014).

Halogen describes their process as follows:

> You and the participants map out the field in general. You discuss different approaches and layout options and create a common basic structure for the diagram. This structure is further explored and detailed in the next phase. This process indicates a draft of the system's boundaries for further examination. This initial mapping also sets an important tone for the shared visual language. It is critical that this step resonates with all parties involved. We often refer to four main types of maps: contextual, relational, sequential and exploratory. In many cases, the map's basic layout refers to one of these four types but sometimes, combinations can be used (Romm, Paulsen, & Sevaldson, 2014, p. 61).

After using Gigamapping as a means of processing insight, framing concepts and facilitating conversations, patterns started to emerge. The following were selected as four stereotypes that made the most sense to the clients in preliminary conversations. Across different projects the conversations with clients and informants tended to take on specific structures or produce patterns. The structures were not mainly discovered based on the sector in which the work took place, but rather as a result of the conversational structure or narrative the people involved were comfortable with. The four types were introduced in the form of short conversations around the following themes, reflecting:

- **Context**: When working with craft-oriented people, or where the space the work is conducted seems important. "I know where my tools are located."

- **Sequence**: With process-oriented people the sequential structured appeared, also were service dominant logic or service design was applied. "I know what part of the process I contribute."

- **Relational**: In projects where human relations or societal perspectives were discussed. "I know who to talk to in order to get things done."

- **Exploratory**: In conversations with a mixed group or no clear conversational structure the exploratory model appeared. "We don't really have a shared model of how we work."

The different approaches represent initial mental models that can support a mapping process in its early and uncertain stages. Especially when involving with participants who had limited experience with mapping, it gave them some guidance and comfort. An important part of using the stereotypes was that they

238

gave a starting point. However, they should not limit the conversation. If the conversation and the mapping moved in another direction or broke the model, the participants were encouraged to break free from the structure or mix them together. This is a very important option and a likely scenario.

The stereotypes were introduced around 2014-15 and in the time since then, the stereotypes have been useful when introducing SOD to new colleagues, clients and partners. The ambition to "dive into the complexity of a topic" can be daunting, but with some structure it is easier to initiate the conversation.

In the following years, Halogen has worked a lot with the public sector, and for this type of work, a new structure has been added, built around "pace layers" (*Figure 13*) (Brand, 1994) and the hierarchical logic of the public sector. The pace layering was useful to relate with the politicians at the top and the different layers of bureaucracy, ending with the citizens at the bottom. (Note: many of the clients agreed that turning the hierarchy upside down and placing the citizen on top was a more useful model, which influenced their own mental models and perception). When initiating any work within the public sector, it is critical to establish a shared sense of ownership, capacity, capabilities, and flexibility the involved actors have. Although the work might later on build arguments to challenge the frame, this agreed understanding gives the work a starting point.

Another aspect of introducing gigamapping through particular models or stereotypes with clear predefined structures is that they can generate bias. The stereotypes are centred on narratives or conversations as a useful framing when the process is organized around or initiated for individuals or prioritized groups. This is efficient and motivates the group, but it has a trade-off where the narrative starts influencing our worldview and data sorting. For example, when drawing out a sequence, the people providing us with data will provide data that supports the chosen storyline. If they are asked to add more information, they will most likely add data that strengthen the narrative. For a consultancy, this efficiency can give value for both our clients and our own business, although the risks of overlooking blind spots needs to be addressed and managed. A returning effort to reduce the risks would be introducing iterations of the map, and establishing a clear communication on what up- or downsides this edition of the map had.

Gigamaps data with a narrative / boundary object constructed to match with a task through iterations becomes more efficient and focused. It filters away info that burdens the conversation or the eye, but it comes at a cost.

Therefore, when engaged with either a topic where one type of storytelling is dominant or if the project has, for example, a mandate to look for innovation potential, trying to postpone developing a dominant narrative and a dominant visual profile can be helpful. Delaying the structuring and visual profile of the map is taxing for the people involved with the mapping process, both as informants or as facilitators, mainly because it forces the group to stay "lost in the woods" for a longer time. Therefore, some projects would lead to the stereotypes being utilized from the start, with the awareness of the trade-off in order to get the needed efficiency.

Collection of Gigamap Exemplars

The intention with this collection is to inspire and make you aware that there are many ways to design a Gigamap, and that the maps can have many uses and functionalities. The maps collected here are therefore not selected because of their quality, but to demonstrate as many different arrangements as possible.

Each map involves a design process to reach something that is bespoke and most useful for the problem situation at hand. The maps are design artefacts produced in nested design processes. They are expressions of the designer's constructed (or designed) knowledge. This implies a reference to constructionist learning, which means that learning is not a one-way process; it cannot be compared with filling a vessel with wisdom or a hard disk with information. Constructivism implies that learning is a process where we actively construct our individual knowledge (Vygotsky, 1997). We suggest a move from the notion of construction to the idea of designed knowledge. Learning is considered a design process (Rowland, 1999). The Gigamaps are devices for actively designing your knowledge. This does not mean that knowledge is constructed freely. Rather, designing implies involving stakeholders, affected bystanders, nature, etc. Designing means increasingly a process of engagement, learning, and co-designing. While the Gigamap is the central device for designerly learning, learning as design implies the development of Gigamaps according to the needs of the individual designers, experts, and stakeholders involved, as well as to the needs of the project.

This map collection is organized according to two groups. The first group displays different organisational or structural principles to inspire you to develop your own and most suitable organisation and structure. The second group displays Gigamaps designed for special functions, to inspire you to design the maps specially made for specific purposes. The samples are collected from the Oslo School of Architecture and Design, The Oslo and Akershus University College of Applied Sciences, and the Chalmers Technical University and others. This collection of exemplars with high-res images can be found on the SOD webpage.

Relational Maps

We tend to be object-oriented and less oriented towards relations. This map (*Figure 108*) demonstrates a relations-oriented mapping. The map is developed according to the library of systemic relations. This map was made by Young Eun Choi.

This Gigamap shows several of the mind switches of SOD. It started with the entities or objects that are networked with relations. From the start, the objects were written down in relatively small text. This first object-oriented network map was then dampened with a layer of transparent foil. Further analyses of existing relations and newly created relations were done with colour-coded threads as a new layer, indicating a move from object-oriented to relation-oriented design. At this stage, the map no longer emphasizes a reading of the singular elements. Instead, it indicates a holistic reading of the picture or figure of the system–the Gestalt. The map is a process tool, and not meant for communication beyond the two students who produced it. For them, the map is familiar also on a detailed level[75].

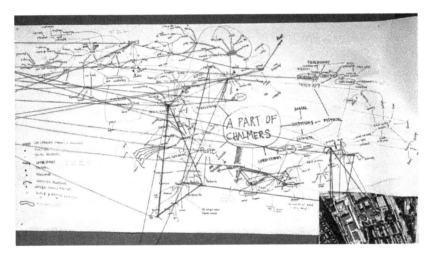

Figure 108: A Gigamap dominated by relations (by Karin Backlund, Maxwell Kevin Otieno, Evelina Peterson, 2015).

Timeline Maps

This map is inspired by service blueprints. It is very detailed and is also generative, depicting a redesigned process. The theme of this investigation is caregivers–the family and friends of severely ill people, and how to build services to support them.

---

75. See also *figure 171*.

Figure 109: Timeline map (by Ingrid Herigstad and Marianne Sælensminde,, 2014).

Semi-Spatial Map Combined with Timeline and Network

This project developed innovative interlinked resolutions for a regenerative future of the municipality of Vevelstad in Norway. The map is a mix of diagrammatic spatial map and network diagram.

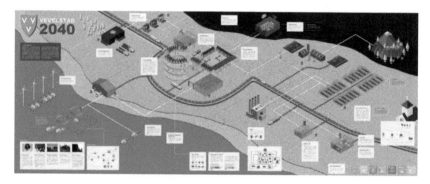

Figure 110: Semi-spatial map. Gigamapping a future scenario of a municipality (Malin Emilie Hoff, June Steinhovden, Kristin Brudeseth, Andreas Offenberg Kristoffer Steen Langvik 2020).

Network Map

This map was made in the process of developing a concept for redesigning the Norwegian Immigration Authorities' front-line offices. This map is network and object-oriented. It shows a balance between the objects and the relations, though the relations could be better diversified.

Figure 111: Network dominant map. Gigamap of the Norwegian Directorate of Immigration (UDI) remapping it as a service for immigrants with the user in the centre (by Lea Brochard, Nicoletta Aveni, 2011).

Object-Oriented Map

This is an object-oriented map where relations are missing. Not all Gigamaps are developed to be systemic. This map puts together different aspects and perspectives to draw a sufficient knowledge base.

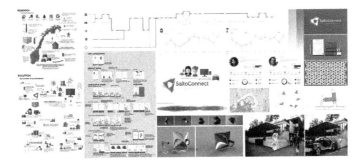

Figure 112: Object dominant map. Mapping out the components of a home charging system for electrical vehicles. There is less emphasis on the interconnected relations than for example in figure 111. (Salto Connect by Marie Frogner, Trym Abrahamsen, Oda Heier, Torgeir Hæreid, Julie Sandvoll, 2017).

Composite Map

Here, the map consists of four different parts that are displayed together to help create a reading of the information from four different perspectives. The map essentially assembles four different systemic maps.

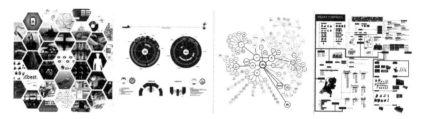

Figure 113: A composite map made out of four separated mapping and illustration areas, all showing a different perspective of the system. Redesigning handles for azimuths for ship control. (For Kwant Controls by Jan Kristian Strømsnes, 2011).

Mixed-Relational Map

This is a mixed map of information fields that are related through drawing relational connections. This map is information-oriented where "information containers" like lists, statistics, references, and diagrams are interrelated within an overarching network.

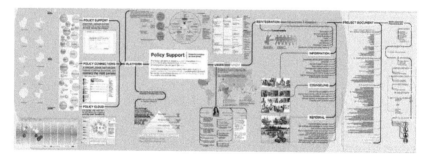

Figure 114: Mixed-relational map where content "containers" (mostly in the left half of the map) are connected by drawing overall relation between them and singular entities in the network (mostly in the right half of the map). Concept for a system to support policy decisions (by Linda Blaasvær, Renata Mikalauskaite, Manuela Aguirre Ulluoa, 2011).

Mixed-Composite Map

This is a mixed information-oriented map where some sub-fields are developed more like systemic models.

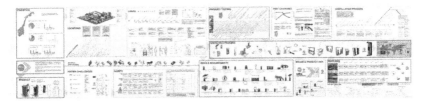

Figure 115: A map with a composite overall design divided into clear compartments but where some of them are developed as systems maps, timelines and flow diagrams. Development of charging system for electrical cars. (For SALTO by Christian von Hanno, 2011).

Layering

This type of map is interesting in the way that it creates sub-fields of layered information sets.

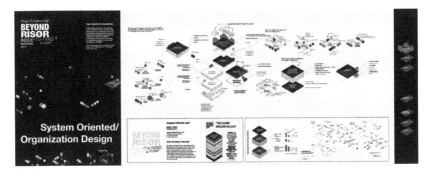

Figure 116: A gigamap where the central information is organised in blocks of layers. (For Risør Municipality by Linn-Hege Øverstad, Rebecca R. Larsen, Ulrikke Pedersen, 2011).

Axial-Relational Map

This is a clearly structured map that builds an ordered model of the information. The structure imposes a strongly guided interpretation, which has its advantages, but also comes at a cost. The structure gives the shared picture a strong and recognizable, as well as easy navigational, "Gestalt."

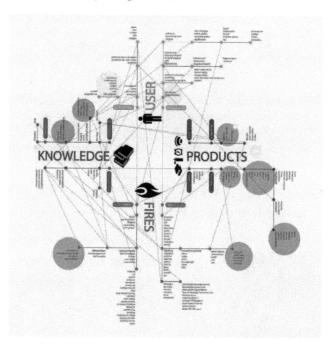

Figure 117: Axial-relational map unfolding the possibilities and relation in a product service system for firefighting equipment. (For RED By Phuc-Tan Nguyen, Pia Fleng Sandal, 2011).

Special Functions Maps

The following section presents some special uses of gigamapping.

Value Map

This is a map that defines a set of core values (for the Norwegian police) and maps out how these core values are related to the global system.

Figure 118: Mapping out the values of the Norwegian Police Force (Bente Moen, 2014).

Evaluation Map

This map is made to evaluate the systemic impact of a long series of ideas in relation to a range of personas that represent different customer types for a ban service.

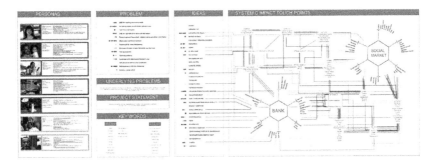

Figure 119: Personas (to the left) are mapped into a proposed new bank service system depicted in the systems map to the right. (For DNB bank by Anna-Lisa Skoog and Beate Romslo, 2014).

Total Organisational Map

This map was designed to give a total overview of a company's organisational structure and activities.

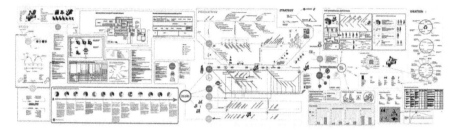

Figure 120: Gigamap showing a whole picture of a company producing electrical mobility scooters. The map shows brand, product, and competition (left) production facilities (Upper mid left, the retail ecosystem, (Centre) and future scenarios and concepts (right). (For MEDEMA by Julian Guribye and Christian von Hanno, 2011).

Comparative Map

This map compares two different businesses along a timeline with major operations. One company is represented in the upper half of the map and the other in the lower half. Despite the density of identified relations, the map is still very easy to navigate because of the distinctive colour-coding. You do not need to follow the lines to see the connections; you just need to follow the colour. The lines are still needed in order to show the strength of the relation. The map is displayed both in its hand-drawn draft version (*Figure 121*) and in its digital version (*Figure 122*).

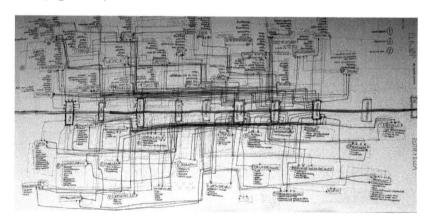

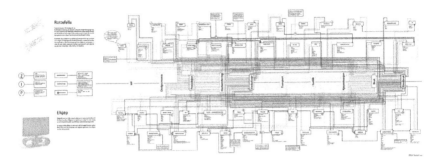

Figure 122: Comparative map refined digital version. (Jane Domaas, Jarnal Kassarna, Kathrine Høgh 2012).

Implementation Maps

Ideally, implementation is an integrated part of a systemic process from the beginning. If the whole system is understood well enough, implementation should go by itself or at least very easily. In reality, this is rarely the case. There are always things that are missing in the understanding of the system, things that emerge when the focus is turned towards implementation. A natural turn of events is when the process turns from imagining possible futures to working with real life implementation. Implementation can be seen as a complex process itself, and is well addressed with particular Gigamaps.

This first implementation map serves as a guide for implementing a teaching collaboration coupled with an aid program (*Figure 123*). The map is circular, indicating that the program is run in cycles and that it needs to be re-implemented for each cycle. A critique of a circular implementation plan is that it does not distinguish the repetitive elements from those that would change for each cycle. Since there is learning involved, the third and fourth cycles will be different from the first. A spiral model would cater for both cyclic processes and how they change over time for each repetition (*Figure 124*).

Figure 123: A detailed implementation plan for establishing an international aid system catered towards disabled children, which involves Norwegian health care student exchange within a learning system in order to educate and empower local self-help processes. (Therese Charlotte Aarland, 2009).

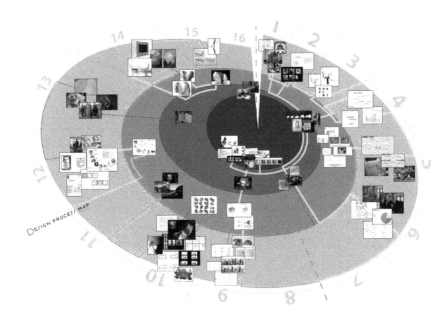

Figure 124: A spiralic development of a process. In this case, it is a design process integrated with implementation. The process resulted in highly innovative and experimental media stations for the Deichmannske Library in Oslo. (AHO / HFG 2007-2008).[76]

The last example of implementation maps is a advanced and complex map of implementation portfolio, the eventual resistance to change and actors involved. The case is a study of a possible future for the municipality of Hemsedal in Norway developing towards a regenerative future.

---

76. See also A. Menges "Systemisches Denken und Integrales Entwerfen, System thinking and Integral Design" (Menges, 2008) for full project description and credits.

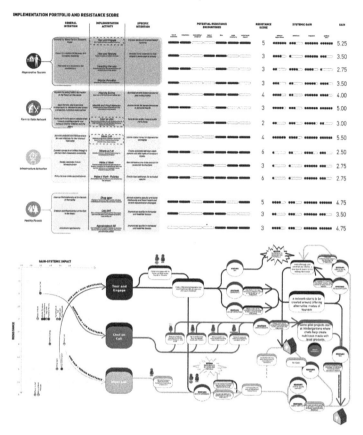

Figure 125: Implementation of a local regenerative program for Hemsedal Municipality in Norway. Top left, an analyses of intentionality. Top right and bottom left, an extensive impact and threshold analyses. Bottom right a detailed implementation strategy for three chosen concepts. See also Figure 35 for another example of implementation mapping. (Janina Sánchez Cárdenas, 2021).

A Process Map and "Discussion Board"

The next map systematizes, develops, and interrelates a documentation of the many activities in a building process for an experimental installation, the LOOP pavilion, constructed in Prague (*Figure 126*) (Davidová, 2014). It functioned as the central communication device and as a continuous discussion board. This physical Gigamap is a teamwork design tool. It is also timeline-based and keeps track of responsibilities while using printouts to highlight particular questions about the design of the pavilion.

Figure 126: Process map of a process unfolding along a timeline from the left to the right. The map functioned as a discussion board, keeping all participants informed and providing them an shared overview [Marie Davidova, Šimon Prokop, Martin Kloda (Tutors)], [Jiří Pokorný, Anna Hrušová, Alena Novotná, Antonín Hůla, Barbora Slavíčková, Jakub Kopecký, Jiří Fáber, Petr Tůma, Tereza Jílková, Radim Sýkora, Eliška Antonyová, Tereza Lišková, Filip Janata (Students), 2014].

Action Map

From the same project of building an experimental pavilion, we have this map, which puts in context and relates the many different actions to be taken in the project (*Figure 127*). This map organizes a design and construction process, showing computational processes and other actions.

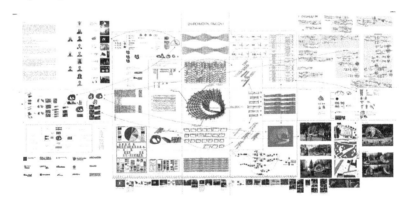

Figure 127: Action map showing all activities in an interdisciplinary collaborative process of designing an experimental pavilion. The activities are both physical and computational (Marie Davidova et. al., 2014).

Figure 128: The LOOP pavilion, Prague 2014 (Photo: Osamu Okamura, 2014).

Gigamapping Components

The following is a list of visualization components and media, which do not themselves constitute a Gigamap, but might be included in the Gigamapping process. A Gigamap would always combine different kinds of information in different forms of representational models.

Possible mappings include:

- Hierarchical maps: Mind maps

- Non-hierarchical maps: Concept maps

- Time-based maps: Gantt

- Time-based maps: Timelines (non-Gantt)

- Time-based maps: "Key Frame Mapping"

- Time-based maps: Flow charts and similar

- Time-based maps: Digital animated maps

- Time-based narratives: Story boards, cartoons, texts

- Image maps: Qualitative information in maps, images, videos, soundtracks

- Spatial maps: Geographic maps or construction plans, flow patterns

- Intensity maps: Gradients and interpolation of continuous intensity fields

- Mixed maps

Usage of Gigamapping

The Gigamap has several functions and purposes. Our bottom-up and practice-based research on Gigamaps led to a compiled list of the following functions:

- Learning: Mapping and coordinating pre-existing knowledge. Zooming into white spots on the map. Strategizing further investigations including desktop research and addressing stakeholders and experts. Inducing a very rapid learning process.

- Research: Including and organizing knowledge gained from targeted research. Organising authors in a field according to a knowledge network rather than reading lists. Understanding cross disciplines.

- Imagination: Generative, iterative design. Creating scenarios, narratives and storyboards and imagining in detail how they might effect the system. Creating imagined design interventions to see how they fit and effect the system.

- Management: Working with the involved organisation as a complex social organism. Bridging ruptures and silos in organisations. Redesigning organisations and create organisational innovation.

- Event mapping: Working with orchestrating of complex events. Understanding the ecology, emergence, and pace of an event.

- Planning: Registering, describing, and modifying complex processes. Producing timelines and action plans while maintaining flexibility and alternatives for action.

- Innovation: Defining areas and points for intervention and innovation. Finding leverage points for interventions. Changing the structure of the system.

- Implementation: Engaging in all details and agents' ecologies and environments within complex implementation processes

- Sensemaking and sharing. Increasing the shared understanding and communication between involved actors.

A Matrix of Gigamaps

The matrix below shows how the different mapping types have been preferably combined with the different uses of Gigamapping:

	Learning	Research	Imagination	Management	Eventmapping	Planning	Innovation	Implementation	Sense making sense sharing
Mind maps	X	X							
Concept maps	X	X				X	X		X
Gantt diagrams				X	X	X		X	
Timelines	X			X	X	X	X	X	X
Key frames	X		X		X			X	
Flowcharts						X		X	X
Animations			X		X			X	
Story boards			X	X	X		X	X	
Image maps	X	X	X					X	
Spatial maps		X	X		X	X		X	X
Intensity maps		X	X		X		X		X
Mixed maps	X	X	X	X	X	X	X	X	X

Figure 129: The matrix shows the different types of design activities and types of maps, and provides suggestions for what type of map is best suited for what activity. This is suggestive and not to be taken as a rule. (Birger Sevaldson, 2018).

The matrix is far from being exhaustive of gigamapping's functions. Many functions are generic and applicable across most types of maps. Amongst them are, for example, building expert networks and communicating with them, and mapping a field involving stakeholders. The Gigamap can be used to define where expert knowledge is needed.

Other generic uses along the process are defining and remodelling the boundaries of a system in an informed manner. Towards the implementation of a project, communicating externally becomes more important and the Gigamap can help visualising and communicating the systemic aspects of a process.

Systemic Relations

The description of systemic relations in systems theories is relatively limited. Most often we talk about causalities and quantitative relations or hard relations and structural relations. The relations are often not described in depth. For example, in systems dynamics-based models, they are reduced to two types: positive relations and negative relations. Most often, maps drawn to understand the relations between entities only show a line between the entities. Sometimes there is an arrow indicating a direction for the relation. However, in human activity systems, this is far from sufficient. I will illustrate this with a simple example that everybody can relate to through what I call the Grandmother Model. Imagine the relation between you and your grandmother (or another very close relative). There are many different types of relations at play (see *Figure 130*). The relation between the two of you is indeed very complex. There is obviously a biological relation in the form of information travelling down generations via genes (pink), but there are also emotional relations (orange). There might be an economic dependency (red) such as if the grandmother is supporting a grandson's studies. There are also action-based relations in the form of the grandson helping the grandmother tend to her garden, or other such activities (ochre). As well, there are entangled and complex cultural relations (yellow). Your grandmother might be part of a bigger social context within the family, the community, and society at large. There is an educational relationship as well. Most often, it is very hard to untangle and map out the entire complex network of relations that may exist even in seemingly simple situations. Such is the nature of all human activity systems as well as that of many other species.

257

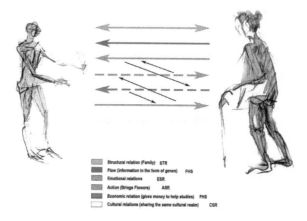

Structural relation (Family)   STR
Flow (information in the form of genes)   FHS
Emotional relations   ESR
Action (Brings Flowers)   ASR
Economic relation (gives money to help studies)   FHS
Cultural relations (sharing the same cultural realm)   CSR

Figure 130: The relation between a grandmother and her grandson is complex. The colour coding and tags follows the Library of Systemic Relations described below. The model describes, in a simplified way, the complexity of relations between a grandmother and her young adult grandson. (Birger Sevaldson, 2017).

Furthermore, there are also interrelations between relations. In this sense, they are bundled, or they influence, reinforce, or weaken each other (indicated by small black arrows above). For example, the grandson's action of bringing flowers to his grandmother would influence the emotional relations. As in all models, this is not a clean, clear-cut model. For example, the grandmother's financial support is both an economic relation through the flow of money, but it can also be defined as an action or a cultural expression.

The Grandmother Model's sole purpose is to be an eye-opener for helping us understand that there is rarely only one relation between two things. It is the norm for countless relations to be at play, relations and interactions that we do not have the capacity to fully grasp. It is a futile task to capture all that is at play. However, it is useful to distinguish between some of the types of relations as far as our resources allow sometimes on a superficial level, and sometimes we need to dive into the details.

The relations are so complex that it would be more useful to talk of networks or fields of relations than lines and arrows. Maybe lines and arrows are an insufficient way to define relations that seem more like webs or force fields of influences. Interestingly, this complexity is rarely described in diagrams. This might be because of the powerful simplification rule of the schemata. The relation between you and your grandmother is reduced to a simplified symbolic entity. When asked, the relation is briefly described as "good," "ok," or "problematic," etc. Taking into account the large complexity of such relations, it is no wonder that some parts of it may work nicely, while others may not. Realizing this would help to better understand such dynamics and to accept that not all parts of a relationship will work equally well. It is also useful to understand why relations between people, for example, are sometimes problematic, and why it is difficult to untangle such situations.

However, the dramatic reduction and abstraction of relationships symbolized with one singular line might be fine for some systems models, and could work to build insight in other systems practices, but for SOD, this generic level of abstraction and lack of precision in describing the relations is often inadequate. When looking carefully at the types of relations, we can find a long list of different types. When we want to design for complex systems, it is a constant challenge to keep focus on the relations and to design with relations in mind. Design attention constantly gravitates towards the objects and away from the relations, which are often overlooked. To turn relations into design material, we need to be more accurate in describing them, and to build a catalogue of the types of relations in order to objectify them and find ways to articulate them in detail.

Realization of richness in relations led to the construction of the Library of Systemic Relations. It is a library, not a typology, because it is hard to claim that it ever will be complete. It is, therefore, under constant development.

The Library of Systemic Relations

In the following, we will give an overview of the library including mentioning fields that are relevant to the library. This has to be very brief to fit the frame of this book.

The library consists of two main groups:

1. Relations that are depicted with nodes and connectors

2. Relations that defy being depicted with nodes and connectors

Group 1 is sorted into four sub-groups, all with a main colour and a tag:

- Structural relations, hierarchies (Green) (SR)

- Semantic, thematic and associative relations (Blue) (SA)

- Social relations (Yellow) (SO)

- Hard relations, causal relations (Red) (HR)

Each tag contains two or four letters. The first two letters stand for the main group, the last two for the sub-group.

1. Relations in systems that are depicted with nodes and connectors (typically objects connected with lines or arrows)

1.1 Structural relations, hierarchical supra- and subsystems (GREENS) (SR)

Structural relations are discussed in many fields, and the way these are discussed varies from field to field. Examples of fields are Linguistics, Economics, Statistics, and Organisations. Here we use it in generic terms, as the structure of the relations and connections. These can be hierarchically ordered in supra and subsystems, or in flat order or messy networks where it is difficult if not impossible to single out supra and subsystems as, for example, in the salamander food web discussed before (*figure 68*). Structural relations is a generic class or perspective that is applicable to all other types of relations. Though a structural relationship is not necessarily, for example, causal, social, or semantic, all relations can be seen as structural or the structure of all kinds of relations can be investigated as such.

Very often, systems are described as the assembly of parts where the sum is more than its parts. This is not a cause and effect relationship; rather, it is a structural relationship.

> Example: There is no causal relationship between the wheels and the frames of a bicycle. They are assembled in a structure where what they generate together creates a surplus output. The whole is more than the sum of the parts.

> Example: Think of the relations in the air traffic system between the planes and the control system. The number of planes does not automatically decrease if the control system is reduced. They are entities that are in a structural relationship rather than a cause-effect relationship.

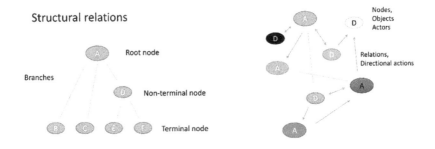

Figure 131: Structural relations. To the left ordered hierarchical structures, to the right messy non-hierarchic structure. (Birger Sevaldson, 2016).

1.1.2. Macro-Systemic Relations (SRMA)

These are relations that are caused by the entities being sub-systems in the same "supra-system," but without necessarily being in direct contact with each other.

> Example: Bikes and cars are related because they share the same macro-system: the roads. (They are related in additional ways beyond this of course.)

> Example: A winter coat and swimming suit are both part of the clothing wardrobe of the same person.

1.1.3. Micro-Systemic Relations (SRMI)

These systems are related because they share a relation through a sub-system:

> Example: The rubber in the tires of cars and bikes comes from the same producer.

Example: A Mixmaster and a hair dryer can share identical electronic parts from the same manufacturer.

1.1.4 Horizontal Structural Relations (SRHO)

These are relations between branches in a hierarchical tree structure.

Example: The doors of a car are on the same level of the structure of the car.

1.1.5 Vertical Structural Relations (SRVE)

Structural relations between suprasystems and subsystems.

Example: the dynamo of a car engine is a sub system of the car engine, while the car itself is a suprasystem of the engine.

1.2 Semantic (semiotic), associative and representational relations (BLUES) (SA)

1.2.1. Semantic Relations (SASR)

Semantic relations are entities connected through a sentence, where one word indicates the relation.

Example: Fish — lives in — water. Fish and water are the entities while 'lives in" is the relation connector.

Example: Cow — is a — mammal.

One definition of semantic network is as follows:

> A **semantic network**, or **frame network** is a knowledge base that represents semantic relations between concepts in a network. This is often used as a form of knowledge representation. It is a directed or undirected graph consisting of vertices, which represent concepts, and edges, which represent semantic relations between concepts, mapping or connecting semantic fields. A semantic network may be instantiated as, for example, a graph database or a concept map. (https://en.wikipedia.org/wiki/Semantic_network).

1.2.2. Categorical Relations (SACR)

Categorical relations are entities that are part of the same thematic field or category. Themes and categories are manmade sorting devices, and there does not necessarily have to be a causal relation between the members of a category.

> Note: Categorisation has its own problems, especially when it comes to borderline cases and items that fit into multiple categories. See also thematic relations because the term is used in linguistics.

> Example: The relation between universal design and ergonomics.

> Example: Genres of music. There are many possible relations between genres of music, but if we think of the relation between the music of Australian indigenous people and a symphony by Bach, we can only think of a few relations, such as biological (music being programmed in our genes) and thematic relations (both being music).

1.2.3. Associative Relations (SAAR)

Metaphors and analogies: These are the types of relations that pop up during brainstorming because of associating one thing with another.

An associative relation is a cognititve connection between two concepts that do not belong to the same system athough they have apparent similarities. The associative relation exists purely in the observer's mind and should be treated critically.

> Example: If two people are very similar to each other in appearance, yet they do not have any other connections, we associate them. This is an associative relation.

> Example: If I say bird, you say fish....

For semiotic definitions on associative relations, see Ferdinand Saussure.

1.2.4. Representational Relations (SARR)

These could be images, representation, videos, simulations, VR and AR etc.

> Example: The relation between a map and landscape.

> Example: The relation between a diagram and the reality it represents.

> Example: The correlation between a VR environment for virtual prototyping and the reality it represents.

Representation is defined in the following way:

> **Representation** is the use of signs that stand in for and take the place of something else. It is through representation that people organise the world and reality through the act of naming its elements. Signs are arranged in order to form semantic constructions and express relations
> (https://en.wikipedia.org/wiki/Representation_(arts)).

1.3. SOCIAL RELATIONS (YELLOWS) (SO)

Social relations are here defined as relations between two or more individuals but expanded also to groups or social "ecosystems". This view emphasises that social relations rarely are the question of two individuals only but that pairs play out in larger networks of social constructs. This interpretation refers in a limited degree to sociological models. It is rather based on practical understanding of relations making them workable for systemic designers.

1.3.1. Structural Social Relations (SOSR)

These are relations between people that are driven by or influenced by the way we have organised society through work, religion, cultural segregation, and other institutions.

> Example: Family, friends, etc.

> Note: There are always multiple relations between, for example, the members of a family; some are given, while others are optional. The structural (biological) relation between family members is given (constant), while the social relation is optional or conditioned. One can choose to have a social relation with a relative. But it is not possible to have a social relation with your ancient ancestors.

1.3.2. Institutional Social Relations (SOIR)

These are relations between people that are driven by or influenced by the way we have organised society through work, religion, cultural segregation, and other institutions.

> Example: Work, municipality, nation, culture, language, laws and regulations, money, contracts, etc.

1.3.3. Actions (SASR)

These are relations between people that are created through their joint actions or counter actions.

> Example: Volunteering. Planting a field together. Participating in a demonstration or counter demonstration. This often feeds into emotional relations between people who do not know each other.

1.3.4 Emotional Relations (SAER)

Emotions are a major driver in social relations. Often emotions are triggered by other relations and events but sometimes they are emerging on their own. Dealing with emotional relations in SOD is important.

1.4. Hard relations causal relations, flows, etc. (REDS) (HR)

Hard relations are here understood as cause effects relations, material and energy flows, and flows of other resources that are quantifiable and of which effects can be observed and measured directly.

1.4.1 Causal Relations (HRCR)

Cause and effect models: The nodes depict what entities cause an effect and what entities are being affected; the relations (normally arrows) depict the effect.

> Example: If the heat is turned on, the kettle starts to boil.

Example: If the tolls for entering the city by car increase, the passengers using public transportation go up.

1.4.2. Qualitative Causal Relation (HRQR)

The amount or intensity will not be influenced, but the quality will be changed.

Example: The relation between architectural space and the micro-climate.

1.4.3. Relational Tools (HRRT)

Tools that typically modify and influence the relations, not the entities directly.

Example: AR used to increase a cultural understanding of biological systems.

1.4.4. Flows in Human Systems (HRFH)

These are the concrete flows of values in society. They are driven by needs and economic forces.

Examples related to human society: Material flows, energy flows, information flows, knowledge, economic flows, and stock markets.

Examples: Traffic flow and crowds of people.

1.4.5. Flows in Natural Systems (HRFN)

These are driven by pressure differences (field conditions) or by nuclear processes. At one level, these might be understood as causal relations, but on a more detailed level, they need to be understood as differentiations in uniform fields, such as flows in water, which are caused by the impact of heat causing internal differentiation of pressure, but the shapes of the flows themselves are generated by internal chaotic principles that resist simple cause and effect analyses.

> Examples related to natural phenomena: Water, air, magma, cosmic particle flows, etc.

1.4.6. Variables, Stocks and Flows (HRSF)

This is the normal way of describing systems in systems dynamics. Variables are nodes that might change under the influence of other nodes. Flows are the flows of the content of the nodes from one node to the other, or the influence from one node to the other. Stocks are the storing capacity of the nodes.

> Example: A classic example is a bathtub. If the inflow of water is more than the flow out of the drain, the bathtub will fill up too fast and flood. If the flow out of the tub is larger, the tub will eventually be empty.

> Example: The relation between the price of goods and the availability of them especially with regards of goods on stock.

1.4.7. Negative Relations (HRNR)

If node A increases, node B decreases.

> Example: The fox and rabbit example. Imagining a green island with only foxes and rabbits, the two species would control each other. As

rabbits' population increases, foxes live well and increase until they have eaten so many rabbits that they will starve and decrease in population. Then the rabbit population will start to grow again. This tends to be a fluctuating but self-stabilizing system.

1.4.8. Positive relations (HRPR)

If node A increases, the node B increases, or if node A decreases, then node B decreases.

> Example: A company showing increased profits on the stock market leads to an increase in the number of traders. This tends to be an unstable system that has the potential to spin out of control.

1.4.9. Feedback loops (HRFloop)

The effect of a chain of causal relations between variables that returns to the 'starting node'.

> Example: On the mentioned island of foxes and rabbits, When the foxes increase the rabbits decrease (Negative relation). When the rabbits decrease, the foxes decrease (Positive relation). When the foxes decrease the rabbits will again increase (negative relation). This forms a simple feedback loop. It is balanced because it has one negative relation, and the populations will fluctuate because of delay but regulate each other

Positive feedback loop (HR+Floop)

The sum of the relations is positive, so the system is unbalanced. In the loop there are balancing (negative) relations missing. One needs at least one balancing relation to avoid feedback loops that spiral up or dawn into eventual self-destruction of the system.

> Example: Hostile negotiations accelerating into war.

> Example: The housing marked having to few balancing relations.

Negative feedback loop (HR-Floop)

The sum of the relations is negative, and the system is balanced.

> <u>Example</u>: The fox and rabbit populations regulate each other.

> <u>Example</u>: If the price goes up, the sales go down (-), then the price goes down (+) and the sales go up (-) and the price goes up (+). This is a self-stabilising system, but it works only well on paper because of all kind of actions that exploit the system. Therefor a totally free marked does not work. Reality is rarely captured in simple models.

2. Systemic relations that resist the model of nodes and connectors

Not all systemic relations can be abstracted to nodes with connections. They must be diagrammed with spatial maps, intensity maps, or along timelines.

In many cases, we should challenge the predominant systems model of entities and relations. Often, it is more useful to use a model of continuum. When mapping out the myriad of relations, they will generate a weaving that is so dense; it creates a sense of a field more than an overview of a large amount of relations.

> <u>Examples</u>: Schools of fish or flocks of starlings, the phenomena called hive minds, collective intelligence or continuums as in oceans and weather systems.

2.1. Spatial proximity (SP)

Elements sharing the same space within an operational proximity for the agent (e.g., the user).

> <u>Example</u>: The relation between a chair and table. Of course, there is also a thematic relationship because they are both furniture and also may have a historic relationship because both could belong to the same style. There is also a functional and structural relationship. (Who said this is simple?)

> <u>Example</u>: The proximity between a neighbourhood and a park.

> <u>Example</u>: The proximity of same shops in specialised shopping streets, for example the textile quarter in Istanbul.

2.2. Temporal proximity (TP)

Elements share a temporal proximity in relation to an agent (e.g., the user).

Example: Traffic regulation systems that are timed according to rush hours, which of course are caused by the working hours, which again are influenced by the planetary system (day length).

Example: A cafe serving lunch at lunch hour.

2.3. Spatial distribution (SD)

Intensity fields, variations, and differentiation of the distribution of similar elements in space.

Example: Temperature across a room with a stove in one corner.

Example: The density and distribution of sunbathers in a park.

2.4. Temporal distribution (TD)

Relations play out over time as singular events related to other events or in patterns rhythms and variations in intensity.

2.4.1. The distribution of elements over time

Describes how elements and actions are distributed over time either through orchestration or through self-organisation.

Example: The distribution of intensities in a music composition.

Example: The distribution of traffic density over the course of one day.

2.4.2. Timing, rhythms, and repetitions (TRR)

The same elements are appearing in a recognisable pattern.

Example: The repetitions in a music composition.

Example: The rhythms of intensity in the density of traffic.

Example: The rhythms and patterns of usage of the rooms in a house.

Using the Library

One shift in mindset for becoming a systemic designer is to turn your attention from the object to the relations. This is not only a question of awareness, but it is also about practice. In gigamapping, this can be done through designing the relations. As mentioned, relations are most often depicted with simple lines or arrows. But there are many graphical ways of distinguishing relations. The colour-coding we already introduced for example. In addition, we can work with the format of the line, or line fonts.

- An important relation can be depicted with a thick line.

- A less important relation can be depicted with a thinner line.

- A relation that is unbalanced, e.g., it is more important for one entity than the other, can be depicted with a gradient or a tapered line.

- Relations that are constant can be depicted with a continuous line.

- Relations that kick in regularly can be depicted with a dashed line.

- Relations that were present in the past can be depicted with a fading gradient.

All these graphic treatments of the connectors can be combined. For example, very important relations that function only rarely can be depicted with a thick dashed line.

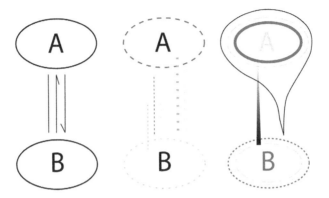

Figure 132: Diagram of different ways to graphically visualizing relations between two entities. Line fonts and weights are used to codify the relations (Birger Sevaldson 2013, first version: 2001).

Another issue that is rarely addressed is the boundary quality of the entities described in the mapping. They are normally drawn all in the same way as nodes. The boundaries could be varied in similar ways as the connectors to depict the nature of the entities (*Figure 132*).

All of these considerations are cumbersome if not impossible to carry through on all levels of the Gigamapping process. For some interesting zoom points or leverage points, however, it might be worthwhile to use these microscopic analyses to find relations that are intertwined and that might turn out to be very important bases for innovation.

Understanding the Relations through Designing

The design process of coding the relations is an analytical process. This analytical process is done during mapping, maybe after the first sketch is finished and the first iteration is being refined; for example, when a hand drawn Gigamap is redesigned with digital media. The tools at one's disposal are as mentioned: colour coding, tagging, and line fonts. Below is an example of a map using the library.

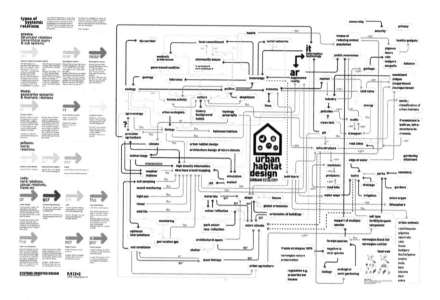

Figure 133: Relational map of urban habitats involving urban ecology. The library of systemic relations is in the legend to the left. Black connectors are unsorted in relation to the map. The tags do not correspond with the current state of the library (Young Eun Choi, 2013).

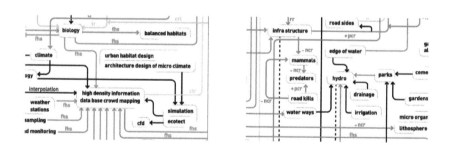

Figure 134: Two details from the map in Figure 133. The details show on the left, weather and climate, and on the right, parts of the water system. The colour coding and tagging are explained in the Library of Systemic Relations above (Young Eun Choi, 2013).

274

Analyzing, Ideating, and Evaluating

Concepts and ideas might emerge in a spontaneous manner when working with large amounts of information. In the early stages of such a process, the ideas might be unrealistic and unrooted. Later, when insight and knowledge grow, they might become more realistic and rooted in the system. Also, seemingly good ideas might turn out to be impossible to implement while seemingly obvious and unimportant ideas might develop to become ground-breaking.

We will now return to the ZIP analysis, and introduce some other tools for the evaluation of concepts and ideas.

ZIP Analysis

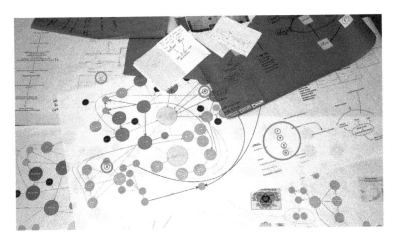

Figure 135: Example of ZIP analyses of multiple smaller scale maps. One can spot the ZIP points as small black circles with the letters, ZIP emphasised with red circles (Photo: Birger Sevaldson).

ZIP Analysis is a simple method for developing Gigamaps in order to find potential areas for interventions and innovations. ZIP stands for Zoom, Innovation, Problem or Potential.

You apply the analyses by marking spots and areas in the Gigamap with one of the three points (*Figure 135*). You can do this while developing the map and / or in separate analysis sessions where you investigate the map to search for these points.

Often, the order of the process is that we start with Z-points to zoom in on white spots on the map, then look for P-points to identify potentials and problems, and eventually search for I-points of innovation or intervention. A zoom can progress to become a potential, and in the process of finding a resolution for a potential, it becomes an intervention or innovation. This is not meant to be a prescriptive approach. I-points might pop out immediately, and the order might be changed.

There are other points that could be used also. Pain-points, for example, are frequently used in service design; risk-points have been suggested by Elisabeth Skjelten (Bjørndal Skjelten, 2014); and leverage-points are used to identify points where a systems intervention would have a greater impact on the whole system (D. Meadows, 1999). I have also used the term Intersection-points. An Intersection-point is where two or more systems intersect, such as the point where the system of coffee growth, trade, and refinement intersect with the system of forestry, paper, industry, and chemical technology for the production of a simple paper cup (*Figure 16*).

Use the ZIP and additional analysis points in your gigamapping process as a starting device to initiate a generative process and ultimately find innovation in the map that is truly rooted in the system. The effect of the ZIP analyses is not so much to generate ideas and solve problems as it is a device for thinking through issues in the map. The dialogue generated through the ZIP analyses when conducted between collaborators is as important as the output.

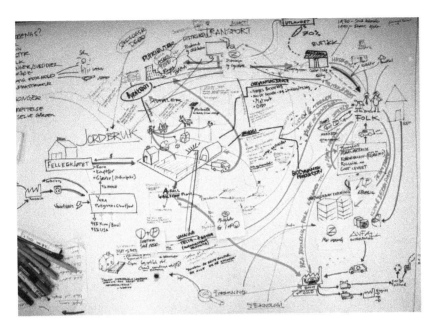

Figure 136: A Gigamap. In this case, the theme is agriculture and autonomous technology. ZIP points are marked with post-its (By Geir Hutoft, Alvilde Jerpseth, Elias Olderbakk, Martin Bøckman, Thomas Wang, Gustav Traberg, GK6 Oslo School of Architecture and Design, 2018).

ZIP Analysis in Detail

The ZIP analysis can be done individually or in groups. It is especially beneficial to do this with interdisciplinary teams so that you can utilize different expertise and avoid wasting time on knowledge that is already represented in the team.

Z: Zoom is used to mark areas or points in your map that need more research. It is a reminder for you that there is a lack of information and a catalyst for zooming into these specific areas of the map. The Z-points help give your investigation and inquiry needed structure and direction. First, you establish an overview of all the gaps (indicated by white or blank spots on the map) in your knowledge of the environment and landscape. When you have established this overview, you can plan activities to improve your knowledge. The overview of blank spots gives you a chance to sort and prioritize them, so that you can start with the most crucial ones or the ones that block further progress. At the same time, you have a clear documentation of the blank spots, and you can return to them later if needed.

P: P stands for potential, problem, problematique, or pain-point. If there is an obvious problem, then there is potential for improvement. On the other hand, something that works very well has the potential to be learned from, and it might reveal principles that can be used elsewhere in the system. There could be big potential within things that work very well. They can be used as inspiration to improve similar situations that are not working, or to link them in new ways. Typically, if you spot a potential or problem but you do not know what to do with it yet, it is a P-point. You can also think of the P-points as leverage points or potential actors, e.g., in the sense of "Enablers" and "Blockers."

I: I stands for idea, innovation, inventions, or intervention. If you get an idea, find something new that you can do, find a solution to a P-point, or find connections to link things in a new way by creating new relations, then you have identified an I-point. Interventions are not necessarily new and innovative, but they are actions that change the system. Tweaking the system to fine-tune it or to remove a bottle neck does not change the structure or topology of the system. Instead, it is an intervention that changes the performance of the system. When you change the topology of the system by, for example, adding new functions entities or operations or adding new relations then we call it an innovation. However, often ideas that are badly rooted in the system pop up in our minds. Still, such ideas have value because they can be used to pose "wht-if" questions. Even if such ideas normally do not turn out as sustainable and realistic, they help us to learn more about the system by imagining how they fit and how they might perform.

When gigamapping, you perform the ZIP-analysis by consciously searching for ZIP points. Identify and mark these points with a Z, P, or I on the map. However, we can also conduct the ZIP analyses as separate activities, where all focus and attention is given to the conducting of the analyses. It is very beneficial to perform ZIP-analysis in teams, because the discussions induced by the process.

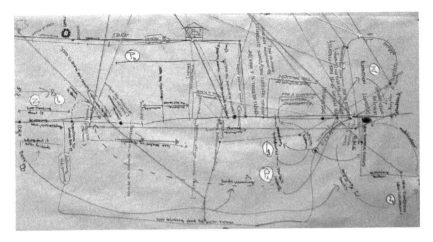

Figure 137: ZIP-points are marked with the respective letter, a circle, and a number. (To see the whole map, see Figure 32 and Figure 33). (Photo: Birger Sevaldson)

How to work with the ZIP-points

Though we do not impose methods in general it has shown to be beneficial to follow a certain convention when conducting the ZIP analysis.

Z-points:

Identify the Z-points or areas on the map. As mentioned, these are "white spots" (or blank spots) where your knowledge is insufficient. The Z-points mark the immediate learning process needed for our project. Instead of diving into these spots right away by conducting web searches or reading up on the issues, postpone further investigation and simply mark them with a Z. The convention we use is a circle with the letter Z and a small number. The number allows us to create a list with short descriptions of all the Z-points. The list will help to prioritize and allocate different ways to gather the needed knowledge. Only after having generated this list can we prioritize which points to zoom into first and which are less important at the moment. Some Z-points can be dealt with by a quick web search, while others require more in-depth literature research, and there are also cases that call for the involvement of experts. So, dealing with the Z-points according to their importance and ease of investigation, we can plan our learning process. To further develop a Z-point, you can make a separate map of that specific point or area with a very high level of detail. An additional benefit with creating a list or other overview is that you always can return to points that have not been prioritized at the moment.

P-points:

Identify the P-points on the map. Start by searching for obvious problems or things that work very well, the potential we can learn from. Use the same convention as for the Z-points. Circle and number the P-points to make a list and prioritize them. To further develop a potential or to better understand a problem, make separate maps of those points, and / or consult stakeholders that are influenced by the problem. Investigate singular problems and potentials by exploring how they are related to other problems and potentials. Maybe some of the P-points need to be solved in synergy or sequence? Maybe one problem needs to be solved first to utilize a potential? Create P-maps out of relationships between P-points so that they become problematiques or fields of interrelated problems or potentials.

I-points:

During the ZIP analysis process, ideas will emerge naturally. Solutions might also pop up as you deal with the P-points. In addition to these naturally emerging ideas, you should search for I-points in the map. Look for interventions, and not only ideas and innovations. An innovation can be about relations rather than the entities. Look for missing relations that connect seemingly disconnected things that should or could be connected. Look for relations that are not beneficial. Disconnect things that disturb each other and reconnect them at needed points. To find points of intervention, search for leverage points. These are points in the system where small changes will have a great impact. Use the same convention as for the other points and make lists of I-points. Make detailed maps to investigate their impact, effort, and their consequences. Strategize their development and bundle them as needed.

I-Point Check List:

1. Find resolutions to P-points.

2. Look between the objects and be relation-focused. Find and / or create new relations.

3. See if you can combine elements in the map in new ways.

4. Check if you should disconnect things.

5. Check for synergies.

6. Check back with the whole system to foresee and avoid unwanted and negative effects.

7. Search for interconnected P-points so-called problem fields or problematiques. Be mindful that solving one problem might make others worse. Avoid unintended bad consequences.

8. Orchestrate the sequence and development of solutions so that they prepare the ground and support each other.

9. Allow any idea that pops up to be registered in the ZIP analyses.

Generating Ideas, Interventions, and Innovation

The ZIP analysis works nicely with Gigamaps to move from descriptive to generative design. The move from a descriptive mode of gigamapping to a generative mode often happens seamlessly and naturally. Ideas might emerge during the process, and scenarios might be a natural part of the mapping process. However, the ZIP analysis is a leap forward into generative mapping. Making the I-point maps and connecting them back to the system will eventually lead to a redrawing of the Gigamaps according to the imagined changes. This brings the mapping process from a state of how things are to how they ought to or might be.

Impact and Threshold Analyses

It is often difficult to evaluate ideas. This is because they are usually personal, and it is hard to let go of a seemingly good idea for a less attractive idea that might result in greater impact. We discuss ideas without having good evaluation criteria.

The Impact and Threshold Analysis (IMP-analysis) is a simple evaluation tool for further investigating Z and P-points, so that it is easier to prioritize and select which I-points should be chosen for further development. The tool presents clear variables to rank the ideas. It contains five main groups of variables:

Impacts: Systemic impact, impact radius e.g., ripple effect, leverage.

Thresholds: Economic, technological, cultural/ social.

Synergies: Multiple effects from an intervention.

Counter-effects: Unexpected side-effects.

Resilience: Resistance towards systemic change.

The analysis framework involves a great amount of detail that will make a full-fledged analysis quite laborious. Like with any other SOD methodology, it is advised to choose the variables relevant to the case at hand. Other variables, even bespoke ones, can always be added to the evaluation to fit and adjust to the case.

The list below can be used as a scaffold for Impact and Threshold analyses:

1. **Systemic Impact** (Leverage)

   This group of factors deals with the effect of a systemic intervention, innovation, or idea. How far reaching is the impact? How long will its effect remain? How fast will its effect kick in?

   1.1 Radius of ripple effects

   This defines how far the effect can reach. How many sub-systems are affected? How many actors and stakeholders benefit from or are negatively affected by the intervention?

   1.2 Short-term effect

   This defines how fast the effect of the intervention will kick in.

   1.3 Long-term

   This defines how long the effect of the intervention will last. Will this have substantial effect to change the system and bring it into a new stage or seed a lasting change process?

   1.4 Platform effect

   This defines to what degree the intervention is creating conditions for further interventions. How can this intervention prepare a platform for other interventions?

2. **Thresholds**

   This group of variables deals with the thresholds that have to be overcome to realize and implement systemic change. How hard is it to realize this intervention?

2.1 Economic

How expensive will it be to realize the intervention?

2.2 Technological

How technologically difficult will it be to realize the intervention? This is partly connected to the economic factor.

2.3 Cultural

What cultural challenges will emerge in the implementation of the systemic change?

2.4 Organisational

What organisational challenges will emerge when one implements the systemic change? This is partly connected to the cultural factor.

3. **Synergies**

This group of variables addresses synergies between elements that are influenced by the intervention. How can the idea, innovation, or intervention support other functions, activities, or elements in the system, and how can it be reinforced by other elements?

3.1 Synergies between intervention and existing system

3.2 Synergies between interventions

3.3 Orchestration effects (combined effects, high-level synergies)

3.4 Orchestration thresholds (how easy is it to orchestrate the implementation?)

4. Counter-Effects (Unwanted and counter-intuitive effects)

One of the difficult tasks in systemic design is to foresee the unintended side effects of our designs. This task requires imagination and good systems thinking. Look back at the Gigamap to find interdependencies that were not obvious at first sight.

4.1 Short-term

4.2 Long-term

4.3 Counter-effects between intervention and existing system

4.4 Counter-effects between interventions

5. Resilience

In this section, we look for the robustness of our designs.

5.1 Resilience towards micro fluctuations

5.2 Resilience towards macro fluctuations

5.3 Resilience towards extreme scenarios

5.4 Black Swans. The ability to survive very unexpected events.

To compare the score of the different I-points, it is best to set up the analysis in a diagram. These can be simple tables like the ones shown below (*Figure 138*).

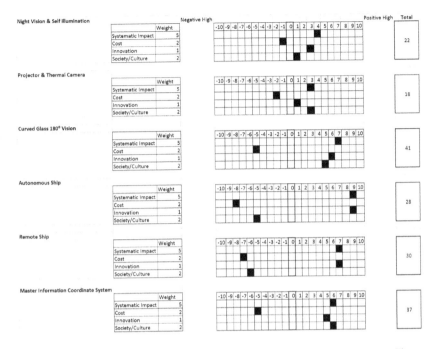

Figure 138: A simple I-point evaluation, customized a bit for the application. This evaluation looks at different main concepts. The different variables are weighed differently according to the perceived importance of each variable. Systemic impact is weighed highest. The graphical representation shows the total score to the left, but it is also easy to see how the score is achieved. A big spread in the scores like in the second last case will indicate that there might be problems to overcome. In this case, the challenges are the high costs and high cultural thresholds required for implementation (Zhongkai et. al. HiALS, 2015).

However, the impact and threshold analyses can be conducted in many ways, for example with stickers on the map as shown in *Figure 139* and *Figure 140*. The examples shown also demonstrate different ways of customization of the impact analyses. In *Figure 138*, only four variables are used for each idea; on the other hand, the importance of the variables is distinguished by weighting them differently. In *Figure 139* and *Figure 140*, the variables themselves are changed and adapted to the project.

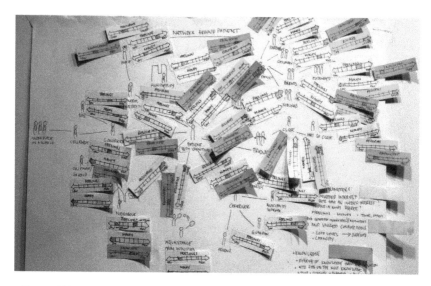

Figure 139: A different way of using the evaluation method combined with a map to contextualize the points that are evaluated. In addition, this evaluation looks more at details, e.g., cultural thresholds that are localized in the network (Natalia Tunheim, AHO, 2013).

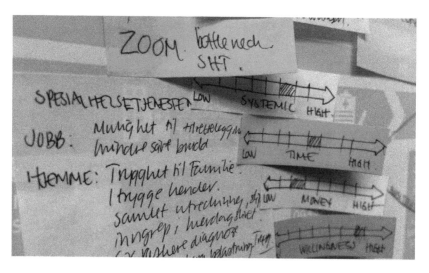

Figure 140: A third version of evaluation where a printed background map is used as a basis for developing judgments around zooming in (Z-point) on a defined bottleneck (P-point) in the care of patients who suffer from dementia (Natalia Tunheim, AHO, 2013).

The Impact and Threshold Analysis gives an indicator for and an informed judgement of the I-points. Yet the highest scoring idea is not automatically the best result. The setup of the scoring system is important.

In the end, this analysis is a decisions support tool rather than a bulletproof decision-making instrument. It needs to be used with care and with common-sense judgment. The most valuable asset of this analyses is the dialogue and discussions it systematises.

Other Types of Analyses and Evaluation Tools

In the following, I will shortly go through a few other simple tools that might be useful in the evaluation of the Gigamaps. It is advised that these tools should be redesigned according to the situation. The evaluation process should also be done in groups where there is a reasonable representation of different expertise.

Leverage Points

The concept of Leverage points implies that there exist certain points in a system where an intervention has especially great effect and impact, and easily ripples through the system (D. Meadows, 1999). Finding and defining Leverage points is a good way of understanding the system better and to induce systems change. For this, the ZIP analyses can be used efficiently.

Intersection Points

Intersection points are where different systems meet. A classic example is the paper coffee cup described earlier (*Figure 16*). Intersection points are not necessary good points for intervention, as the example of the coffee cup demonstrates. However, they are very useful for investigating relations between systems and for learning more about how systems behave and interact. They are also very useful to unpack objects, to look beyond them, and to reconceptualise them. This is helpful for arriving at new creative solutions.

Pro-Et-Contra Analysis

Pro-et-Contra analysis is an efficient tool to check the robustness of a design intervention and to design for resilience. The Pro-et-Contra analysis also helps to break schemata and to voice other opinions. The pro-et-contra analysis is conducted as an argumentation-tree (Førland, 1996).

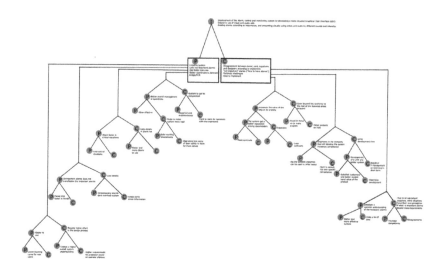

Figure 141: Pro-et-Contra argumentation tree (Stig M. Henriksen NTNU, 2016).

To conduct a Pro-et-Contra analysis, it is recommended to work visually by developing the argumentation in the tree form as deep as needed. Start with following these steps:

- Make a list of the pro arguments that support your idea.

- Make a list of the counter arguments to your idea.

- Select the most important pro- and counterarguments and develop pro and counter arguments for each of them. Repeat this to a level where you think it is sufficient to have some well-supported arguments.

If this analysis results in heavy counterarguments against your project, you should tweak, redesign, and reform it to address the issue(s). If this is not possible, and you still want to continue with the project for specific reasons, you need to honestly flag the issue(s).

Worst Case Scenarios:

Imagination and Phantasy are extremely important in understanding how our systems interventions might play out. We need to imagine what can happen as a result of our interventions, and the most likely scenario is the least useful. This is for several reasons. Firstly, the most obvious scenario will rarely happen. There will always be unexpected events and surprises. Secondly, the most likely scenario does not challenge us to learn anything. More extreme and unlikely scenarios will help us to imagine how the system might respond and eventually survive.

Create a minimum of two different extreme scenarios that are at the rim of what is probable. Develop the scenario so that it shows how your system will survive or adapt to a new situation. For example: the bridge of a ship has burnt down. A small emergency bridge at a different place on the ship allows for emergency operation. The system will survive even in a reduced state of operation. Ultimately, these scenarios are about the resilience or robustness of your intervention.

A "Black Swan" is a scenario that describes something unthinkable happening to your design. It could be useful to think of Black Swans when developing an extreme scenario. The contradiction is that in the moment you are able to think about a Black Swan scenario it is not a Black Swan anymore. Nonetheless, reflecting about this and creating very unlikely and heavy-impact scenarios is helpful in developing your system.

Back-Checking:

Back-checking means controlling how your intervention is tied and related to the system. In periods of a design process, one will lose touch with the big picture. This is natural, but to reduce the risk of errors and disconnected design proposals, one needs to check them back to the system at check points. Using the Gigamaps and rich design space for this purpose is advised. Here are some guidelines for conducting a back-checking process.

Back-checking for synergies: Check your idea and intervention regarding the ripple effects on the system. Try to find synergies. Are there new possibilities that have been opened up by your intervention or idea?

Back-checking to the Gigamap: Draw your idea or intervention back onto the Gigamap, and draw out its relations to everything on the map. How is it influencing or changing other elements? What is needed for your design to work? This allows you to develop design solutions early, and check back later to see how they fit into the system and what impact they would have.

To do this, one has to use the Gigamap and draw in the design sketch directly to see how it relates. Then, run an Impact and Threshold Analysis of the design proposal.

Back-checking is particularly useful because it allows for a more free and unsequenced design process where early design sketches can be facilitated to further learn how the system would behave.

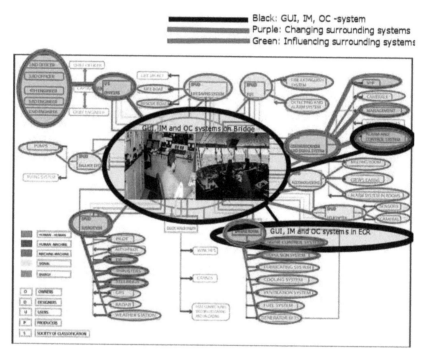

Figure 142: A map showing a back-checking process (Stig M. Henriksen NTNU, 2016).

Counter Intuitive Analysis:

This is a version of back-checking, but it addresses preconceptions and unquestioned assumptions of how the system will work and react. Systems act counterintuitively. The question is how can we capture the counterintuitive effects of a systemic design. In particular, it is important to find and imagine the unintended side effects of the design.

Step 1: Define all assumptions of how the system will work. What is your intuition and gut feeling? Be critical with your intuition as systems might react in counterintuitive ways.

Step 2: Choose the most crucial assumptions and produce network maps of the assumed effects of the design. Create worst-case scenarios. Also, look for possible unintended effects on seemingly disconnected parts of the system. For that, you can use the Gigamap to look back on the whole landscape.

Step 3: Search the Gigamap for potential unintended effects.

Step 4: Select the most crucial effects and create network maps of how these effects might play out. Judge the trigger conditions and dampening effects.

Step 5: Readjust the design or scrap it if this is not possible.

Risk Analysis:

Further down the road, one should do a risk analysis. This can be done by identifying risk points in the system (map), developing scenarios that would play out the consequences of the risk, and developing scenarios for human error. The different risk scenarios are plotted into a simple two-axis diagram where one axis depicts the seriousness of the consequences of a triggered risk factor, and the other depicts the probability of a risk factor being triggered.

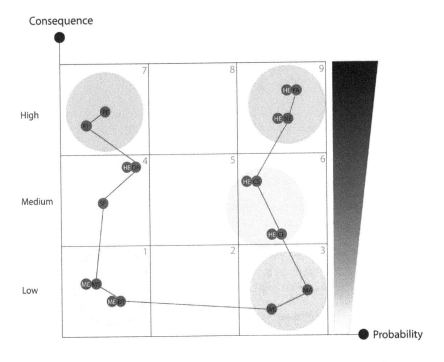

Figure 143: A simple diagram structure is helpful for analysing risks (Jan Kristian Strømsnes, 2011).

291

Pace Analysis:

Another small tool to develop the understanding of how your system intervention might play out is related to time. The pace analyses helps you to imagine how the system might operate and act over time.

PA1: In the Gigamap, depict relations according to time, velocity and acceleration criteria in order to understand the heartbeat of the system. Use timelines.

PA2: Finding and designing the time horizon for an intervention both in terms of implementation and orchestration, as well as operation. As Stuart Brand demonstrated in his pace layer diagram, systems can be seen as having layers that operate with different speeds (1994).

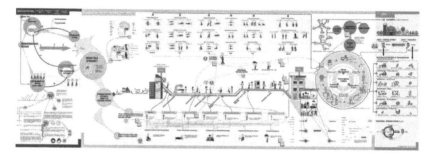

Figure 144: A timeline-based map of the treatment process of a patient suffering from a stroke. Keeping track of what happens when in a scenario is crucial for designing a systemic intervention (Cong Li OlsoMet 2016).

From Descriptive to Generative

Although I am distinguishing between descriptive and generative processes, in SOD practice, we want these processes to blur. This is obviously an artificial divide. A descriptive process will often also be generative by simply generating new insight, "picturesque" richness, and patterns of interrelations that were not visible before. Describing a complex situation is a constructive or designerly process. We are constructing our reality (constructivism). In that sense, all designed descriptions are generative. But the distinction is still needed. A design process naturally starts with learning how to describe a situation, if its only a short brief or idea. In SOD processes, the descriptive part is very extensive, rapid, wide, and deep, and always involves co-learning. The gigamapping typically starts with describing, interpreting, and sensemaking, putting together a picture of the situation. This process naturally changes to become increasingly generative. Some ideas and visions of the future might come very early, but the resolution of the situation at hand develops over time and gets more intense towards the end of the design process. This happens naturally in the Gigamap, when one moves from describing relations to drawing new ones, from describing new entities in the system and to generating scenarios. We can look upon the move from the descriptive to the generative process more as a gradient than a phasing.

Descriptive Tools Include:

- Externalizing and sharing pre-existing knowledge

- Learning: Mapping and networking new knowledge

- Research: Including and organizing knowledge gained from targeted research

- Internalizing large amounts of information, both qualitative and quantitative

- Internalizing relations and networks

Gigamapping as a Generative and Creative Tool

The Gigamap is a shared, designed picture. It is in fact a design artefact. This implies that interpretation and imagination are at play very early on in the process. We start naturally to map out not only how we think things are, but how they could be. This seamlessly integrates description with imagination. This is fortunate because it un-phases the design process. We need to allow this drifting towards the generative to happen and not suppress it. It is easy to mark the prospective elements of the map graphically, such as through the I-points in the ZIP analysis or through other means.

Scenarios

Another engine for innovation and creativity in systemic design is to work within and with time. Naturally this happens when using timelines in gigamapping. Most obviously, it involves imagining how things work and how they might work better or differently. Narratives are central for all these techniques. They include timelines, storytelling and other narratives, key-framing, cartoons, videos, and roleplay.

All these approaches are central to building worst case scenarios, to communicating how things work, and to arriving at systemic design solutions.

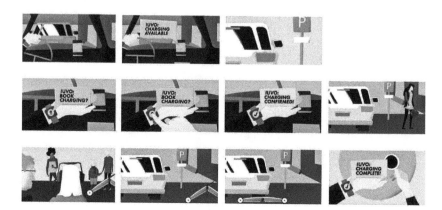

Figure 145: Storyboard for a scenario with an autonomous charging robot for electric cars (Iuvo, by Ofte Solås, Helene Falstad, Tord Stenstavold, Raoul Ronald Antoni in collaboration with SALTO, AHO, 2016).

The relationship between the descriptive and generative will be discussed further in the next section.

SOD Process Frameworks

The SOD frameworks are scaffolds for the application of the SOD tools. They vary from being generic concepts for strategizing a process, such as the hybrid, layered, and media-rich design process, to what we could call meta-tools, tools to organise the use of tools, such as the Rich Design Space and the Creative Process Framework.

The Layered and Nested Design Process

The SOD design process is typically composed of parallel design processes and nested processes inside the main design process. The main design process, or the process encapsulating or circumscribing all others, is similar to a traditional process where the result is a product, system, service, or the design of organisations, activities, and social change. This main design process might consist of layers of parallel or sequential sub-processes, and involve the implementation of different knowledges, methodologies, and people. Nested further inside this processes, like an onion, is another set of design processes: the design of knowledge, or more precisely, the design of the understanding of the situation and the systems involved.

This onion of processes bridges the divide between the research phase and design phase. This divide originates from old models of design methodology where the design process was split into clearly defined phases, which had to be followed in a fixed sequence.[77] Yet, SOD imposes an intensified early process of investigation. Without doubt, if not done thoughtfully, this could lead to reinforcing the divide between researching, designing, and reflection. It is a misunderstanding if we think that SOD increases the divide between a research phase and a design phase. This is despite the fact that what seems to be the research phase in SOD, the gigamapping and adjacent activities, tend to be slightly longer and deeper than in "normal" design processes.

In SOD, we counter the divide in two ways to avoid phasing the design process. First, it is utterly important to start designing at a very early stage, even from the very beginning. "Folding" the design process so as to achieve a laminar rather than sequential process is essential to reach a good synthesis of new design resolutions. More importantly, however, is the effect of investigating a system through the lens of its projected future and imagined design resolutions. Imagining and testing these future states early on will help us learn how the system might react to the suggested designs. It is through imaginative investigation of the reaction of the system that we can learn more of its dynamic nature. This is how designers normally learn; by suggesting a design solution, the client can react to the suggested technological requirements, the marked potential, the usability, etc. Often it is not possible to tease out these issues simply by asking and researching. One needs a concrete design suggestion to get at more concrete issues to discuss and resolve.

Gedenryd has shown that the phasing of the design process is partly an illusion since we tend to imagine solutions very early (Gedenryd, 1998). We need these visions and visualizations early to break the linearity of the design process and to test them in relation to the system (as depicted in the Gigamap) in order to start the process of iterations and to populate the field of possibilities (*Figure 7*) with concrete solutions. Early design solutions will also feed back to the Gigamap, and add to the accumulation of knowledge. This is also an indicator of the fact that there is no straightforward derivation of design interventions, innovations, or solutions found in the Gigamap or in any other systems model. Despite this, the

---

77. Ref. Cross (Cross, 1984), and Gedenryd's critique of product-process symmetry (Gedenryd, 1998 at 23).

Gigamap has a great advantage. It can seamlessly integrate descriptive and generative modes. In the Gigamapping process, it is a seamless step from drawing the system as it is to how it should or could be. Though leaping from a current situation to a preferred one is always challenging and difficult, the smooth transition from descriptive to generative makes it easier. It is a relative easy step from describing relations to adding missing links, and to finding problems and points of intervention. The step between the descriptive and the generative are seamlessly bridged. This does not mean that Gigamapping effortlessly leads to great ideas. We are still dependent on the creative mind and imaginative investigation. Often people feel that there is still a big leap between describing the system to finding good concepts and ideas. Gigamapping is a great technique to reach deep innovations quickly through ZIP analysis, but designing out the generated ideas, interventions, or innovations is another jump. Designing is always a generative process and not an automated derivative from some abstract process. Therefore, designing and prototyping should go parallel with other activities that are informed and inspired by the Gigamap and the findings in it. However, they should also inspire the map and drive its development forward by posing questions.

Still, there is more to this. The early design sketches have the potential to fail early. Failing early is important because this is valuable learning. Failing early is made more probable through the gigamapping process, because it unfolds many aspects of the system, hence presenting many challenges in the design process at an early stage. This presents opportunities to change the system in ways that would be beneficial to adapt to new design solutions. The design solution is contextualized and embedded in necessary and orchestrated systems changes to provide for its implementation, as well as in its synergies to other aspects of the system. Early designs can contribute to insights into the systems at hand that feed back into the gigamapping process. When designing for insight rather than result we call it **imaginative investigations**.

The last reason for designing early addresses the very nature of wicked problems. Conklin formulates this reasoning in the following way:

> You don't understand the problem until you have developed a solution. Every solution that is offered exposes new aspects of the problem, requiring further adjustments of the potential solutions. Indeed, there is no definitive statement of 'the problem.' The problem is ill structured, an evolving set of interlocking issues and constraints (Conklin, 2005).

By designing early, we can use the designs to generate scenarios and develop our knowledge of the system as well as our interpretation of the wicked problem through design.

There is, of course, a risk in designing early. Early design solutions tend to stick, to heavily bias further investigations, leading to "cherry picking" of data and insights. It might be hard to "kill your babies" when needed. To avoid these traps, it is important keep this in mind and always critically scrutinize emergent ideas and visions so that they can instead be used as triggers for investigations and discussions in relation to the Gigamap. To nurture criticality in the process, we can stick to always working with several contradictory design ideas simultaneously and to develop a reflective dialogue between them. Co-design processes are hard places where ideas are scrutinised and criticised. Another important factor to avoid biased design solution is using the evaluation tools frequently. Amongst these tools, the IMP analysis and the pro-et-contra analysis are important to avoid skewing the process.

Another way we counter the divide of the design process in SOD is by looking at the mapping process as a design project itself. Gigamapping is a learning process through designing. As mentioned, this designerly learning process is nested inside of the main design process. Referring to the systemic sensemaking model (*Figure 98*), the main design process is concerned with designing the system we design and at best, the system we design for. The designerly learning process is concerned with designing the system we design within. It is concerned with designing the knowledge about the system, not only as an accumulation of facts and experiences, but also as the Gestalt of the system.

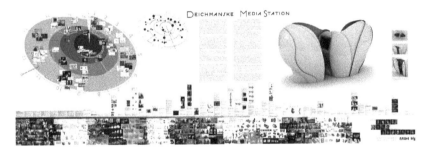

Figure 146: The organic design process of a media station (right) for the Deichmanske Library in Oslo. The process included distant and on site collaboration between a Norwegian and German Design school, and a ship builder in the south east of Norway. It involved observation of how the library was used as a social space, ergonometric experimentation, material experimentation and development, digital as well as manual manufacturing and digital collaboration via blogs. Close examination of the map reveals a large amount of information of the process, captured in the process map to the left and the timeline at the bottom (AHO / HFG 2007-2008).

Referring to SSM and its position on "systemness" being a feature of the systems thinker rather than the real world (Checkland, 2000c), we can similarly think of information-handling and mapping as designed artefacts. We design our picture of the system, its environment, and its surrounding fields and landscape (*Figure 146*). By superimposing different information, we design relations. We consciously design synergies and new relations in the design suggestions. The ways that these maps are drawn, the way information is rendered, and how these are designed and redesigned are influencial for the construction of the information. Several iterations and redesigns of the information are essential to the principles of the Hybrid Process, where switching between design media is important (Sevaldson, 2005b, pp. 317–343). For example, the redesign of an initial paper map made with markers as a new digital version is not only a simple redrawing of the same information. This stage of redesigning is highly cognitive and creative. Redesigning the map is closely tied to reflection through sorting, colour-coding, dimensioning, considering proportions, and reorganising the information. For example, designing a system of colour coding is a highly analytical process. Scaling proportions also indicates a process of sorting according to importance or priorities, and so on. This redesign into digital media also results in an even better internalising of the information. Designing is a very efficient method for remembering large amounts of complex information.

In SOD, we regard this parallel and nested design process of designing and redesigning the information in different iterations of the Gigamap as crucial. We use designerly-thinking and designing as ways for analysis and reflection. Here, designing and thinking are totally integrated. This process is only fruitful when we work through several iterations using large-scale plots with small phases of digital and manual drafting, and the adding and sorting of information.

In the end, we look at the whole design process as a design artefact. It is guided by principles of design rather than methodology, which explains why we like to emphasise praxeology.

The final presentation, documentation, as well as look and feel are not only a question of communication, but also an expression of the total design, its atmosphere, ethics, social position and perspectives. Thinking and designing is again even and totally integrated on the final level.

The final result is not just an accumulation of facts, but more importantly in an overall and holistic conception of the system, a Gestalt of the system. The Gestalt represents its nature, organisation, and place in the world. We will return to this in the section about sense-sharing.

Media-Rich Design Processes and How to Proliferate Them

In the following, we will dive a bit deeper into the issues of media regarding the design process. The perspective discussed here borrows ideas from Media Richness Theory (MRT), developed by Daft and Lengel (Daft & Lengel, 1983). Suh explains MRT and the relation between media richness and information processing as follows:

Task performance will be improved when task information processing requirements are matched with a mediums ability to convey information richness. A lean medium (e.g. a memo) is sufficient to exchange an unequivocal message (e.g. a routine communication), while a rich medium (e.g. face-to-face meeting) is recommended to resolve an equivocal situation (e.g. negotiation) (Suh, 1998).

Simply put, MRT states the information rich processes require rich media, something that is obviously resonant with the concepts of SOD. However, Suh (1998) did not find any support for the concepts presented in MRT, and was critical of the approach. Generally, the theory is criticized for failing to take situational conditions, such as social factors, into account. There is also a criticism of the methods used to measure performance. Yet, MRT is valuable for having highlighted the relation between information richness and the media used to communicate it. This is highly relevant to the design process. The handling and communication of information is central to the design process, both between participants and stakeholders, but also on the individual level at which the designer communicates with the design space.

If we move the focus from information communication to information generation, the idea of media influencing the process becomes even more valid. The design process is media-based and media-dependent. There is valid evidence that the medium influences the design process. McLuhan (1964) discusses the influence of media on culture in general, while McCullouch (1996) considers its influence on design in particular. Both Allen (1999) and Lynn (1999) have demonstrated how media is intertwined with new thinking in design. The importance of media richness in the design process has become more evident over the last few decades as digital media significantly changed the way we work.

The MRT approach compares singular media in communication. The design process normally engages several media in sequences or in parallel. Even a traditional product design process might begin with hand-drawn sketches and continue with 3D CAD, for example. Meanwhile, a video production could start with text, hand-drawn sketches, and storyboards, continue with 3D animation tools, and finally, end with digital video-editing. Such a production involves numerous forms of interaction and communication, including face-to-face meetings with visualisations and physical models involved, as well as remote collaboration using video-conferencing, email, telephones, and file-sharing. Very often, the different media overlap and users jump back and forth between them. A typical CAD process among advanced design students involves a range of different 3D applications, each selected for its ability to perform special tasks (modelling, animation, rendering, parametric design, Virtual Reality, and Augmented Reality, etc.). These jumps and switches between media are not only becoming more normal, but can be beneficial for increasing the capacity to handle very complex design problems and finding solutions when there is an impasses in the process (Sevaldson, 2005a). The jumps between media and representations, and the shifts in social constellations can transform the interpretation of design information. More complex design tasks need multiple interpretations that accumulate to result in a deeper understanding of the task. The creative process from generation to synthesis is partly an explicit reflexive discourse and partly a tacit or intuitive one, all based on a holistic understanding of the task. The ability to generate a rich and manifold understanding from which to synthesize systemic solutions is developed as a skill that goes beyond explicit prescriptions and methods.

A complex design project would benefit from the implementation of a wide range of design media, such as hand-drawn sketches, different 3D-design packages, text, video, design manuals, physical mock-ups, RP-models, simulations, prototypes, Virtual Reality and Augmented Reality, social networking, and different research modes such as participatory research, action-based activities, etc. To research this process, an equally rich and diversified set tools and methods are needed.

It is impossible to draw a sharp line between the media and, for example, the social aspect, because these are closely intertwined. A participatory design process is heavily dependent on media since not all participants are design professionals, and will thus have a limited ability to visualize design suggestions. Even collaborations between professionals in product development are heavily dependent upon the use of media that ensures a common understanding. Capjon (2004) suggested the use of Rapid Prototyping models and other physical representations as especially well-suited to design for collaboration (Negotiotypes). From this perspective, while MRT only has a very limited and fragmented understanding of "media," here we are expanding the term to include all information-carrying elements, including physical spaces and human networks.

The Switching Effect in Hybrid Design Processes

The layered, media-rich and hybrid design processes open up space for strategizing how the different modes of the process are applied. The benefit of this is not so much found in making a process plan that applies each and every mode at the right time. Rather, the benefit is mostly found in triangulation between the different modes. Two or more processes dealing with the same issues will generate different contrasting or reinforcing outputs, helping to reach a deeper level of thoughtfulness. Interestingly, it is the switch between the modes in itself that seems to have especial powerful effect on the process.

The benefit from switching between different design processes, media, and modes becomes especially evident when one gets stuck. Any design process that deals with complexity will encounter substantial resistance One can get the feeling of being "lost in the woods" or "hitting the wall." However, there are certain tricks that can help us get unstuck. Changing the way we work will change the process and unavoidably accelerate the process into new directions. If you are stuck, change the way you work. If you work alone, change to co-design. If you are stuck in a group work, switch to working alone. If you are stuck at a specific level of detail, change to more detailed work or change to more large scale. If you work with manual tools, change to digital tools and vice versa. For example, the conscious staging of shifts between individual design periods and collaborative design in group work has an accelerating and reconfiguring effect. Switching between media, digital design, manual drawing, tape drawings, mock-ups, and prototypes, etc., has a similar accelerating and perspective-changing effect. I call this effect the "Switching Effect." It usually has a crucial influence on the design process.

When working with complexity, the hybrid design process helps to embrace the richness of the challenges. It helps one to investigate, unfold, and design for diverse aspects by shedding light on the problematique from many different angles. The hybrid design process is closely linked to design thinking and reflexive practice.

Very Rapid Learning Processes

Designers often find themselves in situations where they are designing for or with others who are more knowledgeable in the problematique of the project. Most, if not all, design projects involve some degree of learning. This learning is generally done on the fly in a non-systematized way, and accumulates on top of the tacit and explicit experience of the designer. This unstructured way of gaining knowledge is not sufficient when designing for very complex systemic change. The amount of information on the system itself can be overwhelming for the designer who needs to investigate and enrich their understanding of the system environment and the bigger landscape. Also, for most of these projects, we often work with people who have rich experience and expertise in one or several areas of the complex problem. It is crucial to understand both the depth and the limitations of the experts involved. We need to learn to understand enough, to engage the experts (users, inhabitants, stakeholders, agents, field-specific experts, etc.), and to create shared pictures to coordinate the understanding. Co-understanding and sharing a picture of the system create the precondition for understanding each other's viewpoints and for empathy. Empathy amongst the actors is essential to design systems that fulfil multiple stakeholder needs.

In addition, we need to get a fair hold on data and information that are essential to the field. This implies learning about multiple areas simultaneously and within a very short time span. It is possible to achieve this learning through the gigamapping techniques and the ZIP analysis suggested in SOD. This creates a type of knowledge that is superficial in details but holistic enough to grasp the whole. It also points out any weaknesses, blank spots, or limitations in the designer's knowledge. We call this learning process the Very Rapid Learning Process (VRLP).

VRLP enables us to become sufficiently informed so that we know how and when to depend on experts and what limitations our current positions and knowledge bases have. It also guides us to plan the involvement of others for sharing knowledge, judgement, and opinions. It is a technique for quickly achieving an information advantage while knowing enough about what we do not know. This means knowing enough to be humble about one's knowledge. The technique helps us in understanding the limitations of that knowledge. The realistic assertion of your knowledge status is realized because you can feel the boundaries and complexity of the project, and in turn, identify the details and domains that you do not know. You are continuously aware of the lack of complete information.

The methods that make VRLP possible are a designerly approach to learning, gigamapping, co-creation, building expert-networks, and other dialogue-based approaches, in addition to desktop research, field studies and action research. The mapping process has two interesting pedagogical functions. First, it makes things explicit, brings tacit and fragmented knowledge to the table, exposes the relations between such knowledge, and fills in the gaps. Second, while working with different versions of the maps, the redrawing and iteration processes allow the rich information to be internalized. Most people who have been through such processes report that they are able to reconstruct most of the map from memory. Drawing, redrawing, and redesigning are excellent ways for internalizing. It engages motoric and spatial memory. This is at the core of the Rapid Learning Process.

VRLP has been proven to work in many cases during the last years and its relevance has been confirmed by a long list of partners in SOD research.

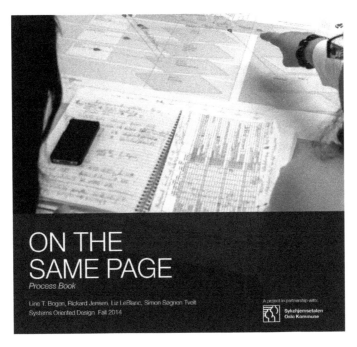

Figure 147: "On the Same Page" was a 2014 master studio project at the Oslo School of Architecture and Design in collaboration with and serving Sykehjemsetaten, the Directorate for Elderly Homes in Oslo. (Students: Line T. Bogen, Rickard Jensen, Liz LeBlanc, Simon Søgnen Tveit).

The before mentioned project "On the Same Page" is an example of a very rapid learning project (Bogen, Jensen, LeBlanc, & Tveit., 2014). This was a one-semester long project with a group of four graduate students in design at the Oslo School of Architecture and Design. It was a student project that became real out of the needs of the collaborating partner. The project was done with the Directorate of Elderly Care in the municipality of Oslo. After a period of rapid learning, the students suggested some early plans for a future change. The office responded by signalling that they would need immediate solutions that would help them with an ongoing change process. The project turned into a real-time process as the Directorate found itself in an urgent and large-scale re-organisation process that involved a large numbers of elderly homes. The project produced graphic and designerly tools for the Directorate to coordinate and communicate between a large number of personnel. Video documentation of planning meetings (not shown here because of confidentiality) provided evidence of the effect of the tools before and after their implementation.[78]

The Rich Design Space

As the gigamapping process unfolds, many generations of maps are created and the zoom maps, sketches, models, images, tables, statistics, sound files, video, and even the people and informants involved all become part of the growing tank of knowledge, experience, information, and data accumulated through rapid learning and the Hybrid Design Process. The information can be so vast and interconnected in so many ways that it is impossible to keep it all in play, or to sort and store it in a reasonable way with conventional approaches like storing and sharing on a computer. To overcome this, we have developed an old principle for collaborative knowledge handling into a new format: the Rich Design Space. This is nothing new, but for years, whenever large amounts of information needs to be shared for collective real-time control and action, it is common to use spaces dedicated specifically for that purpose. These might be control rooms for plants, or mission control rooms like the ones used for space missions (*Figure 148*).

Figure 148: The international Space Station Flight Control Centre (Photo by RadioFan 2016 Creative Commons).

---

78. To see the full process and project reports, go to:
http://systemsorienteddesign.net/index.php/projects/master-projects/aho-2014/on-the-same-page.

One early attempt to design a special space for collaboration and decision-making based on systems approaches is the Cybersyn control room designed by Gui Bonsiepe (*Figure 149*). The Cybersyn system was constructed at the request of the Allende government in Chile. Led by Stafford Beer, the British management professor and systems thinker known for his research in management cybernetics and operation, the Cybersyn room was relatively static and did not include facilities for co-design, but rather it catered for co-decision making. The Cybersyn system attempted to reach a new level of systemic management of a nation's production and resources. It was pre-internet, and communication was largely based on telefax. Unfortunately, the experiment was stopped by the coup. This level of government today seems utopic, but might be what is needed in the future of de-growth and stable ecology.

Figure 149: A unique design by Gui Bonsiepe--a control room for distributed decision-making based on systems thinking models (viable systems model, neural network theory and organisational cybernetics) introduced by Stafford Beer. The room was part of the Cybersyn system built in the Allende period in Chile to monitor and make decisions about the national economy (Image is public domain).

An early attempt of generating a visual space for complex design collaboration similar to a control room was made by prof Jan Capjon and Snorre Hjelseth at the University of Southeast Norway in 2010 (*Figure 150*). The attempt was successful in creating shared awareness of the design space for a large group of attendees.

But as with other such approaches, it was difficult for participants spontaneously to interact with the design material. The effort to pre-program the digital space reduced the usefulness. Unlike a space flight control centre, which is complicated but narrowly framed, a design space is complex and loosely framed. The very purpose of a Rich Design Space is to have the flexibility to integrate new information whenever needed. This flexibility is so far not easily achieved with digital spaces, and the operation of the spaces tends to be monopolized by a few operators. The use of shared digital co-mapping tools like Miro and Figma increased dramatically during Covid and they have shown to be useful and partly filling some of the features of the Rich Design Space.

Figure 150: The SIMSAM design collaborative simulator space at USN Bakkenteigen, Horten Norway. (Photo: Snorre Hjelseth)

The Rich Design Space brings together two ideas. The first one is the idea of the design space. The second is the idea of the richness imperative. The design space is a concept that is normally seen as relatively abstract. It is ambiguously conceptualized as the framing of the possible solutions for a particular design project or design in general (also called solution space) a view that might have stemmed from Zwicky's Morphological Analyses (Zwicky, 1969). In the Rich Design Space, we take this notion quite literally. It is an abstract space aimed at unfolding, mapping out, and constructing the space for possible solutions. Yet, this is done in a concrete space that serves as a huge living diagram.

The Rich Design Space is closely linked to the Hybrid Design Process. The Rich Design Space is where the Hybrid Process plays out. The development of the two concepts has also been interlinked. I first suggested the idea of a hybrid design space in 2004 (Sevaldson, 2004), and later elaborated on this in my doctoral thesis in 2005 (2005b), which was then further developed into two concepts the Rich Design Space and the Rich Design Research Space (2008).

I was partly inspired by Thomas Leerberg and his thesis on Embedded Spaces (2004). Dorta et al. have used the term hybrid to describe design tools, but they suggest a highly specialised set-up, both with respect to the technology and the use, which is limited to sketching (Dorta, Pérez, & Lesage, 2008). In contrast, the techniques that I suggest are easily applicable for all and have a more general application throughout the design process

The Rich Design Space is based on the media richness imperative. Use of the term Design Space was further developed by for example Giaccardi et. al. (2008), who use the term *multidimensional design space* to indicate a multitude of functionality.

Figure 151: A Rich Design Space. (Sofie A. Thomassen and Juan Alberto Soriano Valterra, 2017).

The Rich Design Space, as it is used here, designates the entire setting--spatial, technological, cultural, social, and media-wise--in which the design process takes place (*Figure 151*). This reaches beyond the original notion of the design space, being a space of possible solutions. Instead, the physical representation and richness of the Rich Design Space explicitly embrace the abstract space of possible solutions, but also include, for example, the notion of a social space for creativity, and a sense-making space for coping with large data and complexity. The theoretical inspiration comes from cognitive creativity research where the importance of the social environment is emphasized (Mayer, 1999) as well as from Gestalt psychology, perception theory, and visual thinking (Arnheim, 1969).

Actor Network Theory (ANT) propounds the idea that the "space" in which a research process takes place is of importance. It posits that social networks consist of both human and non-human actors. It maps relations that are material or semiotic, involving people and their ideas and technologies, which together constitute the whole network of relations (Latour, 2005). Certain notions regarding the Rich Design Space are also drawn from Activity Theory as it relates to the production of "tools" through interaction and learning-by-expansion (Engeström, 1999). The Rich Design Space could be seen as a tool for research by design. However, the understanding of "tools" here is more abstract and generative than in the work of Fjeld et. al. (2002) for example, where "tools" are looked upon quite literally. Therefore, the Rich Design Space is regarded here as a complex and manifold framework or environment, as well as an abstract space of possibilities that will enable an inclusive and complex process of inquiry.

The design process that is used to deal with very complex tasks needs to be holistic, detailed, intuitive, knowledge-driven, iterative, and tacit. It should deal with both quantitative and qualitative information. Regarding the nature of the complex design process, the most pressing question is how we can derive knowledge from, through, and by the design process without fragmenting it. Breaking a problem into smaller elements to enhance understanding can be most productive as long as the overview of the context and the interplay between those fragments are maintained. The Rich Design Space enables designers to move between holistic and fragmented approaches.

The Rich Design Space encourages reflexivity, generalisation, theory-building, and communication, as well as the externalisation of results. In the Rich Design Space, design investigations are combined with cycles of observation, fieldwork, information and data, interpretations, and reflection. Reflection aims at a holistic and intuitive synthesis. It alternates between the analysis of particular design actions and an understanding of how they are situated in a larger field. It shifts between post-rationalisation and conceptual forecasting. It feeds from practice and into practice. The different research activities, design, and reflection can be sequential or parallel. They can be interrelated in different ways, or they can be quite independent and feed into each other at certain points.

Figure 152: Rich Design Space in professional context. Halogen, Oslo Norway (Photo: Halogen)

The maintenance of several parallel layers or channels in the design process requires open planning, tolerance of ambiguity, and maintaining multiple models over long periods of time, thereby reducing the need for coordination (Boland & Collopy, 2004). Synthesis is often an individual process or one limited to a few people. For example, Gehri (ibid. 2004), as well as the artist Paul Kaiser (2004), who frequently worked with the choreographer, Merce Cunningham, have described how intense coordination of collaborations can result in a loss of intensity in a project. The need to reach a common ground for interpretation is growing as projects increase in complexity and the number of partners involved. The efforts put into coordination can dilute, delay, or even destroy a project. Therefore, easing the coordination load and making it more fluent and organic rather than based on hard planning and consensus is important. The Rich Design Space provides a means of generating a shared "image" that supports the sense sharing of the design and research process, as well as its goals and intentions. At the same time, it is also the working space for the process. There is no divide between the image of the project and the space for the project to unfold. The Rich Design Space allows uncoordinated threads to be maintained over longer periods. It lessens the energy put into coordination, and encourages individual interpretation by maintaining a common feel, ambiance, and image of the project that is more detailed, visual, and multi-sensory than would be the case if coordination is based on a formal agreement. Coordination is thus performed in synergy with designing. The social dynamics of the Rich Research Space allow the design process to move between large scale group work and small group or individual synthesis and decision-making (Sevaldson, 2008). It is beneficial to use the Rich Design Space consciously for this soft and visual coordination, as demonstrated in the action map in *Figure 153*.

Figure 153: An action map which served as a living Gigamap throughout an ongoing project. The purpose was to coordinate a large group of collaborators with very different backgrounds (Marie Davidova et. al., Environmental Summer Pavillion, 2015).

The Rich Design Space is an artefact that needs to be designed itself to make the designer more capable of coping with very complex and information-rich tasks. This implies that the design space is not only an abstract and potential solution space, but more interestingly, a process space. Andrea Botero et al. have similar ideas and also provide a comprehensive discussion on the theme of the design space (Botero, Kommonen, & Marttila, 2010).

With the Rich Design Space, we add a twist to the idea of the process space by making it into a concrete design artefact. It is made out of both the design media, the physical space (design office), the social space, the electronically networked space, and the cultural space or the creative environment. To cope with such levels of complexity, one needs a concrete representation, as well as techniques and methods to work with in a designerly way.

One important issue is the need to move information out of the computer since the screen has very limited resolution. The surface of a screen is far too small, and the information storage on the computer is organised hierarchically, which is less useful for systemic design projects. Using big physical representation and control room-like arrangements of information is crucial. These strategies enable an extended memory that keeps more information in play for a longer period of time. Think of the Rich Design Space as a dancing floor for your dance with complexity rather as a space to gain control. The Rich Design Space can be seen as a space for designing, for design inquiry, design research, and research by design. These two modes—designing and researching-- are, to an increasing degree, inseparable. Complex design projects tend to have a substantial research component. The relationship between research and design will be further discussed in the following section.

Figure 154: Analysing the Rich Design Space. Two views of the same Rich Design Space. In this case, the Rich Design Space is organized and ordered according to the type of information. (Photo: Henriette Sagvolden Marki, 2014).

The Creative Process Framework

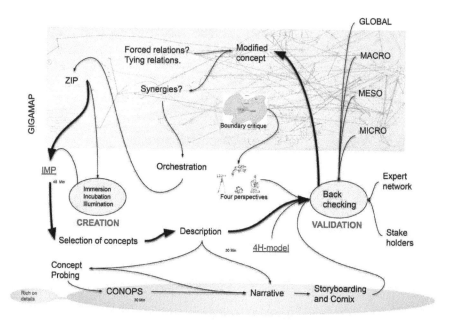

Figure 155: Diagram of the SOD creative process framework (Birger Sevaldson 2019)

Creative processes often live their own lives, and it is not possible to frame them into a methodology that guarantees a creative output. We will discuss the creative process and creativity later. Though the creative process cannot be reinforced or restrained in methods, it is still useful to have some tools that can trigger it. One such tool is the ZIP analyses generating the I-points (ideas, interventions and innovations). Though the ZIP analyses does not guarantee that good ideas are generated, it helps generating some ideas that can function as a platform for further work or as a potential plan B to fall back to if nothing better emerges. The IMP (Impact and Threshold) analyses help with deciding and discussing what a good idea is.

To guide the creative process with these and other tools such as scenarios, storyboards, and concept generation, we created the creative process framework (*Figure 155*). The process represents a loop so that all elements can be repeated as needed. A natural entry-point would be in the upper left corner starting with the ZIP analyses. However, one can apply the process at any level of a project, for example to galvanize and develop existing concepts.

As discussed earlier, ideas emerge at any moment in the design process and have an important role even early in the process. It is recommended to run through the creative process framework at several points, and to do it repeatedly and if possible as a discussion with partners and stakeholders.

Research by Design: The Role of Designing in Understanding Super-Complexity

Recalling the central elements of SOD, including the Very Rapid Learning Process, the Rich Design Space, the interdisciplinary dialogic, as well as reaching into new and unknown realms, we are forced to look at research as an integrated component of SOD. We will look at this from an angle of practice research and research through design dominantly. Therefore, it makes sense to discuss research and knowledge production here in Part Three in the context of the SOD frameworks, rather than in the theory and methodology of Part Two.

The term "research" in design processes is often used as gathering existing knowledge, as in design inquiry. More important, however, is generating new knowledge by putting forward new questions, provoking and testing the system at hand through prototypes and probes, transgressing limitations of the current process, and creating generalization as visions of possible futures. Research by design (research through design) is central in SOD. Therefore, we need to dive a bit deeper into the nature of research by design in relation to SOD.

Design practice as a knowledge-producing activity and its relation to research has been discussed at length (Cross, 1999, 2007b; Dorst, 2008; Friedman, 2003; Owen, 1998; Rust, Mottram, & Till, 2007; Scrivener, 1999; Sevaldson, 2010, 1996, 1999b, 2000b). Though debated and criticized, research by or through design is by an increasing number of authors regarded as the main approach to developing this discussion further. Research by design is seen as new knowledge production within design practice that is documented, scrutinized, and communicated to make it accessible for others. This can take place in any design practice, but the most efficient are those that are rigged for this specific purpose, like design teaching studios with external partners, special experimental practices, or design R&D projects organized though official financing bodies and with close business or organisation collaboration.

Typical of these research by design projects is their closeness to practice. They involve practitioner research, which means that the researcher is normally an insider or a practitioner researcher. Being inside the design process as a reflective practitioner (Schön, 1982) is a unique mode of knowledge production. First, we need to state the type of knowledge that is produced from this position. It is not a descriptive knowledge such as those generated in ethnographies or participant observations. Instead, it is a generative knowledge more closely related to Action Research because it is about change rather than about reading a set situation. However, it goes beyond Action Research because of its generative design intention. It is genuine generative design knowledge that is case-specific, but also has dimensions that can be generalized.

Imaginative Investigations

The design inquiry lies in between the ethnographic, technological, and societal investigations found in other fields, and the purely generative creative work. This middle-ground between those different fields we call Imaginative investigations. Design inquiry is both investigating aspects of the world, yet imagining how these aspects might be changed or how totally new aspects might be introduced, imagining a suggested future.

Through the creation of visual visions, one is able to imagine new types of solutions and create, as well as share, a new mental step for development of hitherto unimagined design solutions. Words fall short in this context because it is not only a question of what is proposed, but also the qualitative aspects, how it is done, and how it is given shape. In the car industry, such imaginative investigations are expressed through the genre of concept cars. A new trend in car design is only imagined through designed examples, but more than that, it is created by early examples that lead the development. Design in new fields is unimaginable before somebody is able to demonstrate not only by words, but through visual visions what role the new design could play, what impact it could have, and what practice this new design might involve. One can debate whether a new type of car design is a type of knowledge or merely a cultural expression. However, in the Ulstein Bridge Vision project discussed earlier in Part Two, the knowledge aspect becomes clearer (Romm, 2010). The project produced visions for the ship bridge of the future. One of its many outcomes was a design of a future ship bridge presented as working demonstrators and a virtual concept design in the form of a video that presented the vision in context. The configuration of ship bridges has developed over many years based on traditions, technical development, research of technologies and human factors, as well as research into safety issues. The design of ship bridges has evolved into a complex knowledge field that involves several different experts with their own respective research approaches and methodologies. These might span from human factors to electronics, safety protocols and regulations. The bridge vision contributed to this knowledge field in a radical way since it opened up and redefined what the configuration of the bridge could be. The video was crucial for the board of the Ulstein Group to make strategic decisions for further development resulting in a (for our context) large design research project financed by the Norwegian

Research Council. This decision could not have been made without the vision of what was possible. The vision opened up the field of ship bridge design to uncover its potential.

Figure 156: The Ulstein Bridge Vision video showing the ship bridge of the future. It sets a new scope to the knowledge field of ship bridge design. (Ulstein Group, 2011).

Furthermore, the project enabled the development of a proposal for Ulstein's new strategic innovation process. This involved workshops with staff, captains, and constructors, and a gigamapping analysis of the existing innovation procedures of Ulstein. This demonstrates that the vision was based on many layers and types of knowledge and design drafts. It was also based on understanding the innovation process as a system of its own. Basing design visions on this type of complex knowledge is important for their potential to be successfully realized. The vision was informed by and dependent on this co-created complex backdrop of knowledge.

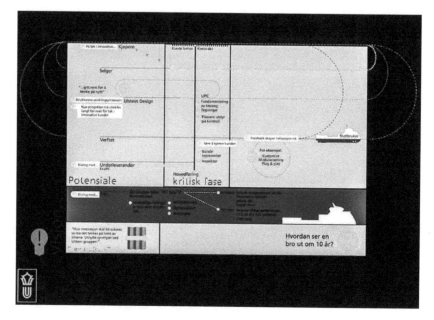

Figure 157: Developed diagram derived from the gigamapping workshop held with three leaders from different departments of the Ulstein Group. (AHO / Ulstein Group, 2011).

Figure 158: Workshop at the Ulstein shipyards for information exchange and co-creation of visions for the ship bridge of the future. (AHO / Ulstein Group, 2011).

The Ulstein Bridge Vision project resulted in a vision of how the ship bridge would be designed if some restraining systemic conditions were solved. Ship bridges were typically composed out of subsystems sourced from a wide range of suppliers each with their own IT system and interface. This fragmented approach resulted in ship bridges that were cluttered and difficult to use. In addition, safety regulations demanded redundancy and imposed requirements that only improved safety in isolation, and lacked any cohesive coordination. One obvious example was the number of competing alarm systems on the bridge. These fragmented designs created unintuitive and ultimately dangerous working environments. For example: The many competing alarms lead to them being ignored or turned off as reported from ship bridge users. The Ulstein Bridge Vision project opened up this problem for discussion on a systemic level, engaging safety authorities to begin exploring how the ship bridge can be better integrated between the many sub-systems.

Another example of the knowledge produced and derived from designing and research by design is from the graduate thesis on sexual violence described in the introduction to this book. When the graduate students first began work with the Sexual Assault Centre (SAC) at the Legevakten Emergency Hospital in Oslo, nobody (professors and students alike) could have imagined the role they could play. It was unfathomable at the inception of the project that the Gigamap of the process at SAC would be immediately adopted by the employees as a tool for dialogue with patients. It was an unimaginable product to both the designers and clients, and would never have been included in the brief of a traditional design project. It was design as a door and eye opener, giving the client a product they did not know they needed, because it was beyond the horizon of their vision.

It also suggests generalizable knowledge. This does not mean that the exact same approach or method can be transformed to other cases. The generalisability of design research is on a higher level. It is the principles, (in this case the principle of an information map of a treatment process *Figure 159*), that can be generalised. It indicates that this type of visualization can be useful in other similar organisations and situations. Further research and development in this realm can be anticipated, and the full outcome yet to be seen. When this is properly documented, analysed, reflected upon, and if suitable, transcribed into generalizable conclusions, or described as unique case studies, it can be seen as research by design achieving its highest potential. None of the knowledge or concepts could have been reached by any other method.

The main purpose of research by design is to imagine things that are yet to exist through concrete design visions based on thorough research and development, co-creation, and systems analysis. This contributes to our knowledge of how to develop human culture.

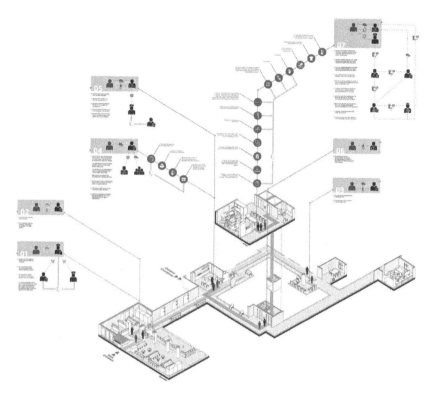

Figure 159: Gigamap of the patient journey at SAC, Oslo (Aguirre and Strømsnes, 2012).

The Vision Horizon

Design visions that are based on technical, social, societal, cultural, economic, ecologic, and other issues; that are analysed and staged in systemic models and contexts; and that are demonstrated and envisioned through storytelling, scenarios, and design visualizations help expand the imagination of what is possible. Being able to set the frame of this space of operation and expand the realm of possibility in terms of how it might be improved, how it can look and feel, and how solutions can be implemented is a core benefit of research by design. We call this aspect of research by design "Vision Horizon". Expanding the Vision Horizon is expanding a type of knowledge. It is not descriptive, deductive, or accurately repetitive knowledge, it is generative knowledge that designers, clients, technologists, politicians, and others can relate to and build upon.

SOD in Design Research

It is beneficial to use the SOD methods in design research. This is obvious given the convergence of design and research, the nature of design research as complex and composed of many perspectives, and that practice-based research in design can be seen as a system of knowledge production. The issues we will discuss here are focussed on research practice rather than theory and methods. The application of SOD as research practice might be equally applicable and useful in projects that are not defined as research per se.

Gigamapping helps us unfold and map out complex relations in research settings, such as the research activities at the institute of design at AHO (*Figure 160*). This exercise helped to get an overview of the overlaps between researchers and themes researched at the institute. It also unravelled white spots, issues, and disciplines where the institute was weak and that should be discussed for further development. The purpose was also improving the communication between the researchers and building a knowledge ecology.

Looking at knowledge production from a systems perspective, as a knowledge ecology, rather than detached and fragmented, is very useful.

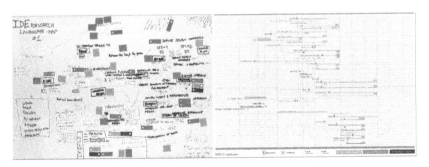

Figure 160: Understanding the design research process at the Institute of Design at the Oslo School of Architecture as a system of knowledge production and as a dynamic process that unfolds over time. To the left, the initial Gigamap with colour coding of projects according to subjects and fields. To the right, a Gantt timeline showing the temporal overlap of the projects (Sevaldson et. Al. 2013).

The SOD approaches can also be used in research projects on a more detailed level. Several examples of how this is done are outlined below.

Gigamapping is very useful to map out the field and literature of a research project. This helps with understanding the different authors as actors in a bigger knowledge production ecology or system (*Figure 161*). In this example, literature in a project overlapping several different disciplines was mapped out and related in a organised map. This helps to remember and relate different authors, to see them in the context of others, and to more easily memorize them. It also helps to plan the reading process and to prioritize.

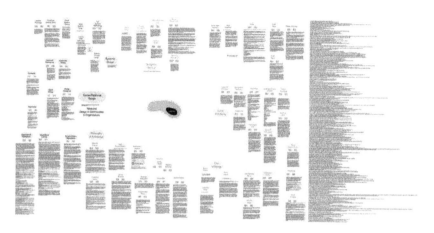

Figure 161: Mapping out a field of references and literature to position a PhD project in the larger context of knowledge production (Manuela Aguirre, 2017).

Another use of the SOD methodologies in design research is when large amounts of data need to be cross-referenced (*Figure 162*) as in this example where a large number of actors were cross referenced.

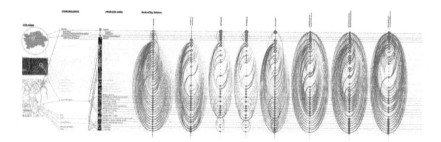

Figure 162: Interrelation of human and non-human actors, actions, and environment in a multi-faceted experimental design research project for a better integration of ecological innovation in an urban setting (Colridor, Marie Davidova, e.al. 2017).

The Rich Research Space

In the following section, we will discuss the *Rich Design Space* as an inclusive methodological framework and scaffold for research by design: *The Rich Research Space*. This constitutes the research component of the Rich Design Space, relating the issues of richness in design processes and design-led research. The two modes of designing and researching are in reality hard to distinguish due to convergence (as previously mentioned). Many aspects of the Rich Research Space are shared with the Rich Design Space.

The biggest potential of the Rich Research Space is to be able to systematically integrate design practice with the research process. The concept of the Rich Research Space as research by design is put forward here as a means for facilitating inclusive, practice-led research into design practices. The concept seeks to include, absorb, visualise, contextualize, process, and reflect on a large number of elements (formal, spatial, social, economic, ecological and technological) through the use of design. The means of design include manifold media representations.

The concept of the Rich Research Space is based on the following:

- The convergence between advanced design processes and research by design that is currently found in the academic realm of design universities, and in innovation and research-oriented design practices.

- The position that the complex design task demands an equally rich and non-reductive design process. To develop and understand such a process, we need an equally complex model for research by design.

- Complex models require increased attention on the research space to describe the total technological, virtual, physical, and social space in which research by design unfolds.

The Rich Research Space embraces and reflects the complexity of the task. It expands itself to the real sites and engages stakeholders, as well as users. It involves field actions, embraces and embeds design practice into research, and delves into design practice. It helps to bridge the gap between practice and theory. Although the Rich Research Space includes descriptive and explorative modes of knowledge production, its main end is a generative mode of research. It is designed for the invention, documentation, and dissemination of new design responses to very complex problems. This dynamic Rich Research Space enables the switching between research modes between exploration, reflection, generative work, description, prototyping, and action.

While the singular elements of the Rich Research Space are well known, what is new here is the more advanced and conscious interlinking of these elements. The different perspectives, research modes, and practices are linked together in two ways:

1. Through the triangulation of design and research data.

2. Through critical and reflexive discourse, activating feedback loops between research, reflection and practice.

The following images show parts of the Rich Research Space of Manuela Aguirre, one of the SOD PhDs (*Figure 163 - Figure 166*):

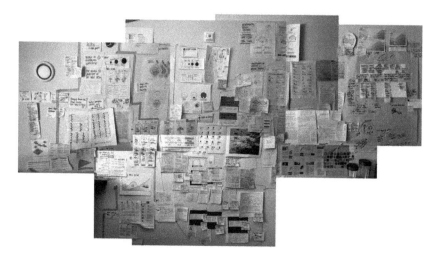

Figure 163: Rich Research Space of Manuela Aguirre. Mapping out and relating the research field, research questions and concepts. (Photo: Manuella Aguirre)

Figure 164: Rich Research Space of Manuela Aguirre. Handling big amounts of data. (Photo: Manuella Aguirre)

Figure 165: Rich Research Space of Manuela Aguirre. Understanding history and canon literature of the overlapping fields involved in the study. (Photo: Manuella Aguirre)

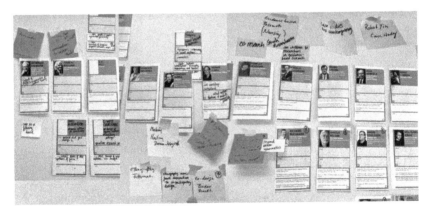

Figure 166: Rich Research Space of Manuela Aguirre. Mapping out and contextualising the central authors in the study. (Photo: Manuella Aguirre)

Praxeology of SOD

In this section we will describe the application of the SOD tools and frameworks.

Design praxeology is the study of the nature, manifestation, and instruments of design in practice (Horvath, 2001). However, it has older roots which we only will mention here like Clemens Timpler in his *Philosophiae practicae systema methodicum,* 1608, and Louis Bourdeau in *Théorie des sciences: Plan de Science intégrale* in 1882

Praxeology is, in short, the study of the practices and processes of a practice, in our case SOD. This implies that praxeology goes beyond methodology. Praxeology is tightly connected to action. It is the study of how to act in the world. The distinction between methodology and praxeology is not a sharp line. In the case of SOD, the limits are especially blurred since SOD methodology only suggests "soft" methods that are to be modified and adapted to practical situations. Hence, the soft methods work as guidelines in praxeology.

I distinguish praxeology from methodology and methods in the following way: A method is a prescription of how to do a thing. Methodology is the study of methods. Praxeology is the study of how methods are applied in practice or in a wider sense all aspects of practice, from properly described methods to tacit and internalised knowledge as well as bodily skills, etc. It therefore adds to, and extends beyond, methods. Gasparski, one of the key figures of praxeology research, describes it this way:

> The understanding of action endeavours to explain the relationship between domains that the mind naturally separates, such as knowledge, science, philosophy, religious beliefs, ethics, justice, and even play or aesthetics (Alexandre & Gasparski, 2000).

We could add to this the rich and most often overlooked repertoire of competencies, skills, tricks, shortcuts, and rules of thumb that are inherent in all practice, and moreover, the design imagination, visualization, and synthesis, and the skilled practitioner's expert intuition for responding to a situation of thrownness (Weick, 2004) and muddling through (Lindblom, 1959). These central elements of design practice are not properly described in methodological terms.

The term praxeology refers to practice, experience, and tacit knowledge that are externalised and systematized in a tool chest or library. It is not prescriptive, but suggestive. It is offered, rather than prescribed. Compared to a methodology, it is not describing procedures that are repeatable. Instead, it describes heuristics, experiences, and problematiques in the practice. Though this term is not widespread, it has been used in that sense by several writers in design (Cross, 1999, 2007a; Gasparski, 1979; Kotarbinski, 2013).

Kotarbinski, the founder of the Polish strand of praxeology, regards it as the science of efficient action (Kotarbinski, 2013). In design discourse, Nigel Cross uses the term praxeology in several places (Cross, 1999, 2007a). Gasparski connects it to a systemic approach to design studies (1979), and describes many of the aspects relevant to SOD.

In this section, we will go through some collected experiences of practising SOD. How can we act purposefully when unfolding a design process, following the general intentions and goals that underlie SOD?

Free-Styling and Untamed Processes

In SOD, we do not prescribe any strict convention when it comes to systems models or system analyses. On the contrary, we encourage a designerly approach that allows for "free-styling" when visualizing and analysing systems. The methodology of SOD is intentionally vague. This vagueness comes from the need to maintain an openness towards bespoke design processes. Every project needs an adjusted variation of the design process. Prescriptions and orthodoxies do not work because they remove the crucial element of sound judgement and sense-making.

The Start Problem

Figure 167: The start problem confronts the designer with a "catch 22." You cannot know the best way to explore an unknown territory if you have not explored it fully. Therefore, the question of how and where to start is of less importance. Grasp a thread and start to unwind and explore from this random position (Illustration by Elisabeth B. Skjelten, 2014).

A common issue when working with complex systems is how and where to start. We will argue that this is not a big problem as long as one allows an explorative and generative approach instead of a pre-planned and deterministic process. Learning to know a complex system by exploring it can be done form any starting point. The start problem exists because there is a lack of an overview over the systems involved in the task ahead. These are the systems we design within and for (Lurås, 2016). Without an overview, you would not know what route to take to start. This problem is more pressing in more innovative projects, or when involving new clients, but it is apparent with any project.

Most design projects will have a learning dimension and an element of exploration. Radically new design fields are like exploring unknown terrain. This involves a "catch 22" situation. One does not know how to explore such terrain in the best way before one has an overview of the terrain. In such situations, it is less important how to start the exploration. One has to start with a thread or detail, and investigate from there as a starting point of the exploration.

After receiving and agreeing on a project, all assumptions should be parked on the side lines for a while. One should be aware that this first phase is a unique learning situation. The start should be uncluttered with preconceptions and ideas. Preconceptions work as strong filters, and prevent you from seeing certain aspects. This becomes another "catch 22." You do not know what is relevant for the project before you know what the project is going to be, and you do not know what the project is going to be before you have learned what is relevant (a wicked problem). It is important to perceive this starting phase as a "naïve," and totally open, exploration.

Externalizing and Activating Pre-Existing Knowledge: Making Tacit Knowledge Explicit

The value of starting with mapping before anything else is that it teases out the pre-existing knowledge of the designer and the team. Even if this is done individually, the result is that pre-existing knowledge is externalized. When working with a group, the common account of knowledge in the group is activated and shared. This helps to trigger the true potential of the group, allowing members to become aware of each other's resources, specialities, and expertise. It also allows them to see what resources and expertise are lacking in the group, so that they can quickly get aligned and share the same picture. This way of starting is as much about building the system we design within as generating and sharing valuable knowledge.

The initial work starts with mapping what we know. We tend to know more than we think, and this "sleeping" knowledge is activated through mapping. In addition, this knowledge is characterized by being a mixture of facts, speculations, and assumptions. We should rate and mark the quality of our knowledge while mapping. Only after an initial mapping, research and inquiry is started in a guided form.

The example below shows the areas that need to be researched in a design process for an electrical car. The diagram does not show the necessary research itself, but it shows the themes that need to be researched. The quality of this map is that it immediately gives an overview of the extent of the task, which then makes it easier to plan the research phase in a more realistic manner and also ensures that the needed knowledge level is achieved as quickly as possible. It also helps to sort and prioritize the research into the areas that need to be researched in depth and those where one can rely more on experts.

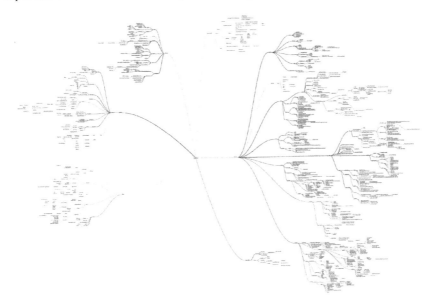

Figure 168: Research mapping; the Gigamap shows the mapping of the needed research areas to design an electric car. The map shows all the market-related, cultural, and user-related inputs to the left, and the technological requirements to the right, forming a double mind map with two focal centres. The map was first developed with the software MindMap and later refined in Illustrator (Students: Thor Henrik Bruun and Fredrik Bostad, 2010).

Knowing What You Don't Know

The initial mapping helps to single out items, issues, and fields where there is missing knowledge. These white spots on the map can contribute to building one's expert network, or be a guide for identifying the issues that need more research and study. Knowledge of these gaps and resources within a group is as important as triggering its resources. The ZIP analysis is a good tool for finding these white spots. The Z (Zoom) points are dedicated to marking missing information.

Building Expert Networks

An expert is any individual who has formal or informal insight, experience, and knowledge about any issue that is directly or indirectly relevant to the project or an individual who has insight on the effects of a system change, having been influenced and exposed to it directly or indirectly. The role of the expert can fall on stakeholders, citizens, refugees, statisticians, social workers, economists, material experts, scholars, and laymen, etc. The idea of the expert network is to bring these actors together to create a dialogue across widely different positions and worldviews.

A systemic design project most likely always revolves around teamwork involving a range of experts. These span from subject experts to users, inhabitants, and practitioners. Note that anybody involved or influenced by the project is regarded as an expert on a similar level as domain experts who are brought in on basis of their earlier experience with similar cases. The systemic designer must design the team so that it fits the process, to cover important fields, but also as a social network well-trimmed to work together and share perspectives.

The white spots on the map mentioned above are very helpful when composing an expert team. The mapping out of the resources and lack of resources in a group are excellent guides to what kinds of experts are needed. Each project demands a particular composition of expertise. The network will most often change during the project period.

Again, the Gigamap plays a central role in facilitating the dialogue among the experts, and also between the experts and the designers. The Gigamapping process bridges fragmented conversations, and helps people stay on track, even when the conversations jump between the experts. Ideally, a collaborative process is preferred over one-on-one connections with the different experts. A process where the different experts sit around the same table will more likely tease out the "unknown unknowns," new questions and perspectives that were not foreseen. However, both modes can be beneficial. A one-on-one conversation with informants can be more guided and targeted. One can also group the experts according to fields to achieve a more specialized uncovering of information.

Acting as a Representative

A representative is an individual who acts on behalf of other individuals (human or non-human), or any systemic entity that is unable to have a voice (for any reason). Typically, a representative would act on behalf of mentally disabled patients, children, future generations, non-human beings, and general perspectives like nature at large, sustainability, democracy, neighbourhood interests, minorities, social fairness, or fair trade.

Representatives seek to represent individuals, organisations, or societies that do not have direct representation in the expert network. The systems-oriented designer should carefully reflect upon what agency is needed in the project. Representatives are experts in their own right, and are a natural part of the expert network.

Shared Pictures and Interdisciplinary Teamwork

While the expert network is built as a social system, one is faced with the challenge of how to bring the experts up-to-date on the project, how to find a common level of understanding, and how to bring them into the mode of transdisciplinarity that is established in the group. This is most efficiently done through visual dialogue with the Gigamap as a discussion object. When initiating experts into the design process, it is vital to share the mapping with them, and to get their input and comments. Further on, one might want to involve them in the continuous mapping processes. Experts are typically introduced to the project at different stages. Some, like users, are included in the group at an early stage and would be a regular part of a reference group for a project throughout its lifecycle. Others, like specialists in particular fields, would eventually be included at a later stage, or in shorter periods.

Figure 169: Different experts having a discussion over a shared visualization. (Photo: Birger Sevaldson)

Being on the Same Page

A SOD process will most likely contain elements of participation. The expert network is not only an information source, but also a source for resolutions and visions. Keep in mind that experts are anybody influenced or engaged by the project. An inhabitant influenced by an urban development is an expert on their own life situation and the nearest neighbourhood. Remember the symmetry of ignorance mentioned earlier.

One of the biggest challenges in participatory design is being able to create a reasonable level of clarity in the shared picture of the complex case at hand. Even in relatively simple collaborative tasks, individuals start with fairly disparate perspectives and preconceptions of the situation. Individuals in the expert network come from highly fragmented and separated starting points. This expands to assumptions of what the others see. This is also the case within groups that have been working together for long periods of time. Typically, we uncover divides in perspectives within leader groups that are seemingly very coordinated. When they start to map out the complexity of their own operation, the differences emerge. Gigamapping processes bring people together onto a more similar page within a reasonably short amount of time.

Figure 170: Team members of the TPG consultancy mapping out their own project process. Slightly different perspectives were aligned, and innovation potentials found in the mapping (Photo: Birger Sevaldson)

Sensemaking and Sense-Sharing

Gigamapping is partly about facts, information, and data, but more centrally, it is about sensemaking and acting from that. This means making sense of a field, a system, a situation, problematiques, relations, etc. and to generate a new state of that field, system, or problematique. Sensemaking is described along a variety of domains. Russel et al relates sensemaking to systems engineering (Russell, Stefik, Pirolli, & Card, 1993). Weick and others relate sensemaking to organisations (Weick, 1995; Weick, Sutcliffe, & Obstfeld, 2005). Meanwhile, Lurås and Aaltonen et al. relate sensemaking to systemics and complexity (Lurås, 2012; Aaltonen, Barth, Casti, Mitleton-Kelly, & Sanders, 2005). In this context, these sources are of less importance than the designerly sensibility and skills that have been inherently and tacitly present in the practice of design from the very beginning of the discipline rooted in the arts and craftsmanship. I argue that sensemaking has been central in design for a long time, even before it was defined and described by Weick and others. Making sense of things through visualization, narratives, and solving needs, problems, and providing experiences have been at the core of design. Design is unthinkable without this component of reasoning.

Kolko describes sensemaking as an inherent part of design synthesis (Kolko, 2010). He also describes how mapping might be central in sensemaking:

> Because of the complexity of comprehending so much data at once, the designer will frequently turn to a large sheet of paper and a blank wall in order to "map it all out." Several hours later, the sheet of paper will be covered with what to a newcomer appears to be a mess—yet the designer has made substantial progress, and the mess actually represents the deep and meaningful sensemaking that drives innovation (p. 16).

Klein and Moon relate sensemaking to a systemic perspective by describing sensemaking as oriented towards understanding relations, but also related to other aspects that are naturally present in the design process:

> By sensemaking, modern researchers seem to mean something different from creativity, comprehension, curiosity, mental modeling, explanation, or situational awareness, although all these factors or phenomena can be involved in or related to sensemaking. Sensemaking is a motivated, continuous effort to understand connections (which can be among people, places, and events) in order to anticipate their trajectories and act effectively (Klein & Moon, 2006).

The Sense-Sharing Model

The sense-sharing model obviously builds on a common notion of sensibility training that is implicitly central in design education. The sense-sharing model is a perspective that describes the shared sensitivities mentioned above. Weick has described sensmaking as a social activity. The proposed sense-sharing model takes this further into some specific issues regarding systemic design and working together on very complex problematiques. The challenges and frustration of working in teams has been proposed to be solved as Team-sensemaking by, for example, Ashmos and Nathan (2002). Referring to the principles of sensemaking described by Weick, they suggest the application of these principles on teams. We will go down an alternative route originating from visual thinking and visual sense making based on the visual dialogue of gigamapping.

Co-designers can share as much information as they want, co-design the Gigamap, and create a shared picture, but they can still have a critically different view on the issue. Total synchronization of internalized and constructed imaginations of complex systems is obviously impossible. We can live with some of these ruptures as long as the mutual understanding and respect is in place. However, others need to be dealt with because they could seriously derail a project. Typically, such disruptive discrepancies are not so much in the details, but more so in the whole picture. Therefore, the attention has to move from information fragments to holistic pictures.

Since the start of the research with Gigamaps, it was clear that there was more to it than the facts only. This has led to a long process of developing insights about this form of mapping. This has developed through two steps of concept development. The first step was the realization and clarification of the Gigamap as a design artefact. This had implications on how the mapping process was seen, and on the relation between the map and the reality that it first depicts, and later redesigns. This realization solved some of the qualitative questions that mapping raised. Nevertheless, there were still more tacit issues or questions tied to it. Intuitively, I was drawn towards certain types of maps that depicted richness and depth at the cost of clarity (*Figure 171*).

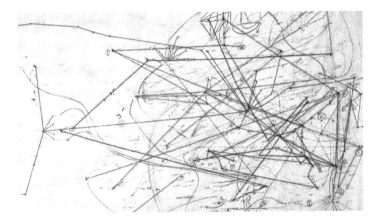

Figure 171: Richness and depth at the cost of clarity. Such maps were intuitively attractive, but what they depicted and emphasised were not immediately clear. (See also Figure 2).
(Photo: Birger Sevaldson)

By studying exemplars of such maps, the realization emerged that what these maps mainly communicated and shared were soft and qualitative relations that were very important and central to bridging ruptures. Instead of dominantly communicating information, these maps communicated and depicted a sense of the qualitative features of the system. These features are the components of the sense-sharing model.[79]

---

79. I relate this theoretically to Zwicky's Morphological Analyses (MA) but a designerly, less ordered, version based on design work. This has some disadvantages compared to MA, but also some advantages, though this discussion would exceed the frames of this section (Ritchey, 1998).

These were defined to include the following features:

- Sense of the field

- Sense of Gestalt

- Sense of degree of complexity

- Sense of timing and dynamics

- Sense of needed effort

- Sense of resistance

In the Following We Will Go Through All of Them Shortly.

Sense of field

This sense-sharing feature generates a shared sense of the field, the environment, and landscape, in which the client organisation or the project is situated. How extensive is it? How solid or blurry are its boundaries? Is it solid and mature or emerging? How enclosed or fragmented is the field? How diverse is it? Failing to share this sense of the field can result in fragmented project work.

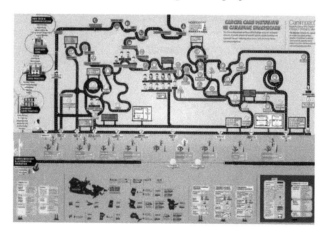

Figure 172: A map that gives a good impression of the field, in this case the cancer care in Canadian Health Care, depicted by patient pathways through the system. (Synthesis map from CanIMPACT research program, © 2016 With permission from Peter Jones, Smriti Shakdher, and Prateeksha Singh).

334

Sense of Gestalt

This sense-sharing feature generates a shared sense of the main figure of the system at hand. Is there a clear head? Is it a top down or bottom-up organisation? Is it old and grown over time? Is it worn and fragile? What shape depicts it best? Failing to share this sense of Gestalt might result in hidden ruptures in the process.

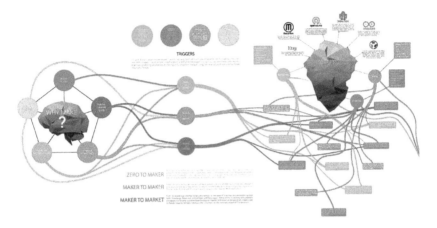

Figure 173: A Gigamap showing a characteristic shape or Gestalt of a system. There is a clear division into two main parts and the connections between them goes through three "hubs" (The Makers: Exploring Ahmedabad as Makerspace, Project guides Praveen Nahar, Mahaan Ghose, with Sahil Thappa, Swapnil Vibhute, Tanisha Vernekar, NID, 2013).

Sense of Degree of Complexity

This sense-sharing feature generates a shared sense of how complex the challenges ahead are. If the team has widely differing views on how challenging the task is, then there is a serious rupture. It is not necessary to understand the system in all its details in order to generate a sense of degree of complexity. Failing to share a sense of the degree of complexity can result in project breakdown when the complexity unfolds as a surprise for some of the participants, even if others are already prepared.

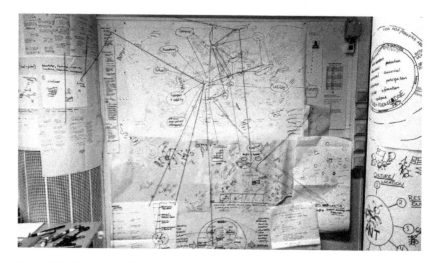

Figure 174: The result of a three-day workshop let the participants develop and share a sense of the complexity of the problem field. In this case, the complexity of embedding social housing in the campus of the Chalmers University, Gothenburg (Chalmers Architecture SOD workshop, 2015).

Sense of Timing and Dynamics

This sense-sharing feature generates a shared sense of how dynamic the system is. Is it changing quickly or slowly? Is it able to absorb change within a reasonable span of time or will change take a longer time? What parts of the system are moving slowly and what parts are changing fast? How is the timing for suggested interventions? Failing to share the sense of the dynamics of a system can result in serious ruptures, as well as desynchronized and erroneous planning. It can make keeping deadlines impossible.

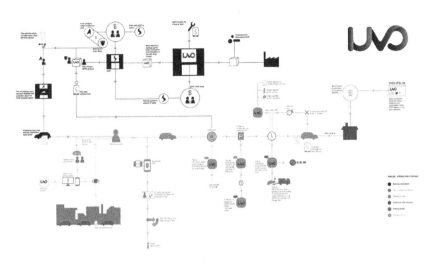

Figure 175: Sharing a sense of sequencing and timing is important in interaction design for example (Suzanne Solås, Helene Falstad, Tord Stenstavold, Raoul Ronald Antoni in colaboraiton with SALTO, AHO, 2017).

Sense of Required Effort

This sense-sharing feature generates a shared sense of the effort needed to successfully implement a suggested systemic design intervention. Is it expensive? Are there technical difficulties? Each actor needs to understand the effort needed particularly by them, but also the shared effort needed to succeed with the project. Failing to share this sense leads to serious implementation problems. Such failures are too normal in fields like IT, for example.

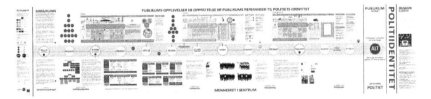

Figure 176: This map shows an analysis of the identity of Norwegian police. This is built up ideals, actions, and communication. Changing identity would require effort in many different places that typically can be seen differently by the various stakeholders in a project (Bente Moen, HIOA, 2014).

Sense of Resistance

This sense-sharing feature generates a shared sense of the inherent resistance to change that affects the systemic design intervention. Resistance can be found on all levels of the system, its environment, the landscape it lives in, and globally. Resistance to change is natural regarding the uncertainty it creates, and that the power balance and benefits might be changed. Creating acceptance of resistance, understanding the objective reasons for it and to co-design resolutions of the contradictions is important. Failing to share a sense of resistance can cause unforeseen delays and eventually stop a project.

Weight of characteristics			Criteria Analysis	Scale	Autonomous Underwater Vehicles	Augmented Reality Overlay	Holographic Alarm System	Sensory Stimulation	VR Robotic Arms	Security Drones
1.1	10 %	SYSTEMIC IMPACT	Radius of ripple effects	6 - big-radius / 1 - small-radius	2	5	5	4	6	3
1.2	10 %		Short term	6 - effective / 1 - ineffective	3	5	5	4	5	5
1.3	15 %		Long term	6 - effective / 1 - ineffective	4	6	6	3	5	4
1.4	10 %		Platform effect	6 - higher / 1 - lower	4	5	6	3	6	3
2.1	15 %	THRESHHOLDS	Economic	6 - low-cost / 1 - high-cost	2	4	1	4	2	4
2.2	10 %		Technological	6 - low-step / 1 - high-step	5	3	1	6	2	3
2.3	10 %		Cultural	6 - low-step / 1 - high-step	6	4	2	5	4	3
2.4	10 %		Organizational	6 - low-step / 1 - high-step	4	4	3	5	4	3
3.	5 %		SYNERGIES	6 - high-impact / 1 - low-impact	3	6	6	3	6	3
4.	5 %		RESILIENCE	6 - higher / 1 - lower	5	4	3	5	4	2
Total of max 100 %					61,7 %	76,7 %	61,7 %	69,2 %	70,8 %	57,5 %
(1.1*10% + 1.2*10% + 1.3*15% + 1.4*10% + 2.1*15% + 2.2*10% + 2.3*10% + 2.4*10% + 3.*5% + 4.*5%) * 16,67%										

Figure 177: The Impact and Threshold Analysis (see page 281) reveals obstacles and needs for resources to realize a project. (NTNU Ålesund 2018)

Action

It is not enough to get the needed knowledge about a system through observation, experts, and data alone. Sometimes we need to "poke" the system to see how it would react to provocations. Acting within the system will reveal how it reacts to our activities. This will give us information on the resilience of a system and different thresholds. How willing is a company to invest in change? These could be both cultural and economic thresholds.

On the other hand, we need to be aware that even observing a system has its effects as an action and provocation of the system. This becomes obvious when we observe small organisations in particular. For example, in a department of an elderly home with a handful of employees, the pure presence of observers would change how people work (*Figure 178*).

Figure 178: Observing a system also changes it. This is most true in the case of a SOD process that includes deep involvement on site and processes of co-creation (From "My Last Home" by Åsne Kydland, Marit Støylen and Emilie Strømmen Olsen, 2012).

Design Action and Action-Design

The dominating conception of planning is that planning and implementation happen separately. The problem with this is that while we plan, the situation we plan for changes. The very process of planning is already an action that changes the situation. Often, we would try to adapt to the changes, but for the most part, we remain in a planning mode of thinking that implies a static and frozen picture of the system we design for.

A different approach is to erase the divide between planning and implementation. This is possible and beneficial for some types of projects that deal with highly unpredictable and dynamic social systems. This could be effective for and with groups that are not guided by a strong hierarchical organisation. Ideally, one could think that a systemic intervention, if done deeply enough, would fit so well with the system that implementation would go by itself, and no particular implementation is needed. Also, the idea of continues change and, for example, versioning, support this view. Yet in practice, continuous designing is rare and is most often executed stepwise, as semi continuous (versioning). Still, even rolling out versions needs particular strategies and planning for implementation, resulting in feedback and learning cycles rather than the perfect system fit that would implement itself. This concept, though logically right remains an idealistic goal that rarely is met in real life situations.

Yet, the new roles of designers as well as the migration into new fields for design also create new situations for engagement and self-implementation. As an example, we can return to the case of the design for asylum seekers by Nilouofar Gharavi and Melina Hozhbari (2018) (*Figure 99*). To quickly recap, the designers worked with asylum seekers at a reception centre in Oslo. The project intended at the outset to coordinate the many public and private services that were planned for the asylum seekers, to make their waiting time at the reception centre more meaningful and bearable. These spanned from education to entertainment. After unsuccessful attempts to bring these actors together, the team decided to work directly with the asylum seekers at the reception centre in Oslo. The concept for the project was to map the resources of the individual asylum seekers, and to create a framework that would enable them to help each other, rather than depend on outside sources. This concept was presented to the users and ultimately developed into a real-time action modus where different options were tested directly. The project resulted in several courses that were held by users according to their competencies and background. For example, these included a first-aid course held by an asylum seeker educated as a doctor, a computer course organised by a programmer, and a training course created by a former boxer.

The project demonstrates how the division between designing and action is blurred when we work very closely within human activity systems. The lack of organisational order makes it easier to implement actions immediately, yet we need to respect this lack of order and leave the belief in top-down planning.

Prototyping

A special form of action is to produce prototypes that are then tested out in the system over time. This allows us to avoid the problem of observation attention biasing an observation situation. One can leave the prototype and ask for people to report on the effects later. *Figure 179* shows such a prototype for a music festival in Oslo. The Recyclomat was built to nudge festival goers to become better at collecting and sorting their garbage. Taking elements from circus fairs and pin ball machines it made it fun to sort and throw the garbage in the right containers. It worked very well. An unforeseen effect was that the children at the festival mobilized to collect garbage just to see the machine at work.

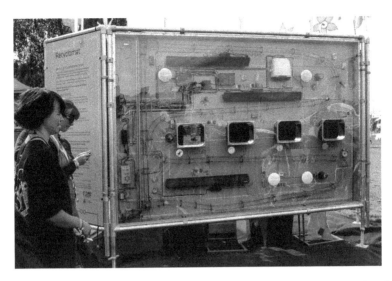

Figure 179: The Recyclomat: A prototype and working installation for a device that should nudge audience at a music festival to handle their garbage better by collecting it and sorting it into four categories. The installation will at certain points of accumulation give a feedback with a pinball-like mechanism. The Recyclomat was very successful for its purpose. (Carmen Bruno and Bo Werenskjold 2010).

Un-Phasing the Design Process

In the following section, we will discuss the phases of the design process. There are basically two extreme positions:

1. A prescriptive view that the design process must be executed in sequential phases.

2. A denial of phasing and the idea that solutions should be designed from the beginning.

I suggest an in-between position, one that strikes a balance between: a) the need for knowledge, and an overview of how the system works and will react to a design intervention through the use of design sketches as probes and provocations to learn more about the system; and b) challenging the false idea that analyses will sooner or later almost automatically lead to solutions.

What are the risks of starting right away with sketching solutions? Jumping to conclusions too early in a design process that deals with complex issues might put the result at risk. Complex systems react in counterintuitive ways when nudged or changed. Therefore, it is important to imagine and analyse the reaction of a system to a design intervention in an extensive way.

So why should we design early? The risk of being biased should not stop designers from developing early, immature design ideas. As long as one is prepared to scrap them, they can be very useful. The role of these ideas is to develop scenarios of how the system would react. They are "what if" questions posted as more than words, and developed almost to the prototype level. This really helps to gain a deeper understanding of the nature of the complex system at hand. To think ahead and ask valuable questions, we need visions that work as creative scenarios of how things could be. Without creative design visions, we are locked in our current framework of what is possible. Facts, data, and evidence are restrained to the current situation. Only design imagination can break these boundaries. Also, a team of experts most likely will not be able to break the given frames. Although they are very knowledgeable in describing what the situation is, most of them are not experts in envisioning what ought to be. This is where the designer's role plays a central role.

Complex real-life human activity systems cannot be tested in laboratories, nor is it normally possible to build simulations. Even if there is the technology and economic backing to make simulations possible, they most often are not inclusive enough. While some aspects of human activity can be simulated on the macro scale, such as for example simulating crowding in fire escape situations, there are currently no technologies that can simulate complex social systems with fair accuracy on a micro or mezzo scale in such a way that would make them useful for systemic design projects. We are thus left with using scenarios. Scenarios are narratives about possible futures of a system. To build relevant scenarios, we need knowledge about the system, and imagination about its future. Design scenarios and inquiries can move forward as iterations. We can envision how the system would react to the design intervention. The more concrete and detailed the design vision, the better can we guestimate the systemic responses it triggers.

Iterations

The phasing and un-phasing of the design process is naturally addressed through iterations. We can imagine a cyclic process where we close in on a resolution through repeated iterations. This iterative nature of the design process has been realized and described by numerous design researchers before.

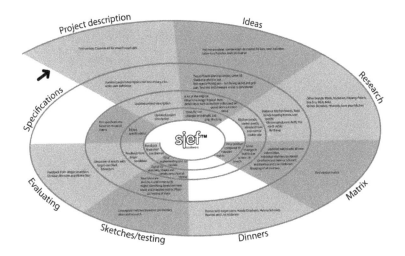

Figure 180: Diagram of a design process with iterations. The spiral diagram indicates how the design process went through four iterations where the same themes or issues were rechecked. These issues were Project Description, Ideas, Research, Matrix (developing the interrelation between things), Having Dinners, Sketches / Testing, Evaluation and Specification. Not all of these were re-examined for each iteration (white fields). Some issues required more reworking in the iteration and the rework would vary in different stages. This diagram was directly used as a process tool to check each stage in iterations (Students: Balder Onarheim, Pål Espensen, 2008).

Systems of Visions

The iterative nature of the design process suggests that a large series of design visions play a central role in systemic design. They can be organized according to how they fit and form their own system of thoughts and resolutions. This helps us avoid the urge to fixate on certain limited and singular ideas, and work instead towards versioning approaches and other dynamic, flexible, and future-oriented ways of generating design output.

Figure 181: Design sketches and models can be systematized to form its own system of ideas and visions (Christian von Hanno and Julian Guribye, for Medema, 2011).

Design Early

Banathy (pointing to Darke and Hiller) states that designers reject the traditional idea of a process that starts from a problem-formulating analysis and ends with a synthesis phase. Instead, he proposes that designers start from "conjecture-analyses:"

> The point of departure of this approach is not a detailed analysis of the situation but the formulation of a conjecture, a contemplation of "what should be" that Drake has termed "primary generator." The primary generator is formed very early in a design process as a set of initial concepts. This primary generator helps designers make the creative leap between problem formulation and solution concept (Banathy, 1997, p. 55).

As mentioned earlier, in SOD, there should be an awareness of how these early assumptions and concepts are both needed, but can also lead you astray. They are both outputs and perspectives that will colour further investigations. There will always be a conjecture about some issues. This is needed to start a project in the first place. If there is no speculation about a potential change that would benefit in one way or another, there is no motivation for the design project. This conjecture can be very vague though, and in most cases, it is an advantage that it has not settled entirely.

We need to be cautious with our speculations; they might turn out to be wrong, and our early concepts might be based on false assumptions, or the consequences of our concepts are not overlooked. In the SOD process, we have assumed that the need for start-up conjecture analyses is less important. We suggest that these are done a little bit later and in several rounds. Nevertheless, it is an important aspect to keep in mind. The design process in general, and the SOD process in particular, is not based on a belief that the analyses will seamlessly and deterministic result in a resolution. Yet, early conjectures and design concepts are needed. They function as probes of the system. They are not necessarily outputs of the process, but might as well function as provocations that help the designer to learn more of the system, and to reach different and better ways forward.

Banathy suggests that the problem and solution are in continuous interaction (1997, p. 31). The design world has continuously been split between analytical approaches and solution-driven approaches. SOD provides a composite approach that is both analytical, morphological, and solution-driven.

The idea of imaginative investigation as drivers in the development of systemic design and conjecture analyses as an iterative process, where imaginations and assumptions of how the system would react, benefit, or perform, are central to systemic design. It is also important that these tools are used very early though critically in a design process. This helps to inform the direction of the inquiry, reformulate requirements, formulate new questions, and search for a main course and direction.

Another point is that descriptive mapping does not automatically result in design. Though the mapping process might flow seamlessly from descriptive mapping into generative mapping, it still does not produce design solutions. Reaching a design phase in the SOD process often seems like a threshold. In observing student projects, one can see a pattern where the students immerse in descriptive mapping and delay designing. This might be less of a problem in commercial projects where deadlines and results are more critical. Still, it is a phenomenon to be taken seriously. It is important to start to design early for the above-mentioned reasons, but also to avoid getting stuck in an endless un-framable "research" process. Early design sketching helps frame the project in periods. The frames can be negotiated or overthrown later. The point is that the boundary critique of the project is triggered and integrated into the process at an early stage.

Intuition and Expertise

Intuition seems both needed and dubious when designing for complex systems. In the following section, we will go through some aspects of intuition and how it might play a role in SOD, as well as how it might cause unexpected results from a design intervention, if not dealt with carefully.

The Intuition Dilemma

A designer working with complexity is dependent upon intuition. Design intuition is important when synthesizing solutions from complex material. In critical systems thinking, Midgley describes the need for including intuition as a part of the methods and approaches (Midgley, 2000, p. 227).

When dealing with complex problems, there is no single right answer, only better or worse solutions. So judgment plays a vital role in planning. Judgment is never entirely based on the weighing of facts because the knowledge about a complex problem is always incomplete. The incompleteness of understanding, and the complex nature of the problem itself means that there are many possible responses, some better and some worth. This is one of the ten criteria of Wicked Problems (Rittel & Webber, 1973). In this complex uncertainty, decisions based on intuition play an important role.

This leads us to discussing intuition as such. Is it just the gut feeling we all can have or is it something more? The Dreyfus and Dreyfus model of skill acquisition describes intuition as a feature of the expert (Dreyfus & Dreyfus, 1980) (*Figure 182*). Only through long practice will one acquire well-developed intuition. The long internalisation of knowledge and experience will trigger intuitive decisions based on the synthesis of all that knowledge without the expert being particularly aware of each source the intuitive decision is based on.

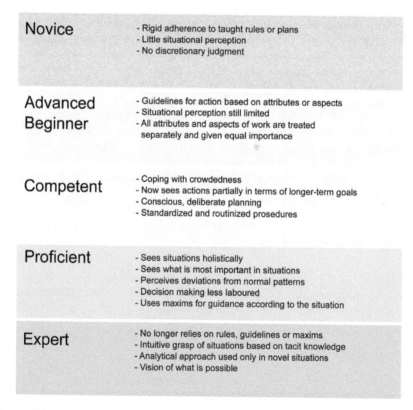

Figure 182: The Dreyfus and Dreyfus skill acquisition model, which proposes intuition as a skill of the expert. In real life skill development, one never follows the indicated steps sequentially. (Redrawn by Palak Dudani after Dreyfus & Dreyfus, 1980).

Forrester describes systems as counter-intuitive (1971) since they often behave differently than what we expect. This confronts us with a dilemma. We are dependent on intuition when designing for complex systems, but they behave in counter-intuitive ways. There are several responses to this dilemma.

First, we need to check if Forrester and Dreyfus and Dreyfus are talking about the same type of intuition. Forrester simply indicates that systems behave differently than we expect from human experience and intuition. He does not define or describe intuition in the article, but states that intuition is formed from experience with simple systems. This is not a convincing argument if we hold it up against the Dreyfus and Dreyfus model, which states that intuition is a result of very long experience, skill development, and learning. It is a feature of the expert.

Forrester's analysis, though partly useful, is insufficient. His analysis of low-income housing problems, for example (p. 8), does not include a whole range of additional dimensions in the system. Forrester describes the systems dynamics of declining building masses:

> As industrial buildings age, employment opportunities decline. As residential buildings age, they are used by lower-income groups who are forced to use them at higher population densities. Therefore, aging buildings cause jobs to decline and population to rise. (1971, p. 8)

The model of systems dynamics and its intention to computerise all systems, which induces the need to describe all systems quantitatively to fit the model, becomes a reductionist mould where reality is squeezed in while macroeconomics, politics, cultural issues, etc. are all left out. Recent years of gentrification have demonstrated how these trends change through rising property prices, at least in European cities where aging and dense buildings have become highly attractive.

A critical application of the Dreyfus and Dreyfus model of intuition, which might involve expert intuition combined with systems approaches that are more inclusive than the traditional models, would be more useful in systemic design. Though such models can be valuable, such as in Forrester's example, they can never be left standing alone. They should be triangulated by contrasting approaches.

The failure of judgment described by Forrester is largely due to a lack of systems thinking. It is also, to a large degree, a question of how the system boundary is conceived. This is often a problem for the layman with uninformed judgments, as well as for the systems thinkers who supports a specific modelling approach without any criticality.

This leads us to the concepts of critical systems thinking and critical heuristics. According to Werner Ulrich:

> In contemporary systems science, the problem of boundary judgments is either entirely ignored (typically in textbook exercises and case studies) or else it is

discussed in terms of formal criteria of modelling, rather than in terms of the normative content of whole systems judgments and corresponding justification break-offs. Frequently, models of 'systems' are presented as if the boundaries were objectively given, and the model itself does not tell us whether the boundaries in question have been adequately chosen. If the problem is discussed at all, it is seen merely from a modelling point of view: to facilitate the modelling task, boundaries are determined according to the availability of data and modelling techniques. But even from a merely technical modelling point of view, this way of dealing with the problem of boundary judgments is inadequate (1983, p. 278).

Ulrich and other researchers from the fields of Critical Systems Thinking and Critical Heuristics address the problem through a critical application of diverse systems perspectives, especially boundary critique. This involves judgment based on experience and is in harmony with the Dreyfus and Dreyfus model of expert intuition.

However well-developed, we need to be sceptical towards expert intuition, especially when reaching into new fields. One could talk of a critical intuition here where the expert skill is the ability to adapt to ever-new situations: the "adaptive expert" (H. G. Nelson & Stolterman, 2012a; Smith et al., 1997). Interdisciplinary, transdisciplinary, and cross-disciplinary work are a natural consequence of the complexity addressed in SOD. We are frequently dealing with unfamiliar realms, and learning becomes a continuous and integrated part of the SOD practice. However, Forrester's claim that systems are counterintuitive leads to a criticality towards intuition and human judgment. Such an observation is valuable in itself. Complex systems indeed often work in counterintuitive ways that escape even the experts' intuition. The judgement of an expert often tends to be too narrow and fragmented to uncover far-reaching effects and consequences from systems interventions. We therefore need judgment and intuition not just from any expert, but also from the "adaptive expert." The adaptive expert is someone skilled in judging new situations, someone with an adaptive intuition and criticality to judge its application, i.e., a generalist with a wide view in their field.

Creativity

Towards the end of Part Three in particular, and of this book in general, it seems nice to return to the issue of creativity.

Systems Thinking is a creative way of working. The intimate knowledge of the systems at hand will reveal opportunities for interventions and innovations. The Gigamap is not only descriptive mapping out myriads of entities and their relations, it is also generative helping designers look for and discover opportunities for creating new design concepts based on identifying new relations and finding synergies. The mapping and systemic insight and awareness of the counter intuitiveness of systems has several effects.

This approach to creativity is based on deep and very informed processes. Creativity is seen as a systemic phenomenon (Amabile, 1996; Csikszentmihalyi, 1996, 1999; H E Gruber, 1988). This model states that creativity is a complex phenomenon found on three systemic levels: the individual, the field, and the domain. While earlier creativity models tend to define creativity as an individual ability, this approach states that all levels--individual, social, and disciplinary-- need to be creative in order to foster creativity. This model is particularly suitable for discussing creativity in Systems Thinking. SSM and similar approaches emphasize social networks and the need for an open ear to stakeholders, almost to such a degree that it wipes out the ground for individual creativity. SSM was not made with the individual creative process in mind, especially since action research, which is so closely related to SSM, opts for social change through systems interventions. As already mentioned, the benefit of Systems Architecting is that it appreciates the individual's creativity and states that a holistic overview are best held by an individual or a very small synchronised group. Synthesis is a mental process that is largely individual or dialogic between a small group of people. Both approaches the community-based and the individual are very much appropriate and should be conducted in a creative systems project, but at different times and for different purposes. Co-designing alone is limited when it comes to synthesis. The systems view on creativity gives a theoretical justification for a process to operate on all three systemic levels of creativity.

The systems approach to creativity and the role of the individual as described by Csikszentmihalyi is one that demands a slow process and concentration over time (Csikszentmihalyi, 1996). This corresponds with Hadamard's model of creativity (Hadamard, 1945). His four-step model consists of:

1. Preparation

2. Incubation

3. Illumination

4. Verification

Particularly interesting are the concepts of incubation and illumination. We can see the connection to Systems Architecting, to intuition, and to the concept of flow and heuristics.

Another aspect regarding creativity in SOD is the aforementioned richness imperative and the shifting use of hybrid media (Sevaldson, 2005a, 317) as well as the Rich Design Space (Sevaldson, 2008). These are all methods or techniques tailored to deal with large information richness in the design process, while also providing a creative boost to such processes.

Yet another aspect of creativity in the context of SOD is the emergence of information visualisation and gigamapping as creative techniques. Points of intervention are discovered in the visualised information. What is originally regarded as the frame of the project is easily redefined. Intentional points of intervention are replaced by other places in the system where the intervention might have much greater impact. In the 2009 SOD studio, the students were asked to come to the first day with a preconceived idea for a product. In their final presentations at the end of the studio semester, all of the finishing students have shifted their focus point from the outset, some towards a radically different point in the system.

SOD opens up creativity because it leads to a shift from the obvious (schematic) initial positions to less obvious positions or entry points in the system that might have a greater impact and a better potential to be realised. In this sense, creativity is closely related to realism since this is not about generating many flimsy ideas in a "brainstormy" way, but is instead a profound type of creativity based on deep understanding of the material, being immersed in the media and information, and having incubation periods from which the most resilient and realistic creative solutions can emerge.

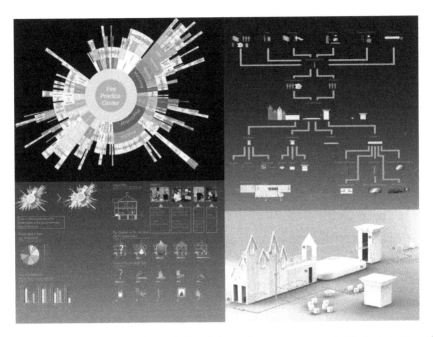

*Figure 183: In the project "Play with Fire," the design student started with the intention of
redesigning fire emergency equipment according to a conventional idea of a design
process. After gigamapping her field (upper left), the psychological issues of the theme
emerged and she shifted focus from looking at the moment of the fire to putting effort into
much earlier phases (analyses lower left), creating a larger degree of security through
training and learning. The result was an innovative concept for a travelling edutainment
centre that caters to learning about fire situations and testing equipment (lower right). She
also developed a financial resourcing plan and an "ecology" of the project, which involved
the expert network and other stakeholder interests like insurance companies (upper right)
(Heidi Borthne AHO master studies, 2009).*

As mentioned earlier, Gedenryd criticises the strict phasing of the design process,
which also implies a criticism of the divide between analysis and synthesis
(Gedenryd, 1998). To recap: While analyses is pulling things apart to look at the
parts, bits and pieces, synthesis is the process where everything comes together in
a new shape, form and structure. It is congruent with the creative process. He
states that designers often have early ideas and that there is no direct relationship
between analyzing and synthesizing. There is no automatic generation of ideas
from analyses (see also conjecture analyses page 344). It is not possible to give an
exact prescription of synthesis and the creativity needed for it. But we can still say
quite a lot about the praxeology of synthesis. This we will go through, but it does
not replace the main requirement for deep systemic synthesis that leads to truly

creative and systems-changing interventions. Instead, long-term engagement and in-depth study of the situation at hand is essential. Without it, sensible synthesis is not likely to happen.

We synthesize through and by:

> **Iterations:** Developing solutions stepwise through and by design and reflection.

> **Heuristics[80]:** Illuminary realizations and discoveries in the design work (Ulrich, 1983) (Ulmer, 1994) [81].

> **Flow:** Closely-related to heuristics. The creative flow in individuals, groups, or domains (Csikszentmihalyi, 1996; Dorta et al., 2008).

The heuristic moment is suggested as a part of a systematized method. The heuristic moment is identical with Hadarmards moment of illumination. Fetterman calls the moment of synthesis "crystallization:"

> The crystallization is typically the result of a convergence of similarities that spontaneously strike the ethnographer as relevant or important to the study. Every study has classic moments when everything falls into place. (Fetterman, 1989).

Harold Nelson uses a similar analyses of a super saturated solution that crystallizes at the insertion of a catalyst.(H. G. Nelson & Stolterman, 2012a)

The most important points of SOD as a deeply creative design technique can be summarized in the following points:

> 1. Breaking schemata. The wide and deep investigations of systems lead to rediscoveries, to review and reconsider how we look at things and the systems behind them. This breaks our simplistic archetypical schemas and opens up for innovations.

> 2. Catering for both individual and collective / social creativity. The systemic model of creativity opens up a space for enhancing creativity not only in individuals but the attention on the systems we design within creates a strong opportunity to reinforce the

---

80. We are not talking of Rules of Thumbs! The term heuristic comes from eureka, expressing triumph of discovery. Heuristic means involving or serving as an aid to learning, discovery, or problem-solving by experimental and especially trial-and-error methods. (Meriam-Webster)
81. Heuristics is a term used for a series of techniques that are highly diverse in their nature.

creative process. It is easier to change the social system than the individual's creativity.

3. Finding leverage points other than where is seems most obvious. Gigamapping helps us look at processes and interconnections beyond the obvious, and to calculate better ripple effects and leverage.

4. Shifting perspectives helps move us out of our accustomed way of thinking and helps us see the systems form other viewpoints.

5. Looking beyond the object: By mapping out the systems behind the objects and regarding them as outcroppings and symptoms of hidden systems we shift our view and the objects become highly interesting and open for innovations.

6. Incubation. Fully engaging with the systems and their complexity leading to deep incubation processes leading to crystallization of possible interventions

7. Awareness of systems of systems engages in the different levels of creativity, the creativity of the social system we design within.

8. Awareness that the systemic change are not singular creative interventions but that systemic change needs multiple action, orchestrated and maintained over time.

9. The realisation that creativity is needed throughout the lifetime of a system and that it is not only a singular delivery from one designer, but rather a result of a collective creative culture.

Summing Up Praxeology: How to Gigamap Rules of Thumb

Below, I present some rules of thumb for the SOD process and gigamapping. These rules have emerged through my years of experience in producing such maps and instructing students and professionals in gigamapping.

Know that nothing is irrelevant: Try to deactivate any filter of relevance and other biases to the task. In fact, forget the task completely and map with the field or the theme in mind rather than the task or brief.

Remember that nothing is uninteresting: All information, even the smallest detail, is interesting in its own right. Search and hunt for it. Be interested in the findings as such. Curiosity is your best friend. Investment of time in this phase will pay back later. You are in the middle of a very rapid learning process that you will benefit from for this project and beyond. As a commissioned designer, investing a few hours at your own cost will be time well-spent.

Strive for information richness: If the map is too simple and contains too few elements, there is something wrong. Often, the problem is an inability to put aside schemata and filters about what is relevant. The other main reason is the lack of ability to increase the resolution of the map. Unpack objects like we did with the paper cup. Silly rule of thumb: you need a minimum of 300 entities on the map.

Use cheap and accessible media: Use low-fidelity media like cheap paper in the beginning. Do not use a computer. Use low-quality, large-format paper rolls. Using the wrong medium in the beginning will hinder the flow. In particular, do not use digital tools when you want to involve stakeholders and experts. Instead, involve everybody by giving them markers and a huge paper surface. Use a table, not a wall. This is better for access and discussions.

Just do it: Do not hesitate to spend resources—there is always more paper available. Do not pre-plan the mapping too much but develop it as you go, and redesign in iterations. Planning the mapping hinders the explorative and generative qualities of the mapping process. You cannot plan for something that is unknown. Yet, in some occasions, pre-planning the mapping can be useful. One can design a scaffold or tables and lead the workshop participants through it in steps. In this case, it is important to consider how this might bias the process. Will this lead to an already presumed direction? The mapping is meant to create an overview becomes a tool to help you plan. Avoid focusing on a central nucleus in the map as this generates a preconceived hierarchy and perspective. First, develop neutral fields with no particular centre of gravity. Centres of gravity are found or even generated in the map later. Just do it and re-do it.

Do not talk too much — write and draw: With group-work in particular, some people tend to get engaged in verbal discussions and forget the visual thinking process. They discuss instead of actually doing the mappings. Visual mapping in dialogues is actually very efficient because you document while discussing. If you fail with the visual thinking, not only you risk a less concise dialogue but you will also loose its richness and detail for later use. The best way to turn such discussions into something useful or to leave them behind is to ask the participants to document their discussions and map it out on the paper.

Facilitate, do not dominate: In group work with experts and stakeholders, do not dominate. It can bias the whole process if you impose your preconceptions. You want to tease out the things you have not even thought of. Therefore, do not interrupt flow. If participants are passive, handing them markers at the right moment can be effective. When they say something, ask them to put it on the map.

Ask them to elaborate when they make a comment. Split into sub-groups when interesting points emerge.

Activate existing knowledge: Do not search for information on the Internet or in books at the beginning of the mapping process. This will stop your flow before you have even started. Use your existing knowledge and map it out completely. Share your tacit knowledge and make it explicit. Then identify what is insufficient and what is speculative, and plan your information-gathering and desktop research accordingly.

Defy filters and schemata: Be aware of your preconceptions and prejudices. Try to put them aside and look beyond them as well as you can. Try to grasp "how the real world really is." Observation is great. A main weapon against preconceptions and schemata is to aim for very high resolution in the visualization of your information. Look for the smallest details in a chain of events. The effect of this is that you rediscover processes since we tend to construct simplifying schemata not only about things but about processes as well.

Avoid hierarchy: Use concept-mapping types of diagrams rather than mind maps. Search out the horizontal relations. We tend to lean on stereotypical hierarchies to help us order the mess. These can be deceiving and we need to understand the non-linear interwoven ecosystems and their detailed hierarchies rather than the stereotypical given hierarchies.

Do not brainstorm: There is ample documentation that brainstorming does not work. We do not need 500 fancy and funny ideas that fall apart when put in the rain. We are happy to find one or two innovations that are thoroughly grounded in the organisation, its environment, and the economic reality. Yet, if ideas pop up make a small sketch or note to maybe investigate it later and use it to learn more about the system.

Messy is good: Do not let your inner designer take over the process too early. Let it be as messy as the reality you are trying to cope with. Overdesigning the map too early turns design into a mould for reality.

Mix it up: Strive to produce a "deep" or "thick" map. This means that the map contains many layers of different information. Finding relations and creating relations between types of categorically different information that are seemingly detached is one of the goals in gigamapping. Therefore, allow for different ways of representing information in the map.

Use timelines: Timeline mapping is very efficient, especially in the co-creation of maps. It allows for open-ended discussions that do not need an agenda to be very focussed. Jumping back and forth on the map does not disturb the focus because everybody is informed about the context of the jumps. This allows for flow and a dynamic discussion.

Never start at the beginning: When timeline mapping, start close to the middle of the timeline so that earlier things have sufficient space to unfold.

Look for relations: Emphasize the relations rather than the entities. Work with defining the relations. A simple line is not sufficient. Arrows indicate directions of relations. Use additional font variations and colour coding to indicate quantitative diversities. Use other types of relations like proximity or sequencing. Put labels with small descriptive texts or other notes onto the relations and not only onto the entities. Avoid sticky notes; they reinforce thinking of the entities rather than the relations. Use materials like threads, stings, and wires, etc. to codify and emphasize relations.

If a group has difficulties focussing on relations, take a time-out at a certain moment and ask them to spend 15 minutes only on relations, finding out what is connected to what and how.

Create relations: Gigamapping is both descriptive and generative. Use the mapping to create relations that are not there today. What relations should be created to make the system function better?

Collaborate: Individual mapping is valuable, but gigamapping is also a very good collaborative tool. Timeline mapping works especially well in groups. Involve experts and stakeholders. You can start by making an individual map and bring it to a short workshop with experts and stakeholders, or to the first client meeting.

Switch media: Start with simple, low-fidelity media like big paper rolls and markers, but switch to other media later. Redraw the mapping on your computer and plot it out in large formats to continue working manually. Then repeat the process with new iterations. Media switches usually accelerate the process.

Display, do not hide: Don't roll up and store away your maps during the design process. They are the centre of your Rich Design Space. One of their most important functions is to make large amounts of information and systems of relations instantly accessible. They support your memory.

Design early: Sketch and draw from the beginning. Do not stick to text, entity symbols, and relations represented with lines only. Combine them with sketches and other visual material in the maps. At the same time, do not get locked to your design ideas too early. Keep them open-ended and avoid letting them become guiding points for the mapping and research process. Do not let early ideas bias your investigations. Instead, use them for testing the system with prototypes or scenarios.

Design and redesign: Gigamapping is a design process on its own, nested inside the design process. The map is a designed artefact. Use your design skills to develop the map through design thinking. Analyses and designing are integrated. Redesign through several iterations where you add missing information, take the design through workshops with experts and stakeholders, reorganize, and systematise the map.

Don't over-design: Be sensitive to moments when designing becomes over-designing. Be suspicious towards overly designed maps where things line up too nicely. Does this really represent the "real world"?

Analyse: Search for points and areas where there are potentialities for doing things better. Search for possible new relations, intervention points, and innovations. Interconnect and orchestrate the design interventions through step-wise implementation, or demonstrate how the design interventions can reinforce each other.

Be critical: Scrutinize your mapping through *pro-et-contra* analysis and your resolutions through catastrophic scenario games, critical foresight, or similar techniques.

Create the meta-information: The meta-information is sometimes the most valuable information you can derive from the map. This includes a sense of the Gestalt of the system, a sense for the level of complexity, a sense of the challenges in a project, numbers and diversity in channels, layers, and actors, etc.

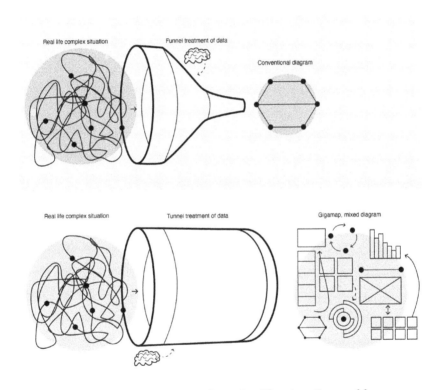

Figure 184: Gigamapping is not about simplification. One could compare simplification with funneling down the amount of data. Gigamapping is more like "tunneling" the information so to reinterpret and redesign it. (Julie Grindland-Sørensen OsloMet 2018)

REFERENCES

Aaltonen, M., Barth, T., Casti, J. L., Mitleton-Kelly, E., & Sanders, T. I. (2005). Complexity as a Sensemaking Framework. *FFRC-Publications*. Helsinki: Finland Future Research Centre.

Ackoff, R. L. (1981). The art and science of mess management. *Interfaces*, *11*(1), 20–26.

Ackoff, R. L., & Emery, F. E. (1972). *On Purposeful Systems: An Interdisciplinary Analysis of Individual and Social Behavior as a System of Purposeful Events*. Chicago: Aldine-Atherton.

Ackoff, R., & Sheldon, R. (2003). *Redesigning Society*. Stanford: Stanford University Press.

Alexander, C. (1964). *Notes on the Synthesis of Form*. Cambridge Massachusetts: Harvard University Press.

Alexander, C. (1965). A City is not a Tree (Part I and Part II). *Architectural Forum*, *122*(no 1 (Part I) and no 2 (Part II)), 58-62 (Part I), 58-61 (Part II. Retrieved from http://www.rudi.net/books/200

Alexandre, V., & Gasparski, W. W. (2000). *The roots of praxiology: French action theory from Bourdeau and Espinas to present days* (Vol. 7). Transaction Publishers.

Allen, S. (1999). Diagrams Matter. *ANY*, *23*(Diagram Works).

Amabile, T. M. (1996). *Creativity in Context*. Boulder: CO: Westview.

Arnheim, R. (1969). *Visual Thinking*. Berkeley: University of California Press.

Arnheim, R. (1974). *Art and Visual Perception*. Los Angeles: University of California Press.

Anderson, P. W. (1972). More is different. *Science*, *177*(4047), 393–396. Retrieved from https://www.tkm.kit.edu/downloads/TKM1_2011_more_is_different_PWA.pdf

Arbib, M. A. (1992). Schema theory. *The Encyclopedia of Artificial Intelligence*, *2*, 1427–1443.

Archer, B. (1979). Design as a discipline. *Design Studies*, *1*(1), 17–20.

Ashby, W. R. (1956). *An introduction to cybernetics*. Taylor & Francis.

Ashmos, D. P., & Nathan, M. L. (2002). Team sense-making: A mental model for navigating uncharted territories. *Journal of Managerial Issues*, 198–217.

Banathy, B. H. (1988). Matching design methods to system type. *Systems Research*, *5*(1), 27–34.

Banathy, B. H. (1997). *Designing Social Systems in a Changing World*. New York: Springer.

Banathy, B. H., & Jenks, C. L. (1990). The Transformation of Education by Design: A Leadership Guide for Educational Decision Makers. Retrieved from http://files.eric.ed.gov/fulltext/ED330034.pdf

Barbero, S. (2017). *Systemic Design Method Guide for Policymaking: A Circular Europe on the Way* (1st ed., Vol. 1). Torino: Politecnico di Torino.

Bateson, G. (1975). Ecology of mind: The sacred. *Loka-A Journal from Naropa Institute. New York: Anchor Books*.

Bateson, G. (2000). *Steps to an ecology of mind: Collected essays in anthropology, psychiatry, evolution, and epistemology*. University of Chicago Press.

Behrens, R. R. (1998). Art, design and gestalt theory. *Leonardo*, 299–303. Retrieved from http://www.gestalttheory.net/cms/uploads/pdf/archive/1934_1960/Principles_Gestalt_Psychology_koffka.pdf

Bergh, J. (2019). Strength in weakness-A new institutional design perspective on the Swedish Trust Reform.

Berkel, B. van, & Bos, C. (1999). Diagrams- Interactive Instruments in Operation. *ANY*, *23*(Diagram Work).

Bertalanffy, L. von. (1969). *General System Theory*. New York: George Braziller Inc.

Bettum, J., & Michael, H. (2000). Channeling Systems: Dynammic Processes and Digital time-based Methods in Urban Design. In *Contemporary Processes in Architecture* (Vol. Vol 70, pp. 36–41). AD Whiley.

Bistagnino, L., & Campagnaro, C. (2014). Systemic design. In *Encyclopedia of Quality of Life and Well-Being Research* (pp. 6563–6569). Springer Netherlands.

Bjørndal Skjelten, E. (2014). *Complexity & Other Beasts: Guide to Mapping Workshops* (1st ed.). Oslo: AHO.

Bloch, P. H. (1995). Seeking the ideal form: Product design and consumer response. *The Journal of Marketing*, 16–29.

Blumer, A., Ehrenfeucht, A., Haussler, D., & Warmuth, M. K. (1987). Occam's razor. *Information Processing Letters*, *24*(6), 377–380.

Bogdanov, A. A. (1913). Bogdanovs Tektology 1996. In P.Dudley (Ed.), *Bogdanovs Tektology*. Hull: Center for Systems Studies Press.

Bogen, L. T., Jensen, R., LeBlanc, L., & Tveit., S. S. (2014). *On the same page*. Oslo. Retrieved from http://systemsorienteddesign.net/index.php/projects/master-projects/aho-2014/on-the-same-page

Bogen, L. T., Jensen, R., LeBlanc, L., & Tveit, S. S. (2014). On the Same Page. Retrieved from http://systemsorienteddesign.net/index.php/projects/master-projects/aho-2014/on-the-same-page

Boland, R. J., & Collopy, F. (2004). Managing as Design. Stanford: Stanford university Press.

Botero, A., Kommonen, K.-H., & Marttila, S. (2010). Expanding design space: Design-in-use activities and strategies. In *Proc: DRS'10* (p. 12). Retrieved from http://www.designresearchsociety.org/docs-procs/DRS2010/PDF/018.pdf

Boulding, K. E. (1956). General systems theory-the skeleton of science. *Management Science*, *2*(3), 197–208. Retrieved from http://www.panarchy.org/boulding/systems.1956.html

Brand, S. (1994). *How Buildings Learn. What happens after they're built*. New York: Viking Penguin.

Broadbent, J. (2003). Generations in Design Methodology. *The Design Journal*, *6*(1).

Broadman, J., & Sauser, B. (2008). *Systems Thinking; Coping with 21st Century Problems*. Boca Raton: CRC Press.

Brown, T. (2008). Design Thinking. *Harvard Business Review*, *June 2008*.

Brown, T., & Katz, B. (2009). *Change by design: how design thinking transforms organisations and inspires innovation* (1st ed.). New York: Harper & Collins Business.

Brown, T., & Wyatt, J. (2010). Design thinking for social innovation. *Development Outreach*, *12*(1), 29–43.

Buchanan, R. (1992). Wicked Problems in Design Thinking. *Design Issues*, *8*(2), 5–21.

Buchanan, R. (2001). Design research and the new learning. *Design Issues*, *17*(4), 3–23.

Capjon, J. (2004). *Trial-and-Error-based innovation*. Oslo: AHO.

Checkland, P. (2000a). Soft Systems Methodology: a 30-year retrospective. In P. Checkland (Ed.), *Systems Thinking, Systems Practice*. Chichester: John Wiley & Sons LTD.

Checkland, P. (2000b). Soft systems methodology: a thirty year retrospective. *Systems Research and Behavioral Science*, *58*, 11–58.

Checkland, P. (2000c). *Systems Thinking, Systems Practice*. Chichester: John Wiley & Sons LTD.

Checkland P., & Poulter, J. (2006). *Learning for Action: A Short Definitive Account of Soft Systems Methodology and its use for Practitioners, Teachers and Students*. Chichester: John Wiley & Sons, Ltd.

Christakis, A. N., & Brahms, S. (2003). Boundary-spanning dialogue for the 21st-century agoras. *Systems Research and Behavioral Science, 20*(4), 371–382.

Christensen, B. B. (2006). Organisasjoner som pågående samtaler.

Churchman, C. W. (1970). Operation research as a profession. *Management Science, 17*(B37-53).

Churchman, C. W. (1979). *The Systems Approach. Revised and updated.* New York: Dell Publishing Co., Inc.

Clatworthy, S. (2011). Service Innovation Through Touch-points: Development of an Innovation Toolkit for the First Stages of New Service Development. *International Journal of Design, 5*(2), 15–28.

Collopy, F. (2009). Lessons Learned -- Why the Failure of Systems Thinking Should Inform the Future of Design Thinking. Retrieved from http://www.fastcompany.com/1291598/lessons-learned-why-failure-systems-thinking-should-inform-future-design-thinking

Conklin, J. (2005). *Dialogue mapping: Building shared understanding of wicked problems.* John Wiley & Sons, Inc.

Cranz, G. (2016). *Ethnography for designers.* Routledge.

Creswell, J. W. (2013). *Research design: Qualitative, quantitative, and mixed methods approaches.* Sage publications.

Cross, N. (1982). Designerly ways of knowing. *Design Studies, 3*(4), 221–227.

Cross, N. (1984). Developments in Design Methodology. John Wiley & Sons, Chichester UK.

Cross, N. (1999). Design Research: A Disciplined Conversation. *Design Issues, 15*(2), 5–10.

Cross, N. (2007a). *Designerly Ways of Knowing.* Basel: Birkhäuser.

Cross, N. (2007b). Forty years of design research. *Design Studies, 28*(1), 1–4.

Cross, N. (2011). *Design thinking: understanding how designers think and work.* Oxford: Berg Publishers.

Cross, N., & Cross, A. C. (1996). Winning by design: the methods of Gordon Murray, racing car designer. *Design Studies, 17*(1), 91–107.

Crutzen, P. J. (2006). The "anthropocene." In *Earth system science in the anthropocene* (pp. 13–18). Springer.

Csikszentmihalyi, M. (1996). *Creativity, Flow and the Psychology of Discovery and Invention.* New York: HarperCollins.

Csikszentmihalyi, M. (1999). Implications of a Systems Perspective for the Study of Creativity. In R. J. Sternberg (Ed.), *Creativity Handbook.* Cambridge: Cambridge University Press.

Daft, R. L., & Lengel, R. H. (1983). *Information richness. A new approach to managerial behavior and organisation design.* Texas A and M Univ College Station Coll of Business Administration.

Davidová, M. (2014). Generating the Design Process with GIGA-map: The Development of the Loop Pavilion. In B. Sevaldson & P. Jones (Eds.), *Proceedings of RSD3, Third Symposium of Relating Systems Thinking to Design.* Oslo: The Oslo School of Architecture and Design.

De Dominico, M., & Hiroki, S. (n.d.). Complexity Explained. Retrieved March 5, 2021, from https://complexityexplained.github.io/

Dekker, S., Bergström, J., Amer-Wåhlin, I., & Cilliers, P. (2012). Complicated, complex, and compliant: best practice obstetrics. *Cognition, Technology & Work, 15*(2), 189–195.

Denis Loveridge. (2009). *Foresight: The Art and Science of Anticipating the Future.* New York: Routledge.

Domingos, P. (1999). The role of Occam's razor in knowledge discovery. *Data Mining and Knowledge Discovery, 3*(4), 409–425.

Dorst, K. (2008). Design research: a revolution-waiting-to-happen. *Design Studies, 29,* 4–11.

Dorta, T., Pérez, E., & Lesage, A. (2008). The ideation gap: Hybrid tools, design flow and practice. *Design Studies, 29,* 121–141.

Dreyfus, S. E., & Dreyfus, H. L. (1980). A Five-stage Model of the Mental Activities Involved in Directed Skill Acquisition. Operations Research Center; University of California Berkley. Retrieved from http://www.dtic.mil/cgi-bin/GetTRDoc?AD=ADA084551&Location=U2&doc=GetTRDoc.pdf

Dunin-Woyseth, H. (2001). Towards a disciplinary identity of the making professions: An introduction. *Research Magazine, 4*(The Oslo Millenium Reader), 1–20.

Ehrenfels, C. von. (1890). Über Gestaltqualitäten. *Vierteljahresschrift Für Wissenschaftliche Philosophie, 14*(3), 249–292.

Eisenman, P. (1999a). *Diagram: an Original Scene of Writing. ANY* (Vol. 23). New York: Any Magazine.

Eisenman, P. (1999b). *Diagram Diaries.* New York,: UNIVERSE.

Engeström, Y. (1999). Learning by Expanding: An Activity - Theoretical Approach to Developmental Research. Retrieved from http://lchc.ucsd.edu/MCA/Paper/Engestrom/expanding/toc.htm

Evans, R. (1997). *Translations from Drawing to Building. AA DOCUMENTS 2.* Carnbridge, Massachusetts: The MIT Press.

Fetterman, D. M. (1989). *"Ethnography."* Sage Publications.

Feyerabend, P. (1975). *Against Method.* London: Verso.

Fjeld, M., Lauche, K., Bichsel, M., Voorhorst, F., Krueger, H., & Rauterberg, M. (2002). Physical and Virtual Tools: Activity Theory Applied to the Design of Groupware. *The Journal of Collaborative Computing, Computer S*(11), 153–180.

Flood., R. L., & Ulrich, W. (1990). Testament to the conversation on critical systems thinking between two systems practitioners. *Systems Practice, 3,* 7–29.

Flood, R. L., & Romm, N. R. A. (1996). Critical Systems Thinking: Current Research and Practice. New York: Plenum Press.

Førland, T. E. (1996). *Drøft.* Oslo: Ad Notam.

Forrester, J. (1989). The Beginnings of Systems dynamics. Banquet Talk at the international meeting of the Systems Dynamics Society, Germany July 13, 1989. Retrieved from http://pagesperso-orange.fr/patrice.salini/Textes /Forrester beginning.pdf

Forrester, J. (1991). System Dynamics and the Lessons of 35 Years. Massachusetts: Jay W. Forrester. Retrieved from http://sysdyn.clexchange.org/sdep/papers/D-4224-4.pdf

Forrester, J. W. (1971). Counterintuitive behavior of social systems. *Technological Forecasting and Social Change, 3,* 1–22. https://doi.org/10.1016/S0040-1625(71)80001-X

Frayling, C. (1993). Research in art and design. *Royal College of Art Research Papers, 1*(1), 1–5.

Friedman, K. (2003). Theory construction in design research: criteria: approaches, and methods. *Design Studies, 24,* 507–522. Retrieved from http://design.osu.edu/carlson/id785/friedman.pdf

Fry, T. (2008). *Design futuring: sustainability, ethics, and new practice* (English). New York, NY: Berg. Retrieved from http://www.loc.gov/catdir/toc/ecip0825/2008035114.html

Fuller, R. B., & Snyder, J. (1969). *Operating manual for spaceship earth.* Southern Illinois University Press Carbondale.

Gasparski, W. W. (1979). Praxiological—systemic approach to design studies. *Design Studies, 1*(2), 101–106.

Gedenryd, H. (1998). How Designers Work. *Department of Cognitive Science*. Lund: Lund University. Retrieved from http://en.scientificcommons.org/7601543

Geels, F. W. (2002). Technological transitions as evolutionary reconfiguration processes: a multi-level perspective and a case-study. *Research Policy, 31*(8–9), 1257–1274. https://doi.org/10.1016/S0048-7333(02)00062-8

Gell-Mann, M. (1995). What is complexity? *Complexity, 1*(1), 16–19. https://doi.org/https://doi.org/10.1002/cplx.6130010105

Geman, S., Potter, D. F., & Chi, Z. (2002). Composition systems. *Quarterly of Applied Mathematics, 60*(4), 707–736.

Gharajedaghi, J. (2006). *Systems Thinking: Managing Chaos and Complexity: A Platform for Designing Business Architecture*. London: Elsevier.

Gharavi, N., & Hozhbari, M. (2018). *@Home in Transition*. Oslo. Retrieved from https://systemsorienteddesign.net/index.php/projects/master-projects/2018/home-in-transition

Giaccardi, E., & Fischer, G. (2008). Creativity and Evolution: A Meta Perspective. *Digital Creativity, 19*(1), 19–32.

Glanville, R. (2014). How design and cybernetics reflect each other. In *Proceedings of Third Symposium of Relating Systems Thinking to Design, Oslo, Norway. October* (pp. 15–17).

Glanville, R. (2008). Designing Complexity. Performance Improvement Quarterly, 20(2), 75–96.

Glanville, Ranulph. (1994). A Ship without a Rudder. Southsea: CybernEthics Research. Retrieved from http://citeseerx.ist.psu.edu/viewdoc/download?doi=10.1.1.37.7453&rep=rep1&type=pdf

Gleick, J. (1993). *Chaos: Making a New Science*. London: Abacus.

Goldschmidt, G. (1994). On visual design thinking: the viz kids of architecture. *Design Studies, 15 no2*.

Gordillo, F. R. (2015). *César Manrique* (9th editio). Teguise: Fundación César Manrique.

Gruber, H E. (1988). The evolving systems approach to creative work. *Creativity Research Journal, 1*(1), 27–51. Retrieved from

http://www.informaworld.com/smpp/content~db=all~content=a916437217

Gruber, Howard E, & Wallace, D. B. (1999). The Case Study Method and Evolving Systems Approach for Understanding Unique Creative People at Work. In *Handbook of creativity*. Cambridge: Cambridge University Press.

Gunderson, L. H., & Holling, C. S. (2002). Panarchy: Understanding Transformations in Human and Natural Systems. Washington DC: Island Press.

Hadamard, J. (1945). *The Psychology of Invention in the Mathematical Field*. Princeton University Press.

Hall, A. D. (1962). *A Methodology for Systems Engineering*. New York: D. van Nostrand Company Inc.

Halpin, C., & Hanlon, P. (2008). Interaction of the legitimate system and the shadow system in organisations.

Hamilton, J., & Jaaniste, L. (2009). The effective and the evocative: reflecting on practice-led research approaches in art and design. Brisbane: Queensland College of Art, Griffith University,. Retrieved from http://eprints.qut.edu.au/29700/1/c29700.pdf

Hegeman, J. (2008). The Thinking Behind Design. *Design, 4*(1), 1–31. Retrieved from http://jamin.org/portfolio/thesis-paper/thinking-behind-design.pdf

Hensel, M., Menges, A., & Weinstock, M. (2004). Emergence: Morphogenetic Design Strategies. (H. Castle, Ed.), *Architectural Design*. Chichester: Wiley-Academy.

Hinte, E. van, & Tooren, M. van. (2008). *First Read This: Systems engineering in practice*. Rotterdam: 010 Publishers.

Hintikka, J., & Remes, U. (1974). *The Method of Analyses: Its geometrical origin and its general significance*. Dordrecht: D. Reidel Publishing Co.

Horvath, I. (2001). A contemporary survey of scientific research into engineering design. In *Proceedings of the International Conference on Engineering Design, ICED* (Vol. 1).

Ison, R. L. (2008). Systems thinking and practice for action research. In P. Reason & H. Bradbury (Eds.), *The SAGE Handbook of Action Research Participative Inquiry and Practice* (pp. 139–158). London: Sage Publications. Retrieved from http://oro.open.ac.uk/10576/1/Ison.pdf

Jackson, M C. (1985). Social Systems Theory and Practice: The need for a critical approach. *International Journal for Genral Systems Theory, 10*, 135–151.

Jackson, M C. (1990). The Critical Kernel in Modern Systems Thinking. *Systems Practice, 3*(4), 357–364.

Jackson, Michael C, & Keys, P. (1984). Towards a system of systems methodologies. *Journal of the Operational Research Society, 35*(6), 473–486.

Jonas, W. (1996). Systems Thinking in Industrial Design. In *Systems Dynamics 96* (pp. 241–244). Cambridge Massachusets: MIT.

Jonas, W. (2001). Systemtheorie und Designpraxis. In *Angewandte Systemforschung: ein interdisziplinärer Ansatz*. Wiesbaden: Gabler Verlag.

Jonas, W. (2005). Designing in the real world is complex anyway-so what? Systemic and evolutionary process models in design. In *European Conference on Complex Systems Satellite Workshop: Embracing Complexity in Design*. Paris.

Jonas, W. (2007). Complexity - Design´s Proper Subject: a foreword, 7 chunks of ideas and an outlook". In *EAD07: DANCING WITH DISORDER: DESIGN, DISCOURSE & DISASTER, 7th conference of the European Academy of Design*. Izmir.

Jones, J. C. (1970). *Design Methods*. New York: Van Nostrand Reinhold.

Jones, P. (2014). Systemic Design Principles for Complex Social Systems. In G. S. Metcalf (Ed.), *Social Systems and Design* (pp. 91–128). Tokyo: Springer Japan.

Jones, P., & Sevaldson, B. (n.d.). Systemic Design. Retrieved January 1, 2014, from http://www.systemic-design.net

Jones, P H, & VanPatter, G. K. (2009). Design 1.0, 2.0, 3.0, 4.0: The rise of visual sensemaking. *NextD Journal; ReThinking Design*.

Jones, Peter H. (2013). Design for Care: Innovating Healthcare Experience. *Innovating Healthcare Experience. Rosenfeld Media, Brooklyn*.

Jordan, N. (1968). *Themes in Speculative Psychology*. London: Tavistock.

Kaiser, P. (2004). On the Design of Creative Collaboration. In R. J. Boland & F. Collopy (Eds.), *Managing as Designing*. Stanford: Stanford university Press.

Kimbell, L. (2009). Design practices in design thinking. *Design*, (May), 1–24. Retrieved from http://www.lucykimbell.com/stuff/DesignPractices_Kimbell.pdf

Kimbell, L. (2011). Rethinking Design Thinking: Part I. *Design and Culture, 3*(3), 285–306.

Kimbell, L. (2012). Rethinking Design Thinking: Part II. *Design and Culture, 4*(2), 129–148. https://doi.org/10.2752/175470812X13281948975413

Klein, G., & Moon, B. (2006). Making sense of sensemaking 1: Alternative perspectives. *IEEE Intelligent Systems*. https://doi.org/10.1109/MIS.2006.75

Koffka, K. (1935). *Principles of Gestalt psychology*. Routledge. Retrieved from http://www.gestalttheory.net/cms/uploads/pdf/archive/1934_1960/Principles_Gestalt_Psychology_koffka.pdf

Kolko, J. (2010). Abductive Thinking and Sensemaking: The Drivers of Design Synthesis. *Design Issues, 26*(1), 15–28. https://doi.org/10.1162/desi.2010.26.1.15

Koss, J. (2009). Modernism after Wagner. *Leonardo, 45*(5), 489–490.

Kotarbinski, T. (2013). *Praxiology: An introduction to the sciences of efficient action*. Elsevier.

Kydland, Å., Støylen, M., & Olsen, E. S. (n.d.). My Last Home. Retrieved June 28, 2016, from http://systemsorienteddesign.net/index.php/projects/master-projects/aho-2012/my-last-home

Lane, D. C. (2000). Should Systems Dynamics be Described as a "Hard" or "Deterministic" Systems Approach? *Systems Research and Behavioural Science, 17*, 3–22. Retrieved from http://wikinator.com/files/Lane00.pdf

Latour, B. (2005). *Reassembling the Social: An Introduction to Actor-Network-Theory*. New York: Oxford University Press.

Latour, B. (2008). A cautious prometheus? A few steps toward a philosophy of design (with special attention to Peter Sloterdijk). In *Proceedings of the 2008 annual international conference of the design history society* (pp. 2–10).

Lavik, M. (2015). Vil ha tillit fremfor detaljstyring. *Stat & Styring, 25*(01), 36–37.

Lawson, B. (1997). *How Designers Think: the design process demystified*. Oxford: Architectural Press,.

Leerberg, T. (2004). Embedded Spaces. *The Danish Center for Integrated Design*. Aarhus: Aarhus University.

Liedtka, J. (2018). Why design thinking works. *Harvard Business Review, 96*(5), 72–79.

Liedtka, J., & Ogilvie, T. (2011). *Designing for growth : a design thinking tool kit for managers*. New York: Columbia University Press.

Lindberg, N., & Nordin, F. (2008). From products to services and back again: Towards a new service procurement logic. *Industrial Marketing Management, 37*(3), 292–300.

Lindblom, C. E. (1959). The science of" muddling through". *Public Administration Review*, 79–88.

Lindblom, C. E. (1979). Still muddling, not yet through. *Public Administration Review, 39*(6), 517–526.

Lissack, M. (2016). Don't Be Addicted: The Oft-Overlooked Dangers of Simplification. *She Ji: The Journal of Design, Economics, and Innovation, 2*(1), 29–45.

Lockwood, T. (2010). *Design thinking: integrating innovation, customer experience and brand value*. New York, NY: Allworth Press. Retrieved from http://www.loc.gov/catdir/enhancements/fy1006/2009026966-b.html

Loiperdinger, M., & Culbert, D. (1988). Leni Riefenstahl, the SA, and the Nazi Party Rally Films, Nuremberg 1933–1934: 'Sieg des Glaubens' and 'Triumph des Willens.' *Historical Journal of Film, Radio and Television, 8*(1), 3–38.

Luft, J., & Ingham, H. (1961a). The Johari Window: a graphic model of awareness in interpersonal relations. *Human Relations Training News, 5*(9), 6–7.

Luft, J., & Ingham, H. (1961b). The johari window. *Human Relations Training News, 5*(1), 6–7.

Luhmann, N. (1989). *Ecological communication*. University of Chicago Press.

Luhmann, N. (1995). *Social systems*. stanford university Press.

Lurås, S. (2016). Systems intertwined. *Design Issues*.

Lynn, G. (1999). *Animate Form*. New York: Princeton Architectural Press.

Maeda, J. (2013). Artists and Scientists: More Alike Than Different. Retrieved February 17, 2015, from http://blogs.scientificamerican.com/guest-blog/2013/07/11/artists-and-scientists-more-alike-than-different/

Maier, M. W., & Rechtin, E. (2000). *The Art of Systems Architecture*. Boca Raton: CRC Press.

Manzini, E., Vezzoli, C., & Clark, G. (2001). Product-Service Systems. Using an Existing Concept as a New Approach to Sustainability. *Journal of Design Research, 1*(2).

Mariussen, Å., & Uhlin, Å. (2006). Trans-national Practices, Systems Thinking in Policy Making. Stockholm: Nordregio.

Marquard, O. (1983). Gesamtkunstwerk und Identitätssystem. *Der Hang Zum Gesamtkunstwerk. Aarau/Frankfurt.*

Martin, R. L. (2009a). *The design of business: why design thinking is the next competitive advantage*. Boston, Mass.: Harvard Business Press.

Martin, R. L. (2009b). *The design of business: why design thinking is the next competitive advantage*. Boston: Harvard Business School Press.

Massumi, B. (1998). The Diagram as Technique of Existence. *Any, 23*, 42–47.

Maturana, H. (2002). Autopoiesis, structural coupling and cognition: a history of these and other notions in the biology of cognition. *Cybernetics & Human Knowing, 9*(3–4), 5–34.

Maturana, H. R., & Varela, F. J. (1980). *Autopoiesis and cognition: The realization of the living* (Vol. 42). Springer.

Mayer, R. E. (1999). Fifty Years of Creativity Research. In R. J. Sternberg (Ed.), *Handbook of Creativity*. Cambridge: Cambridge University Press.

McCandless, D. (2009). *Information is Beautiful*. London: Collins.

McCullough, M. (1996). *Abstracting Craft*. MIT.

McKim, R. H. (1972). Experiences in visual thinking.

McLuhan, M. (1964). *Understanding Media*. London: Routledge Classics.

Meadows, D. (1999). Leverage Points: Places to intervene in a System. *The Sustainable Institute, Hartland.*

Meadows, D. (2002). Dancing with systems. *Systems Thinker, 13*, 2–6.

Meadows, D. H. (2008). *Thinking in Systems*. White River Junction: Chelsea Green Publishing.

Menges, A. (2008). Systemisches Denken und Integrales Entwerfen, System thinking and Integral Design. Offenbach: Präsident der Hochschule für Gestaltung Offenbach am Main.

Metcalf, G. S. (2014). *Social systems and design* (Vol. 1). Springer.

Midgley, G. (2000). *Systemic Intervention: Philosophy, Methodology, and Practice*. New York: Kluver Academic / Plenum Publishers.

Midgley, G., Munlo, I., & Brown, M. (1998). The Theory and Practice of Boundary Critique: Developing Housing Services for Older People. *The Journal of the Operational Research Society, 49*(5), 467–478. https://doi.org/10.1057/palgrave.jors.2600531

Miller, J. H., & Page, S. E. (2007). *Complex Adaptive Systems: An Introduction to Computational Models of Social Life*. Princeton: Princeton University Press.

Ming-fen, L. (2000). Fostering Design Culture through Cultivating the User-Designers' Design Thinking and Systems Thinking. Retrieved from http://files.eric.ed.gov/fulltext/ED455775.pdf

Mitchell, M. (2009). *Complexity: a guided tour*. New York: Oxford University Press.

Morelli, N. (2002). Designing product/service systems: A methodological exploration1. *Design Issues*, *18*(3), 3–17.

Nahman, & ShiftN. (n.d.). Systemic Design Toolkit. Retrieved from https://www.systemicdesigntoolkit.org/about

Nelson, H. (1994). The Necessity of Being "Un-disciplined" and "Out-of-Control"; Design Action and Systems Thinking. *Performance Improvement Quarterly*, *7*(3).

Nelson, H. (2011). The Berkely bubble. Retrieved from

http://accidentalvagrant.blogspot.no/2011/08/berkeley-bubble.html

Nelson, H. G., & Stolterman, E. (2012a). *The design way: intentional change in an unpredictable world: foundations and fundamentals of design competence*. Englewood Cliffs: 1st ed. Educational Technology, 2nd ed. MIT press.

Nelson, H. G., & Stolterman, E. (2012b). *The Design Way: Intentional Change in an Unpredictable World* (second edi). MIT Press.

Nordby, K. (2019). Open Bridge Design System. Retrieved from http://www.openbridge.no/

Norman, D. (2010). Why design education must change. *Core77*, *26*.

OCEAN-NORTH. (1998). Chamberworks. Retrieved from http://www.ocean-north.net/

OCEAN, Bettum, J., Larsen, K. B., & Sevaldson, B. (1998). Synthetic Landscape 3. Oslo: Ocean north. Retrieved from http://www.ocean-north.net/research/synth3

Olsson, M.-O., & Sjöstedt, G. (2004). Systems Approaches and Their Applicaitons: Examples from Sweden. Dordrecht: Kluwer Academisc Publishers.

Online Etymology Dictionary. (n.d.). Complex. In *Online Etymology Dictionary*. Retrieved from https://www.etymonline.com/word/completely

Oster, G. W. (2008). Derailing Design Thinking. *International Journal of Leadership Studies*, *4*(1), 107–115.

Owen, C. L. (1998). Design Research: Building the knowledge base. *Design Studies*, *19*.

Paulsen, A., Wildhagen, B., & Sevaldson, B. (2018). Gearing up the level of systems oriented design in public sector: Case, experiences and learning from Stimulab innovation program.

Pecker, J.-C. (2004). The provocative razor of William of Occam. *European Review*, *12*(2), 185–190.

Pezzi, M. G. (2013). 'We don't need to copy anyone': César Manrique and the Creation of a Development Model for Lanzarote. *Urbanities*, *3*(2), 19–31.

Poli, R. (2013). A note on the difference between complicated and complex social systems. *Cadmus*, *2*(1), 142.

Protzen, J.-P., & Harris, D. J. (2010). *The Universe of Design: Horst Rittel's Theories of Design and Planning*. Oxon: Routledge.

Ramage, M., & Shipp, K. (2009). *Systems thinkers*. Springer Science & Business Media.

Ramasesh, R. V, & Browning, T. R. (2014). A conceptual framework for tackling knowable unknown unknowns in project management. *Journal of Operations Management*, *32*(4), 190–204.

Rechtin, E. (1999). *Systems Architecting of Organisations: Why Eagles Can't Swim*. Boca Raton, Florida: CRC Press LLC.

Reigeluth, C. M., & Garfinkle, R. J. (1994). *Systemic change in education*. Educational Technology.

Richardson, G. P. (1997). Problems in causal loop diagrams revisited. *System Dynamics Review: The Journal of the System Dynamics Society*, *13*(3), 247–252.

Ritchey, T. (1998). Fritz Zwicky, Morphologie and policy analysis. *16th EURO Conference on Operational Analysis, Brussels*, 11.

Rittel, H. W. J. (1972). Son of Rittelthink. *The DMG 5th Anniversary Report, DMG Occasi,* 5–10.

Rittel, H. W. J., & Webber, M. M. (1973). Dilemmas in a General Theory of Planning. *Policy Sciences, 4,* 155–169.

Romm, J. (2010). *Sluttrapport for Design Pilot – U-Bridge Vision (UBV).* Oslo.

Romm, J., Paulsen, A., & Sevaldson, B. (2014). *Practicing Systems Oriented Design; A guide for business and organisations that want to make real changes.* Oslo: Oslo School of Architecture and Design.

Rowe, P. G. (1987). *Design thinking.* Cambridge, Mass.: MIT Press.

Rowland, G. (1999). *A tripartite seed: The future creating capacity of designing, learning, and systems.* New Jersey: Hampton Press.

Rowland, G. (2015). Teaching Systemic Design in the Context of Organisational Communication. *FORMakademisk, 7*(3).

Russell, D. M., Stefik, M. J., Pirolli, P., & Card, S. K. (1993). The cost structure of sensemaking. In *Proceedings of the SIGCHI conference on Human factors in computing systems - CHI '93* (pp. 269–276). https://doi.org/10.1145/169059.169209

Rust, C., Mottram, J., & Till, J. (2007). AHRC Research Review, Practice-Led Research in Art, Design and Architecture. Shefield, Nottingham: Arts & Humanities Research Council. Retrieved from http://www.archive.org/details/ReviewOfPractice-ledResearchInArtDesignArchitecture

Ryan, A. (2014). A Framework for Systemic Design. *FORMakademisk, 7*(4).

Schön, D. A. (1982). *The Reflective Practitioner.* London: Basic Books.

Scrivener, S. A. R. (1999). Design Research as Reflection in Action and Practice. In *Useful and Critical.* Helsinki: UIAH.

Senge, P. M., Smith, B., Kruschwitz, N., Laur, J., & Schley, S. (2008). *The Necessary Revolution: How individuals and organisations are working together to create a sustainable world.* New York: Douobleday.

Sevaldson, B. (1996). Science, Scientific Reasoning and Research on Design. *DEcon '96.* Baden-Baden.

Sevaldson, B. (1999a). Graphical Analyses of Synthetic Landscape Phase 3. Channeling System Animation "Tøyenparken." Oslo. Retrieved from http://www.birger-sevaldson.no/ambient_amplifiers/texts/Channeling_study.pdf

Sevaldson, B. (1999b). Research Design in Design Research. In *Cumulus Conference.* 12-16 April, Rome: Cumulus.

Sevaldson, B. (1999c). Research on Digital Design Strategies. In *Useful and Critical, the Position of Research in Design, conference.* Helsinki: UIAH (Aalto University).

Sevaldson, B. (2000a). Dynamic Generative Diagrams. In D. Donath (Ed.), *Promise and Reality* (pp. 273–276). Weimar: eCAADe.

Sevaldson, B. (2000b). The Integrated Conglomerate Approach: A Suggestion for a Generic Model of Design Research. In D. Durling & K. Friedman (Eds.), *Proceedings of the conference Doctoral Education in Design: Foundations for the Future, held 8-12 July 2000, La Clusaz, France* (pp. 163–170). Stoke-on-Trent: Staffordshire University Press. Retrieved from http://www.aho.no/staff/bs/phd/ica.pdf

Sevaldson, B. (2001). The Renaissance of Visual Thinking. In *Proceedings of Konference om Arkitekturforskning og IT.* Aarhus: Nordisk Forening for Arkitekturforskning.

Sevaldson, B. (2004). Ways of Working. In T. R. Ebbesen (Ed.), *Digitale Designprodukter - vision og virkelighed.* Kolding, Denmark: Kolding School of Arts and Design. Retrieved from http://www.digitaledesignprodukter.dk/

Sevaldson, B. (2005a). *Developing Digital Design Techniques. Investigations on Creative Design Computing.* (1st ed.). Oslo School of Architecture and Design, Oslo.

Sevaldson, B. (2005b). *Developing Digital Design Techniques.* Oslo: Oslo School of Architecture and Design.

Sevaldson, B. (2008). Rich Design Research Space. *Form Akademisk, 1*(1), 28–44. Retrieved from http://journals.hioa.no/index.php/formakademisk/article/view/119/108

Sevaldson, B. (2010). Discussions and Movements in Design Research: A systems approach to practice research in design. *FORMakademisk, 3*(1), 8–35.

Sevaldson, B. (2013a). Can Designers Design Anything? In *2012 Yearbook of The Oslo School of Architecture and Design* (pp. 94–99). Oslo: Oslo School of Architecture and Design.

Sevaldson, B. (2013b). RSD2 Relating Systems thinking and Design, opening lecture. In S. Birger & J. Peter (Eds.), *RSD2: Emerging Contexts for Systemic Design Relating Systems Thinking and Design 2013 Symposium Proceedings.* Oslo: Oslo School of Architecture and Design. Retrieved from http://systemic-design.net/rsd2/plenaries/

Sevaldson, B. (2018). Beyond user centric design. In *Proceedings of RSD7 Relating Systems Thinking and Design.* Torino: Systemic Design Association.

Sevaldson, B., & Duong, P. (2000). Ambient Amplifiers. Retrieved from http://www.birger-sevaldson.no/ambient_amplifiers/competition/

Simon, H. (1969). *The Science of the Artificial* (first edit). Massachusets: MIT Press.

Simon, H. A. (1969). *The sciences of the artificial* (Vol. 136). Cambridge, Mass: M.I.T.

Skyttner, L. (2005). General systems theory: problems, perspectives, practice. Hackensack, N.J.: World Scientific.

Slavin, K. (2016). Design as participation. *Journal of Design and Science.*

Smith, E. M., Ford, J. K., & Kozlowski, S. W. J. (1997). Building adaptive expertise: Implications for training design. *Training for a Rapidly Changing Workplace: Applications of Psychological Research,* 89–118.

Somol, R. E. (1998). *The Diagram of Matter. ANY* (Vol. 23). New York: Any Magazine.

Suh, K. S. (1998). Impact of communication medium on task performance and satisfaction: an examination of media-richness theory. *Information & Management 35 (1999), 35 1999,* 295–312.

Thackara, J. (1988). Design after Modernism: Beyond the Object. (J. Thackara, Ed.). New York: Thames and Hudson.

Tjalve, E. (1976). *Systematisk udforming af industriprodukter.* Copenhagen: Akademisk Forlag.

Tufte, E. R. (1983). *The Visual Display of Quantitative Information.* Connecticut: Graphic Press.

Ulluoa, M. A., & Strømsnes, J. K. (2012). *Design for Dignity in a Sexual Violence Response System.*

Ulmer, G. (1994). *Heuretics: The Logic of Invention.* Baltimoe: John Hopkins University Press.

Ulrich, W. (1983). Critical Heuristics of Social Planning.

Ulrich, W. (1994). Can we secure future-responsive management through systems thinking and design? *Interfaces, 24*(4), 26–37.

Ulrich, W. (1996). Critical systems thinking for citizens. In *Critical systems thinking* (pp. 165–178). Springer.

Ulrich, W. (2000a). Reflective Practice in the Civil Society: the contribution of critical systemic thinking. *Reflective Practice, 1*(2), 247–268.

Ulrich, W. (2000b). Reflective practice in the civil society: the contribution of critically systemic thinking. *Reflective Practice, 1*(2), 247–268.

Ulrich, W. (2002). Boundary Critique. In H. G. Daellenbach & R. L. Flood (Eds.), *The Informed Student Guide to Management Science* (pp. 41-). Thomson Learning.

Ulrich, W. (2003). Beyond methodology choice: critical systems thinking as critically systemic discourse. *Journal of the Operational Research Society, 54*(4), 325–342. https://doi.org/10.1057/palgrave.jors.2601518

Vatn, G. (2018). Troen på tillitsreformen–en studie av sentrale aktørers forståelse av Tillitsreformen i Oslo kommune. OsloMet-storbyuniversitetet.

Vezzoli, C., & Manzini, E. (2008). *Design for Environmental Sustainability*. London: Springer.

Vygotsky, L. S. (1997). *The collected works of LS Vygotsky: Problems of the theory and history of psychology* (Vol. 3). New York: Springer Science & Business Media.

Wagenknecht, S. (2017). Beyond non-/use: The affected bystander and her escalation. *New Media & Society*, 1461444817708775.

Walters, J. P., Archer, D. W., Sassenrath, G. F., Hendrickson, J. R., Hanson, J. D., Halloran, J. M., Alarcon, V. J. (2016). Exploring agricultural production systems and their fundamental components with system dynamics modelling. *Ecological Modelling, 333*, 51–65.

Warfield, J. N. (2003). A proposal for systems science. *Systems Research and Behavioral Science: The Official Journal of the International Federation for Systems Research, 20*(6), 507–520.

Wasson, C. (2000). Ethnography in the field of design. *Human Organisation, 59*(4), 377–388.

Weber, C. (2005). What is "complexity"? In *DS 35: Proceedings ICED 05, the 15th International Conference on Engineering Design, Melbourne, Australia, 15.-18.08. 2005*.

Weick, K. E. (1995). *Sensemaking in Organisations (Foundations for Organisational Science). Star*. https://doi.org/10.1177/009539978601800106

Weick, K. E. (2004). Designing for Thrownness. In R. J. Boland & F. Collopy (Eds.), *Managing as Designing*. Stanford: Stanford University Press.

Weick, K. E., Sutcliffe, K. M., & Obstfeld, D. (2005). Organizing and the Process of Sensemaking. *Organisation Science, 16*(4), 409–421. https://doi.org/10.1287/orsc.1050.0133

Weinberg, G. M. (1975). *An introduction to general systems thinking* (Vol. 304). Wiley New York.

Weinberg, G. M. (2001). *An Introduction to General Systems Thinking*. New York: Dorset House.

Wettre, A. (2012). *Report on experiences with GIGA-mapping with leader groups*.

Wildhagen, B. (2018). Understanding variations of entanglement and complexity: A way to influence expectations of Service and Systems Oriented Design in public sector.

Wilson, J. Q., & Kelling, G. L. (1982). Broken windows. *Atlantic Monthly, 249*(3), 29–38.

Wolpert, L., & Richards, A. (1988). *A passion for science*. Oxford Univ. Press.

Yin, R. K. (1994). *Case Study Research: Design and Methods*. Thousand Oaks: Sage.

Zwicky, F. (1969). *Discovery, Invention, Research: Through the Morphological Approach*. Macmillan.

INDEX

Printed in the USA
CPSIA information can be obtained
at www.ICGtesting.com
LVHW070724261023
761975LV00011B/158

9 780949 313614